Vought A-7
Corsair II

10
AE
NAVY
157485

Vought A-7 Corsair II

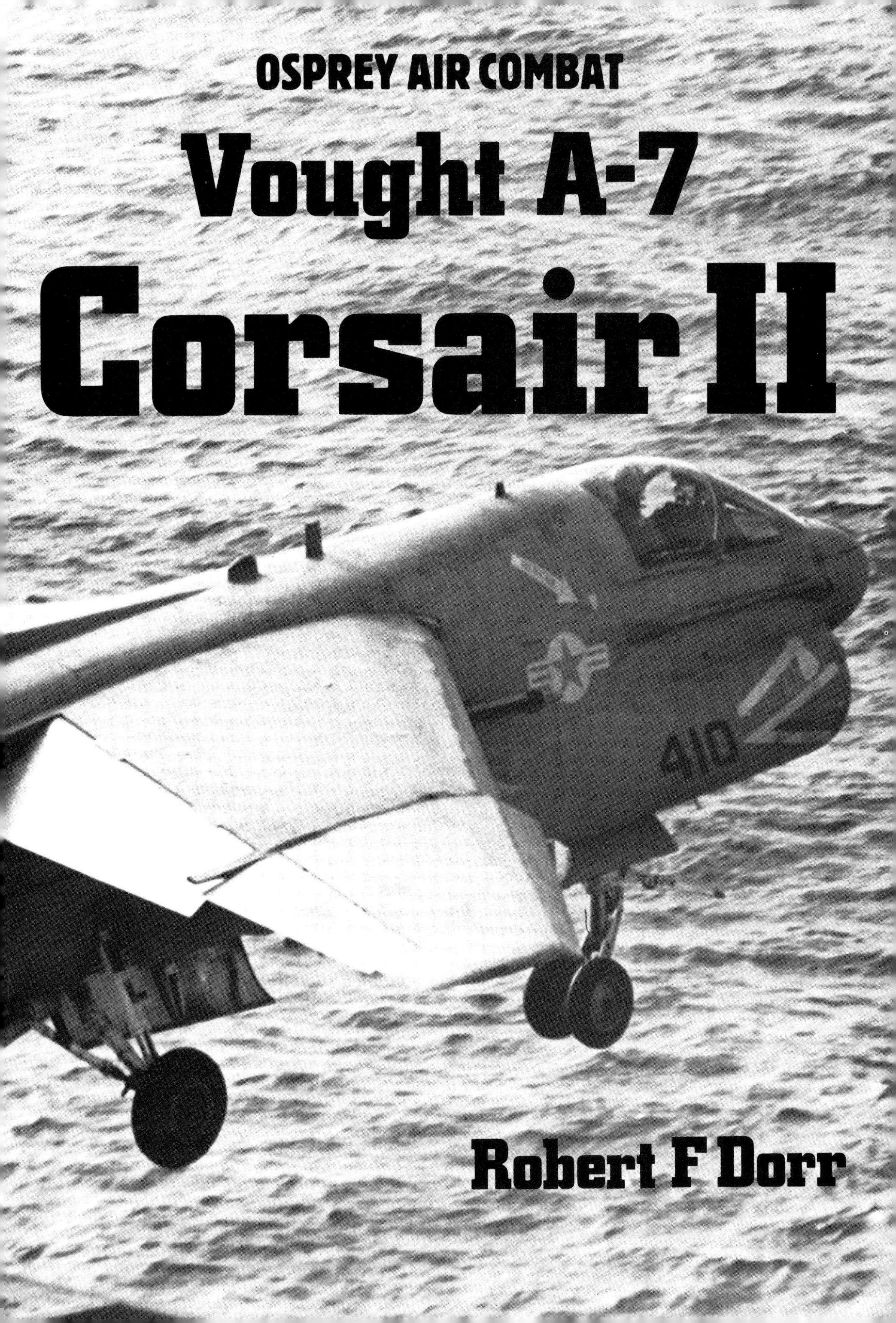

Robert F Dorr

Published in 1985 by Osprey Publishing Limited
12–14 Long Acre, London WC2E 9LP
Member company of the George Philip Group

Osceola, Wisconsin 54020, USA

Sole distributors for the USA

British Library Cataloguing in Publication Data

Dorr, Robert F.
Vought A–7 Corsair II.—(Osprey air combat)
1. Corsair (Fighter planes)—History
I. Title
623.74′63 TL686.C45

ISBN 0–85045–626–6

Editor Dennis Baldry
Filmset in Great Britain by
Tameside Filmsetting Limited, Ashton-under-Lyne,
Lancashire and printed by
BAS Printers Limited
Over Wallop, Hampshire

Contents

For Dad

Introduction

Long after it was over, when there was no going back to change any part of it, I met a pilot who'd almost flown the A-7 Corsair in combat in Iran. Lieutenant (j.g.) Ted Smith had been on deck aboard USS *Nimitz* (CVN-68) that awful night in April 1980 when Charlie Beckwith's Delta Force went in to rescue my colleagues being held hostage in Tehran, when sandstorms, helicopter failure and too many people in charge spelled an end to the rescue before it could begin.

It was a low time for me, a diplomat, and a lower time for Smith, a warrior. Smith had watched the helicopters launch. His A-7E Corsairs, wearing the red-bordered black stripes painted on *Nimitz'* aircraft solely for that Iran operation, had been bombed-up and ready to go. Morale was high. The men were up. In the end they were not needed, not because the mission went off too well but because it was aborted before somebody could decide to throw Vought's very fine light attack aircraft into the fray. Ted Smith and I lamented all of this, and he told me that we could have gone in. Even when Chargin' Charlie was down to five helicopters, it could have been done. 'We could have covered him,' Smith insisted.

'Let's say you've got the hostages, you're loading them into a truck, and some guys are shooting at you from a building a few feet away. With the weapons-delivery system on the A-7E, you could put 20 mm rounds or cluster bombs into the building without touching the people in the street. We could have put the ordnance on a dime for him.' It didn't happen this time, but there were a lot of other times when a brace of A-7 Corsairs made the difference. Not everyone appreciates how many times like that there have been, or how often the A-7 has gotten us out of a tight spot.

Included in his personal album of colour slides, Capt David Moss has an Ektachrome of a gigantic splash in the water. Not everyone would keep a picture of a large plume of salt spray rising up into the air. Dave's picture was taken by his wingman. It depicts the abrupt end in the Gulf of Tonkin of his A-7E Corsair II (156860), side number NK-504, callsign JURY 504 belonging to the 'Mighty Shrikes' of attack squadron VA-94, which Dave commanded at the time.

When the picture was taken, Dave was hanging from a parachute with all sorts of gunfire rushing around him and everybody in North Vietnam trying to kill him. He had just finished mining Haiphong harbour on a combat mission flown from the deck of USS *Coral Sea* (CVA-43). Dave sustained heavy battle damage while 'feet dry' (over land) and had kept his A-7E aloft long enough to punch out only after going feet wet. He'd been hit straight-on by a SAM and believes he might not have survived flying anything but an A-7. Dave Moss is a modest, practical man who flies a modest, practical airplane and if one theme shines through the narrative which follows it is that modesty has prevented the tough, reliable A-7 Corsair from receiving fair credit for earning the love and appreciation of almost every warrior who, like Moss, took it into harm's way.

Just as the mission we never flew in Iran is part of it, shootdowns, ejections and harrowing experiences are a part of the story of the feisty A-7 which emanated from Russell Clark's design team in Dallas. Statistically, however, it is remarkable how few of them there have been. A Pentagon analyst once looked over loss figures for A-7 squadrons, marvelled at how low they were, and thereby came to precisely the wrong conclusion—namely, that North Vietnam's defences weren't nearly as formidable as everybody claimed.

The defences *were* formidable and A-7 pilots weren't merely lucky, not when at the controls of a nimble, load-carrying, phenomenally accurate light attack aircraft which simply thumbed its blunt nose at missiles, MiGs and triple-A. The very success of the

Corsair makes it all the more extraordinary that so little literature has appeared to sing praise of the A-7. Attempting this volume on the Vought A-7 Corsair in a year no earlier than the 20th anniversary of the airplane's first flight, editor Dennis Baldry and I were astounded that no full-sized work on the A-7 had appeared before.

A certain amount of 'gee whiz' encumbers the pages which follow, the inevitable awe felt by this aviation buff toward those who fly and fight. There is, too, some honest mention of flaws in an overall superbly-crafted machine, especially the catapult steam-ingestion problem which proved a real drawback in the A-7's early days. Criticism appears solely to make credible the praise which is repeated again and again.

Any of the thousands who've flown the A-7 in combat might have written this history better than I. They shall, for the Corsair will be with us for a generation yet. This is a start, an attempt to pinpoint the quintessential Corsair for the aviation buff and the A-7 pilot alike. A glossary is appended. Military ranks, hull numbers and other minutia are given for the time period covered. Because this is an 'Air Combat' series, the design work done by Russell Clark, Capt Henry Suerstedt and others is treated only as prelude to the air battles which came afterward.

This volume contains thousands of facts. Any errors are the sole responsibility of the author. But a history like this is inevitably hostage to the help of those who were there, and the effort would have been impossible without generous assistance from many.

This book is dedicated to my father, Lawrence G Dorr, Sr, who got me to look up and who knows why it resembles a Crusader. I am indebted to editor Dennis Baldry, who is both demanding and knowledgeable and has become a special friend, and to James W Croslin of LTV who pulled out all the stops. Dennis, Jim and I talked-up this project at Farnborough 84 where no A-7 Corsairs were present and when Vought was no longer manufacturing airplanes. It came to me, only much later, that A-7s were on battle stations in the Med that day and that we shouldn't use the past tense talking about the A-7, not yet.

Assistance in the preparation of this work was received from the Department of State, the United States armed forces, and numerous American military units. Help came from many at the LTV Aerospace and Defense Company, which retains a proud surname in its Vought Aero Products Division, and from many other firms in the aerospace field. Thanks are due to Reed Duncan for the section on Lebanon.

I especially want to thank Harold Andrews, Robert J Archer, Paul Auerswald, Beetle Bailey, Roger F Besecker, Philip D Chinnery, Eric Cintron, Paul C Clements, Ken De Cell, HM2 Martye Dixon, SSgt Edward K Downs, John Dunnell, Capt Lewis Dunton, Col Erv Ethell, Lt Col Basil Evans, James W Freidhoff, Nelson Gillette, Lt Col Ed Gorman, Maj Jack Hudson, Marty J Isham, Donald L Jay, Jim John, Martin Judge, M J Kasiuba, John W Konrad, Cdr James J McBride, Cdr Dennis V McGinn, Robert Parmerter, David L Perry, Lt Gen Evan W Rosencrans, Cdr Michael A Ruth, Arthur L Schoeni, Capt Benjamin F Short, Don Spering, Richard Stemen, Karen Stubberfield, Jim Sullivan, Douglas R Tachauer, Norman Taylor, 'Deep Throat,' Walter A Trimborn, Commodore Gary F Wheatley, Cdr Howard Wheeler and Nick Williams.

The views expressed in this book are mine and do not necessarily reflect those of the Department of State or of the United States Air Force.

Robert F Dorr
London, April 1985

FRONT COVER
Two A-7D Corsairs of the Virginia Air National Guard in low visibility 'Europe One' camouflage (Va. ANG, Dr Hudson)

TITLE PAGES
A-7E Corsair of VA-87 launching from the USS Independence *is caught by the camera of Kirby Harrison during operations off Lebanon in 1983 (US Navy)*

Chapter 1
Green Ink in Lebanon
Corsairs in Combat in the 1980s

The two A-7E Corsairs loitered in a gentle orbit a mile off the Lebanese coast, ominous and unadvertised, in low-visibility gray paint which blended them into the grey afternoon. Layers of cumulus hugged the green-brown coastline and the narrow defile carved out of the land, leading to Suk al Gharb. A few days ago in September 1983, Syrian artillery positions at Suk al Gharb had fired upon American warships in the Mediterranean—ships standing in readiness at Bagel Station, supporting an international peace-keeping force and the imperilled Lebanese government of President Amin Gemayel. For the first time, US warships had fired back. Now, the A-7E flight leader peered toward the shoreline and raised his gaze until he was looking high against the sun, where a TARPS-equipped F-14A Tomcat was going in.

Dull-gray, foreboding, devoid of distinctive markings, Cdr Kenneth L Brunson's two A-7Es were in position to protect that Tomcat as it began a

Seen from a tanker carrying forward-looking infrared (FLIR) and demonstrating the old and new in US Navy paint schemes, these A-7Es of the 'Waldomen' of VA-66 are veterans of combat in Lebanon in 1983. Before their carrier USS Dwight D Eisenhower *(CVN-69) was relieved at Bagel Station by USS* Independence *(CV-62), Corsair aircraft 157541 (AG-301) and 160736 (AG-302) were used to escort TARPS-equipped F-14A Tomcats in the region around Beirut*
(USN)

Just in time for Grenada and Lebanon, low-visibility camouflage paint helps to shield an A-7E Corsair from enemy view. But the drab paint scheme also makes the aircraft difficult to see on a crowded carrier deck, and deck crews often can't distinguish a bureau number from a few feet away. Aboard the training carrier USS Lexington *(CVT-16) in August 1984, this VA-174 aircraft is visible only because of the dark background and the non-standard use of black paint for its modex number, 422. The 'Hell Razors' of VA-174 landbased at NAS Cecil Field, Florida have been the east coast replacement air group (RAG) for A-7 operations for two decades (Peter B Mersky)*

reconnaissance run. Like much which happened in a bizarre and bitter confrontation where little was as it seemed, this was backwards. Usually, fighters protected attack planes. Now Brunson's attack aircraft were in readiness, laden with Mk 20 Rockeye II CBU bombs and APAMs (bomblets) to engage Syrian AAA if the Tomcat was fired upon. Easy and comfortable at the controls of his A-7E (157452), side number AG-400, callsign CLINCHER 400, from the carrier USS *Eisenhower* (CVN-69), dark-haired Ken Brunson belonged to the 'Clinchers' of attack squadron VA-12, and was a deceptively mild-mannered man, with a resemblance to film actor William Devane. Another officer in his squadron—not Ken—had expressed the hope that they'd get the go-ahead to assault Syrian gun positions. 'You call, we haul,' was the message naval aviators gave to policy-makers who sent them into battle, but this officer had said it more graphically: 'I think it's time we lay some ordnance straight down on top of those mothers.' Americans at this juncture in history were becoming tired of being kicked around.

Brunson's earphones crackled with a report that the recce Tomcat had spotted streaks of light rushing across the cluttered tin rooftops of Suk al Gharb. This had to be a shoulder-mounted SAM-7 missile. In moments, a decision was relayed. Brunson spoke to his wingman: 'We're going in.'

Not far north of them was Beirut, once a shining metropolitan crossroads, the jewel of the Middle East, watering hole for the rich and famous and now a battered, broken city. Ahead, just over the first bare, cumulus-shielded ridgeline, were the first Syrian AAA positions. Ken Brunson took his flight down across the shoreline—anywhere in the world, naval aviators call it crossing the beach—and began his run-in at 2,000 ft (610 m), low enough to hunker down if missiles were fired at him. Not easily aroused, Brunson was merely displeased, not angry, that men on the ridges ahead waited, lurked, with a distinct interest in killing him.

Not everybody believed that the thrust-and-parry of American airpower versus Syrian and Druse

Just back from combat operations in Lebanon is A-7E (buno 160613), coded AG-305 of the 'Waldomen' of attack squadron VA-66 aboard USS Dwight D Eisenhower *(CV-69), at Andrews AFB, Maryland on 17 March 1984 (Joseph G Handelman)*

RIGHT
Close-up of the low visibility tail insignia on A-7E (buno 160613) of the 'Waldomen' of VA-66, just after Lebanese operations, at Andrews AFB, Maryland 17 March 1984. Fillet at upper tail is a radar warning receiver (Joseph G Handelman)

BELOW
Close-up side view of the forward-looking infrared (FLIR) pod carried by Lebanon combat veteran A-7E buno 160613 of VA-66 (Joseph G Handelman)

ABOVE
VA-12 in high visibility . . . A-7E Corsair (156863), side number AG-404 of the 'Clinchers' of attack squadron VA-12 makes a rare visit to RAF Mildenhall, England in 1982 in the readily visible markings of the squadron, including 'kiss of death' head on tail, now toned down. This particular aircraft was still with the squadron at the time of combat operations in support of the Multinational Peacekeeping Force in Lebanon in autumn 1983 (John Dunnell)

ground installations was a sensible way to employ force of arms. 'We were just screwing around, running around in circles,' a Tomcat pilot from VF-142, also aboard *Eisenhower*, would say later. The enemy was dimly defined, the purpose of the American presence in Lebanon susceptible to controversy. Brunson did not believe that naval officers were expected to raise questions on issues of policy. Proud that his had been the first Atlantic Fleet squadron to operate the A-7E, after experience with the older A-7A and A-7B, he regretted only that VA-12's were the *oldest* A-7Es in the inventory and did not have the forward-looking infrared receiver (FLIR) package employed for target acquisition on newer, less ratty E models. Not that FLIR was needed today, in broad daylight . . .

That day in September, Ken Brunson's A-7E Corsairs covered the American presence in Lebanon in what ended up being an uneventful trip over the beach into hostile areas where Syrian forces might

have stirred up further trouble but didn't. The remarkable loitering time of the A-7E, more a function of the fuel efficiency of its turbofan engine than its internal fuel capacity, enabled the Corsairs to guard the F-14A TARPS mission with an admirable show of endurance. Had it been necessary to engage Syrian gun and missile positions, the superb navigation/bombing system in the A-7E and its ordnance-carrying capability would have made the Corsair a potent adversary. Almost twenty years old now, the Vought A-7 had shown enormous growth potential and was slated to remain a front-line, carrier-based attack plane for years to come.

Protecting the American presence in Lebanon on an extended cruise which included a 93-day line period without a port call, *Eisenhower*'s pilots (including A-7E pilots from Brunson's VA-12 and its sister squadron, the 'Waldomen' of VA-66) came under fire and evaded shells and missiles, but were

VA-12 in low visibility . . . A-7E Corsair (157455), side number AG-406 of the 'Clinchers' of attack squadron VA-12 on a visit to Andrews AFB, Maryland on 6 November 1982, a year before the squadron was in combat in Lebanon. Although these toned-down markings are representative of those used in Lebanese operations, this individual aircraft was no longer with the squadron by that time
(Don Linn)

never called upon to engage the Syrians directly—a job which lay ahead for the carrier air wings on *Independence* and *Kennedy*, which relieved *Ike* on Bagel Station in November 1973. Still, *Eisenhower*'s pilots were officially in combat every time they crossed the beach. Their logbook entries for each sortie were made in green ink, signifying combat. The seriousness of their purpose was underlined by the grim undoing of that American attempt to bring stability to Lebanon—the 24 October 1983 terrorist bombing of the US Marine Corps headquarters in Beirut which killed 241 men. When *Ike*'s line period ended and she steamed for home, the situation in Lebanon remained tense. VA-12 and VA-66 had done their jobs, but other A-7 pilots, on another carrier, were going to earn their green ink with great difficulty.

Lieutenant K C Albright lands his VA-12 aircraft, A-7E (157452), side number AG-400, at RAF Mildenhall, England in June 1984. Aircraft wears one variation of current low visibility paint scheme with side number, on nose, in black
(John Dunnell)

Grenada

The Vought A-7 Corsair has been the standard light attack aircraft on US Navy carriers for so long that it has flown in peace and war under almost every possible set of conditions. But not many pilots can match the feat of those aboard USS *Independence* (CV-62) in late 1983 when they flew in combat in two wars on a single cruise. The 'Valions' of attack squadron VA-15 under Cdr Michael F Korda and the 'Golden Warriors' of VA-87 under Cdr Michael F O'Brien departed the east coast home of the A-7 community, NAS Cecil Field, Florida, in early October 1983 just as the missions already described were being flown from *Eisenhower*'s flight deck. The two squadrons were embarked on *Independence* when she set forth from Norfolk a few days later for a planned TRANSLANT (trans-Atlantic crossing)

During operations off the coast of Lebanon on 31 August 1983, two A-7E Corsairs of the 'Waldomen' of VA-66 blend into a grey background. Fuselage Sidewinder stations are empty, external fuel tanks are mounted, tailhooks are dragging, and the aircraft in foreground carries Mk 20 Rockeye II cluster bomb unit on the centre wing station (US Navy)

direct to the eastern Mediterranean—but was suddenly diverted southward to an island most of her crew had never heard of. *Independence* would launch Corsairs against targets in Grenada before arriving half a world away for the controversial 4 December 1983 air strike in Lebanon.

At the very time world attention was focussed on the terrorist bombing of Marines in Beirut, the US moved against a Cuban-backed counter-coup in the West Indies island nation of Grenada with a hastily-assembled task force which included *Independence*'s two A-7E squadrons. At dawn on 25 October 1983, Marines from the assault ship USS *Guam* (LPH-9) landed by helicopter on the northeast tip of the island while US Army Rangers paradropped into Port Salines Airport on the south side. The Rangers had planned to land quietly and take over; they were astonished when resistance proved so fierce that they had to repack their chutes and drop in. Thus began an invasion and a ten-day war fought with no journalists present and no one recording the details for history. Operation Urgent Fury, it was called. It is evident that the close-support capabilities of the A-7E Corsair played an important role in the seizure of the island.

The Rangers, supported by AC-130 Hercules gunships, found it difficult to dislodge Cuban defenders from the airport. A-7E Corsairs from VA-87, accompanied by A-6E Intruders from VA-176, flew repeated strikes to thwart a counter-assault, to

permit the aerodrome to be secured, and to cover the arrival by C-141 Starlifter of additional troops from the 82nd Airborne Division. As Rangers and paratroops broke out and moved north to seize the city of St George, more A-7E strikes were called in.

Pockets of resistance throughout the island were almost tailor-made for a light attack aircraft with pinpoint bombing accuracy. Cdr O'Brien's 'Golden Warriors' continued to cover the two-pronged ground assault. On 27 October, when Marines moved on Richmond Hill in their southward thrust, A-7Es provided close support as they advanced. Later in the day, the 82nd Airborne ran into resistance and A-7Es were called again. Few details have been published but it is easy to visualize a hectic and high-pressure environment on *Independence*'s flight deck with aircraft being armed, launched and recovered around the clock. The men who maintain and service the A-7E, labouring under great difficulty, probably were grateful that almost every inch of the airplane can be reached without ladders or scaffolds. Pilots must have been gratified at the way the airplane can be 'turned around' quickly.

During the 1983 Mediterranean cruise which included action against Syrian SAM sites in Lebanon, an A-7E Corsair approaches Eisenhower*'s deck for landing. Aircraft carries AGM-45 Shrike anti-radiation missile under starboard wing, fuel tank and triple ejector racks (TER) under port wing*
(US Navy)

BELOW
Just prior to the 1983 Med cruise which included action in Lebanon, an A-7E Corsair of attack squadron VA-66 fires an AGM-45 Shrike anti-radiation missile at NAF China Lake, California. High-resolution film gives a mistaken impression of the aircraft's colour, which is actually light, low-visibility gray
(US Navy)

Aside from infantry weapons, the island's defenders were equipped with artillery and anti-aircraft guns including a surprising number of Russian-made ZU 23-2 twin-barrel guns capable of firing 2,000 23 mm shells per minute. These proved deadly against Marine AH-1 Cobra helicopter gunships. Cobras and A-7 Corsairs engaged them repeatedly, one of the gunships being downed by 23 mm fire. By 1 November, six days into the operation, close support flights by A-7Es and other aircraft had proven so effective that a force of Fairchild A-10s, deployed to NAS Roosevelt Roads, Puerto Rico, could be sent home without being used. VA-15 and VA-87 with their Corsairs continued flying strikes until *Independence* was pulled back and sent on its original course for the Mediterranean.

The fight in Grenada made headlines all over the world but there was more to come. An official history published by VA-87 reads: 'The Corsair's timely response was credited with shortening the conflict and saving American lives. In the words of Commander Second Fleet, Vice Admiral Metcalf, 'the A-7 provided the turning point in the battle for St George, allowing the multinational force (Jamaica, Barbados, Venezuela and the United States) to quickly gain the upper hand. Admiral Metcalf had only the highest praise for the pinpoint accuracy of the A-7's bombs and bullets . . .' In fact, of course, the A-7E carries a 20 mm M61A1 gun which fires a shell, not a bullet.

By any standard, it was a modest military undertaking (18 Americans were killed, 119 wounded; the two A-7 Corsair squadrons suffered no casualties). To attack pilots supporting ground troops, Grenada provided an uncommonly permissive environment. There were no enemy radars to jam or deceive, no SAM missiles to evade. The A-7Es could assemble over a pre-selected anchor point, pick up contact with the forward air controller (FAC), proceed at almost any altitude unless ZU 23-2 gunfire was encountered, and make their run-in without any of the concerns found in modern electronic warfare. Some of the VA-15 and VA-87 pilots were seasoned veterans of action against far more formidable defences in North Vietnam. All of them were soon to confront everything they'd missed in Grenada—radar, missiles, electronic thrust and parry. It would happen in Lebanon.

Indy departed Grenada's waters, made the belated TRANSLANT, and arrived at Bagel Station. An unprecedented second carrier, USS *John F Kennedy* (CV-67) with Capt Gary F Wheatley as skipper, also moved to support the US presence in Lebanon. At the time, because of an experiment with a restructured carrier air wing, *Big John* was the only carrier in the Navy without two A-7 squadrons embarked. *Big John*'s Intruders and *Indy*'s Corsairs were going to do it together.

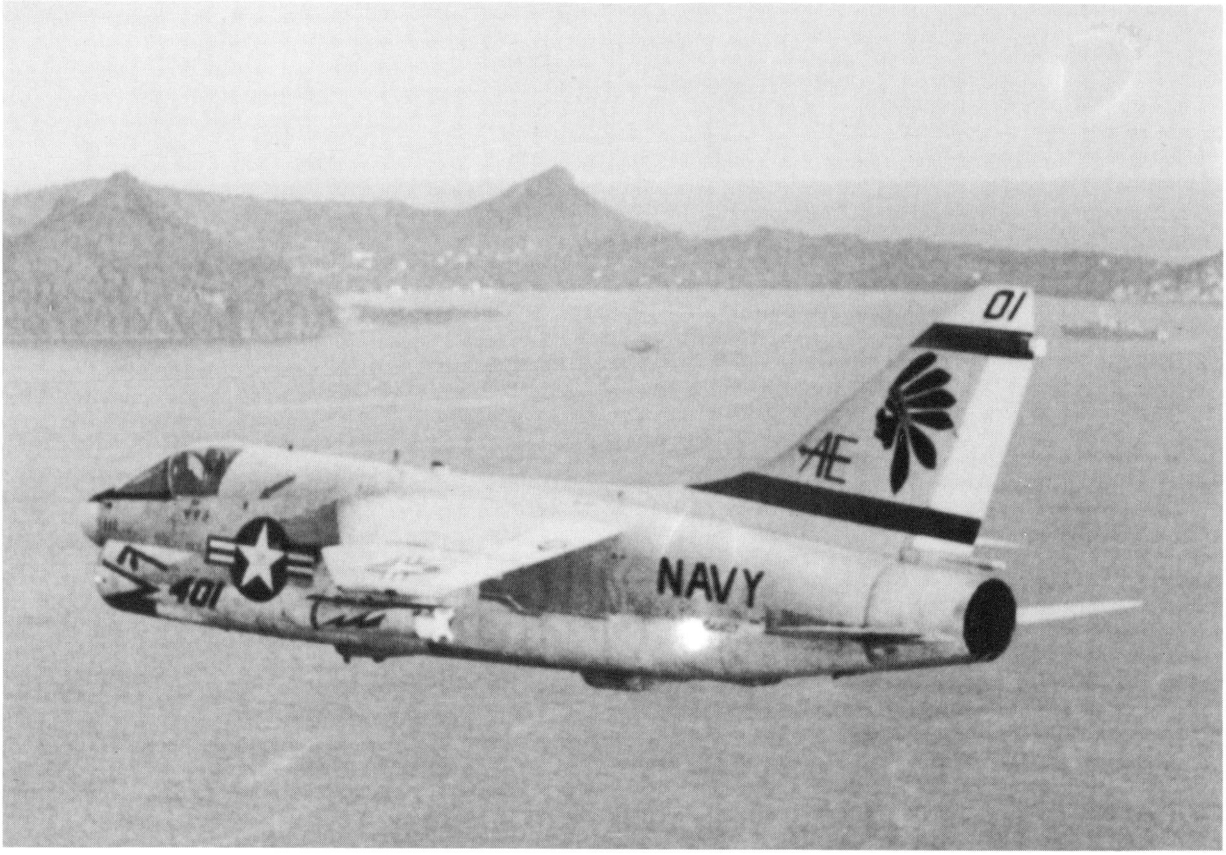
01
AE
NAVY
401

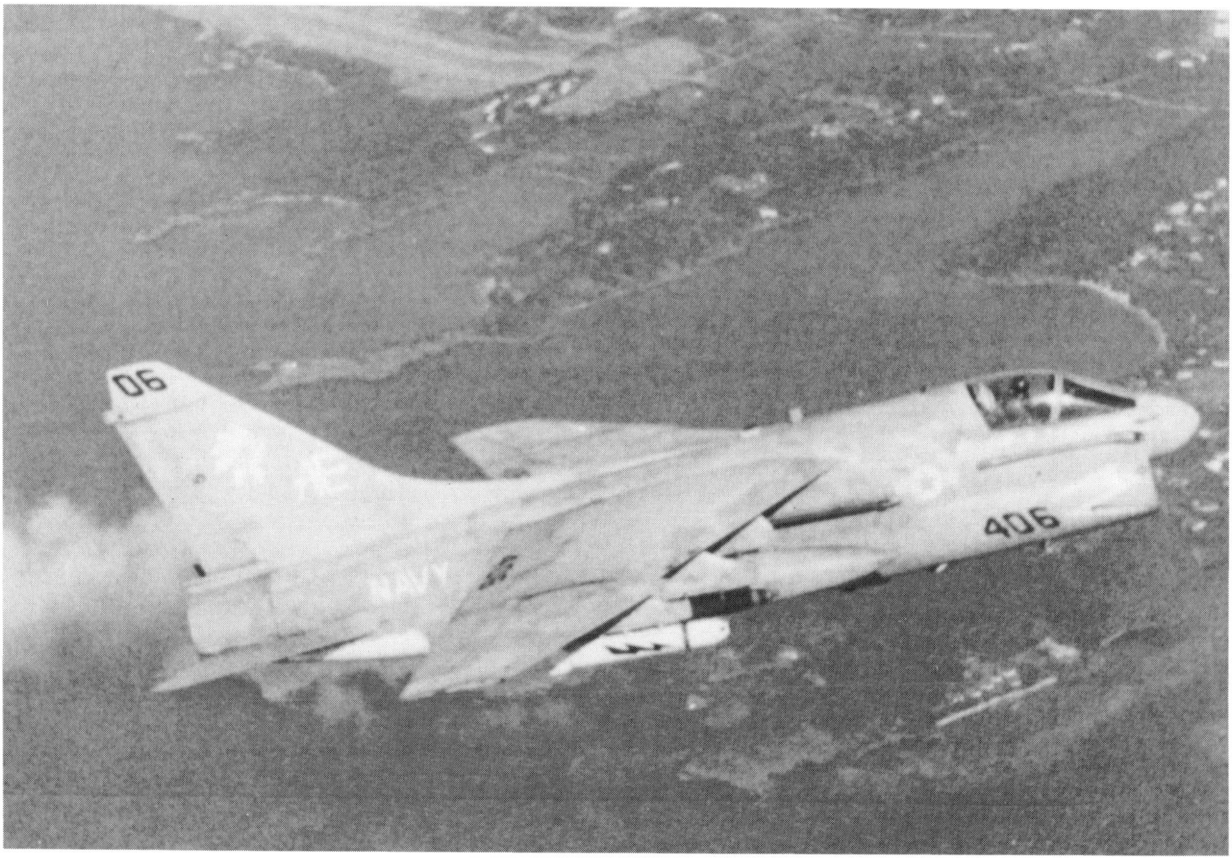
06
406
NAVY

Corsair 406, different location. After dropping bombs in Grenada and Lebanon, attack squadron VA-87 continued with Independence *to the coast of Norway, seen here, where its A-7Es operated in near-Arctic conditions (US Navy)*

TOP LEFT
Grenada in high visibility . . . During the 'ten-day war' in October 1983, A-7E Corsair (156804), side number AE-401, of the 'Golden Warriors' of VA-87 approaches the Grenada shoreline, ready to go in over the beach with Mk 20 Rockeye II cluster bomb units. Few A-7Es were still painted in these old-style markings on the Independence *cruise which took VA-87 to Grenada and Lebanon (US Navy)*

BOTTOM LEFT
Grenada in low visibility . . . Banking over Grenada's Point Salines Airport in October 1983, A-7E of the 'Golden Warriors' of VA-87 wears subdued gray paint scheme and carries Rockeye, Mk 82 bombs, and external fuel. VA-87 and sister squadron VA-15 dropped bombs in Grenada and Lebanon, then went on to operations in Norway, all in the same cruise aboard Independence *(US Navy)*

4 December 1983

Looking back at the 4 December 1983 air strike flown by *Independence* and *Kennedy* in Lebanon, it is difficult to know why the strike needed to be flown that day and not the day before or the day after. It is equally unclear whether the mission was a success or a failure. For the Vought A-7E Corsair, it was an introduction to the kind of high-intensity fighting which Israel, Syria and others had frequently experienced in the Middle East.

The day before, the Syrians directed heavy ground fire and ten SAMs at a pair of F-14A TARPS Tomcat reconnaissance flights, apparently launched by the 'Swordsmen' of fighter squadron VF-32 under Cdr J C Sherlock. The earlier quote by an F-14A pilot denigrating this mission was only one man's opinion. VF-32 was proud of supporting US Marines and the international peace-keeping force in Beirut and VF-32's Tomcats flew 20 such missions, several of which were subjected to confirmed hostile fire from Syrian and Druse positions.

The air strike was launched in the full knowledge that the Syrian positions were heavily fortified and that Syria possessed SA-5 missiles within its own territory that could in theory hit American airplanes taking off from *Independence* and *Kennedy*. The attack force comprised 28 aircraft. Its precise composition has not been disclosed but it included seven A-6E TRAM Intruders from VA-85 on *Kennedy*, seven A-7E Corsairs with Mk 20 Rockeye II CBU bombs and Sidewinders from VA-87 and an unknown number of A-7E Corsairs from VA-15, both from *Independence*. The strike was led by *Indy*'s carrier air wing commander (CAG), Cdr Edward K Andrews, flying an A-7E (160738), side number AE-300, belonging to the 'Valions' of VA-15. Andrews was a well-known pilot more often at the controls of

Seen through the camera lens of the US Navy's JOCS, Kirby Harrison, arguably the widest-travelled photojournalist in the world, A-7E Corsairs of VA-15 and VA-87 line up on the deck of Independence *ready for operations in the Beirut area on 6 December 1983 (US Navy)*

RIGHT
Two days after the 4 December 1983 air strike in Lebanon, Naval Aviation News' *globe-girdling JOCS, Kirby Harrison, was on the flight deck of* Independence *to photograph this A-7E Corsair of VA-87 preparing for another mission near Beirut. With a AIM-9L Sidewinder casting a silhouette against the fuselage, pilot looks down for a signal from the deck crewman (US Navy)*

an F-14A who had once had a role in the making of a Hollywood motion picture on carrier aviation, *The Final Countdown.*

President Reagan had authorized the attack and was monitoring it from Camp David, although he wisely left tactical decisions to Andrews and other commanders in the field. As they crossed the beach and rolled in, the attack pilots faced some of the heaviest missile and AAA fire Americans have ever encountered. It can be assumed that the A-7E Corsairs were using Goodyear ALE-39 flare and chaff dispensers as well as more active ECM measures to make the task of Syrian defenders more difficult. The Lebanese state radio said the Intruders and Corsairs struck at Jabal al Knaisse and Mghite, 19 miles (30.5 km) east of Beirut. It is thought that a covering force of F-14A Tomcats was led by *Kennedy*'s CAG, Cdr J J Mazach, although no Syrian MiGs rose to challenge the attack force.

OVERLEAF
Typical of the subdued paint scheme on today's naval aircraft is the light gray of these A-7E Corsairs of the 'Clansmen' of attack squadron VA-46, an east coast unit flying temporarily from NAS Fallon, Nevada and photographed in 1984 by Robert L Lawson of The Hook, *journal of the Tailhook Association (Robert L Lawson)*

404

VA-46
301
306

301
306
NAVY

NJ
00
40
NJ
VFA 125
NAVY
540

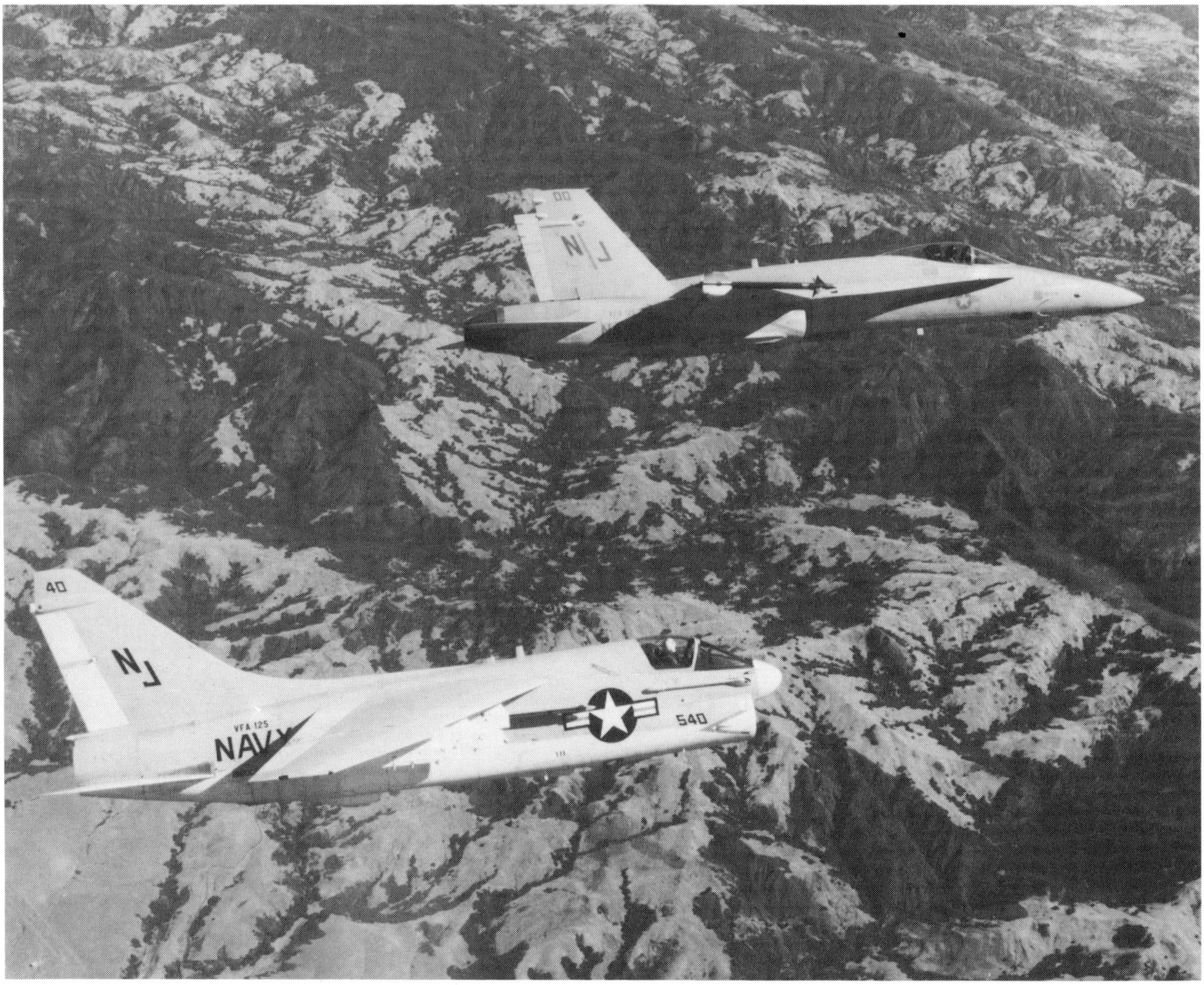

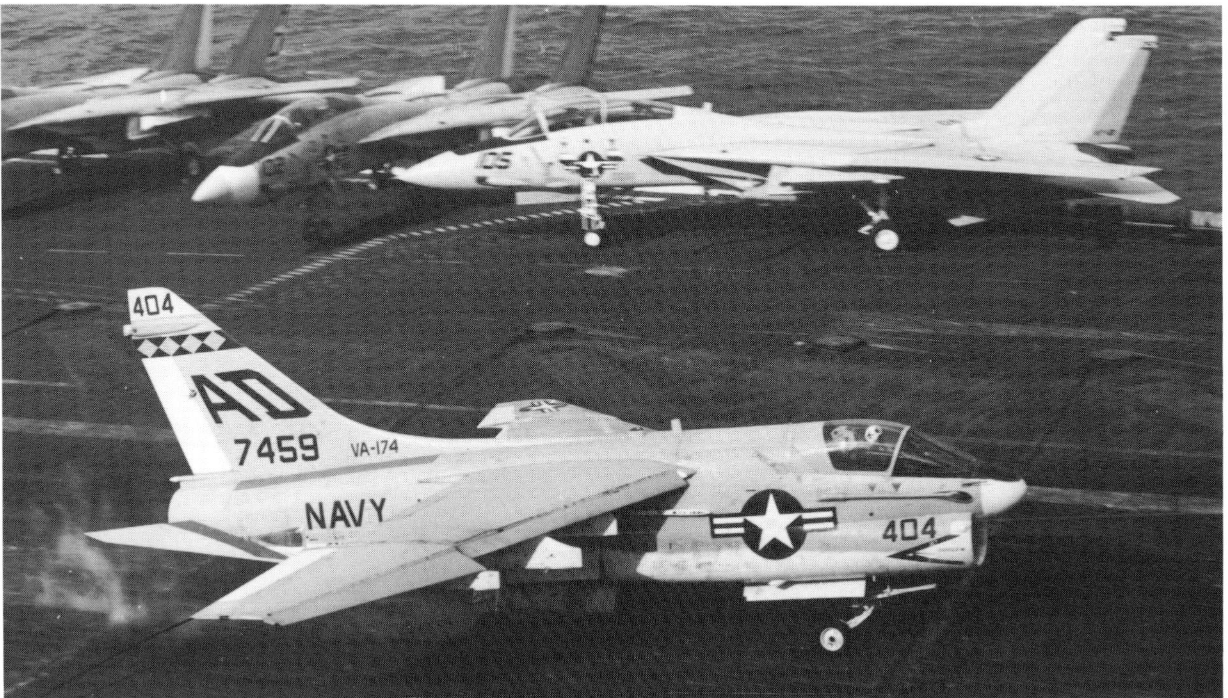

404
AD
7459
VA-174
NAVY
404

LEFT
While strike fighter squadron VFA-125 becomes the west coast RAG for the F/A-18A Hornet, it also operates A-7E Corsairs for transitional purposes. Skipper Cdr Dennis McGinn has flown both, praises both. F/A-18A (161250) side number NJ-500 is trailed over the California mountains near Lemoore in 1981 by A-7E (158009), side number NJ-540
(MDC)

BOTTOM LEFT
Tomcats in the background may symbolize a new era, but the veteran Corsair still remains at the front lines. A-7E (157459) side number AD-404 of the east coast RAG, attack squadron VA-174, catches the wire in the early seventies
(Don Spering)

A-6E Intruder No 556 of VA-85 was hit by a SAM. Forced to eject over Syrian territory, pilot Lt Mark Lange died from injuries sustained while punching out. Lt Bobby Goodman, the Intruder's bombardier-navigator, parachuted safely but was captured—and held until his release weeks later during a visit to Damascus by presidential candidate Jesse Jackson. Hostile photos of the mangled tail of the downed Intruder were widely published to suggest that the American air strike had been a failure.

It apparently was not. Despite withering gunfire and criss-crossing SAMs, CAG Andrews kept his strike aircraft in the region for some time and attempted to mount an SAR (search and rescue) effort for Lange and Goodman while continuing to pound Syrian emplacements. Once out of ordnance, Andrews defied the Syrian defences by zooming down over their heads again and again, popping off quick bursts with his 20 mm M61A1 gun.

Then Andrews, too, was hit. He banked toward Beirut and ejected over the troubled city.

His A-7E kept flying for a few moments and went down in the village of Zuk Mkayel a few miles northeast of the capital. The Corsair crashed into a villa where a mother, three daughters and two sons were sleeping. A villager said later, 'There was a horrific noise, as if the devil was coming to visit.' No one was killed by the plummeting A-7E and Cdr Andrews, fortunately, was picked up by the wind. His parachute was carried out to sea within eyesight of Beirut's Casino du Liban and he was quickly rescued.

Two aircraft lost out of 28. One man killed, one captured, one rescued. Undisclosed damage to Syrian gun and missile emplacements. It was an ambiguous end to an isolated air action. The peacekeeping effort in Lebanon also ended in ambiguity, as modern situations often do.

Whatever else may be said of abbreviated air combat in Grenada and Lebanon, it proved again the mettle of the Vought A-7 Corsair II, an accomplished weapon of war which has received far too little attention and never enough praise. Lt K C Albright, one of *Eisenhower*'s VA-12 pilots who used green ink in Lebanon, says that, 'The A-7 is a good aircraft. It performs a diverse mission. You feel good flying it and you know you have an excellent chance of surviving out there.'

Not everyone does survive. Over the years, a share of men who work on the Corsair, and who fly it, have taken the last cut. The final page of a cruise book for a US Navy carrier deployment which included two A-7 Corsair squadrons contains a sobering message in memorium to those claimed by air, sea and enemy. IN ANY ARMED CONFLICT, MANY OF A NATION'S FINEST SONS ARE LOST. The carriers which fought in the Mediterranean in 1983 left some men behind. The finest tribute that can be paid to the A-7 Corsair is that, with due recognition that all carrier operations are dangerous, A-7 squadrons have lost no more men on extended combat cruises than on extended cruises in peace-time. In Grenada and Lebanon at least, while inflicting heavy punishment on its adversaries, the A-7 Corsair left no one behind. The ultimate aim of any carrier cruise is to bring back every man who went out, and Vought's gifted designer Russell Clark must have had that in mind when he put the first A-7 sketches on paper two decades before Lebanon.

Chapter 2
'Devil's Advocate' in Dallas
Design, Development and Flight Test

This time someone really *had* stepped on the blueprints.

In September 1965, when the prototype Vought A-7A Corsair II (152580) was rolled out into the Texas sunlight, the new US Navy attack aircraft looked like a shortened, scrunched-up mutation of the manufacturer's better-known and long-established Crusader fighter. It was a year now since the Crusader had gone into combat during the Gulf of Tonkin incident and it would be another year, yet, before the Crusader began chalking up its tally of twenty MiG kills over North Vietnam. Americans were at war. The open-mouthed, high-wing Crusader was the principal cause of Vought's reputation as a builder of carrier-based combat aircraft able to fight and win wars.

The new plane was something else. It wasn't true, of course, but the A-7A gave the distinct impression that somebody had taken a Crusader, sat on it, and compressed it in accordion fashion. The Crusader was sleek and fast. The A-7A was chunky and subsonic. 'The A-7 did not initially arouse a whole bunch of enthusiasm,' confesses Cdr James J McBride, who knows.

Years later, an A-7 pilot would speak of how crestfallen he'd felt on being assigned to the short little ugly f**ker (SLUF), as the A-7 is known in pilot circles. Before that, the pilot had flown supersonic jets. 'I was demoralized. I had been a blazing jet jock

A-7E (buno 157443), coded AG-300, of the 'Waldomen' of attack squadron VA-66 carries practice ordnance accompanying sister squadron A-6E Intruders on a Mediterranean flight from USS Independence *(CV-62) in 1976. This aircraft was assigned to the carrier air wing commander (CAG). VA-66 later moved to the decks of USS Eisenhower* (CVN-69) *and some of its pilots were credited with combat missions operating from Bagel Station off the coast of Lebanon in November 1983 (LTV)*

and now I was pilot of a slow, ugly beast. But my unhappiness lasted only until my first mission. Suddenly, everything was different. Suddenly, we were navigating with pinpoint accuracy and our bombs *were actually falling right on target*. After that, SLUF became a term, to me, not of derision but of endearment . . .'

152580, the first Corsair, hadn't even flown yet but Vought and its wiry director of flight operations, John W Konrad, were under some pressure. The Pentagon's aircraft-purchasing procedures had been tightened and toughened in the early 1960s, and tightened still farther by 1965 when Americans were in battle. The new plane had an uncommonly rigid set of requirements to live up to, and fast. Says Konrad, 'The . . . flight test demonstration program, by contract, was required to be completed one year after the first flight. This meant that all formal demonstrations, structural, flutter, spins, carrier suitability and ordnance separation and accuracy tests were to proceed separately at three different test sites.'

Much later, Konrad would be enthusiastic about the new attack plane: 'Early in the flight test program, the aircraft showed great promise as a light attack airplane with virtuous flying qualities, long range, and exceptional capabilities to handle heavy external loads.' But at Vought's Dallas plant in early September 1965, no one could know yet that the A-7 Corsair II was at the beginning of a long and phenomenally successful career. No one could know that the new airplane would not merely fly well but fight well, and that a knock-down, drag-out slugfest lay in its immediate future. In Dallas in September 1965, John Konrad had no way to know that the maiden flight of 152580, progenitor of Corsairs to follow, would last exactly five minutes and accomplish exactly nothing.

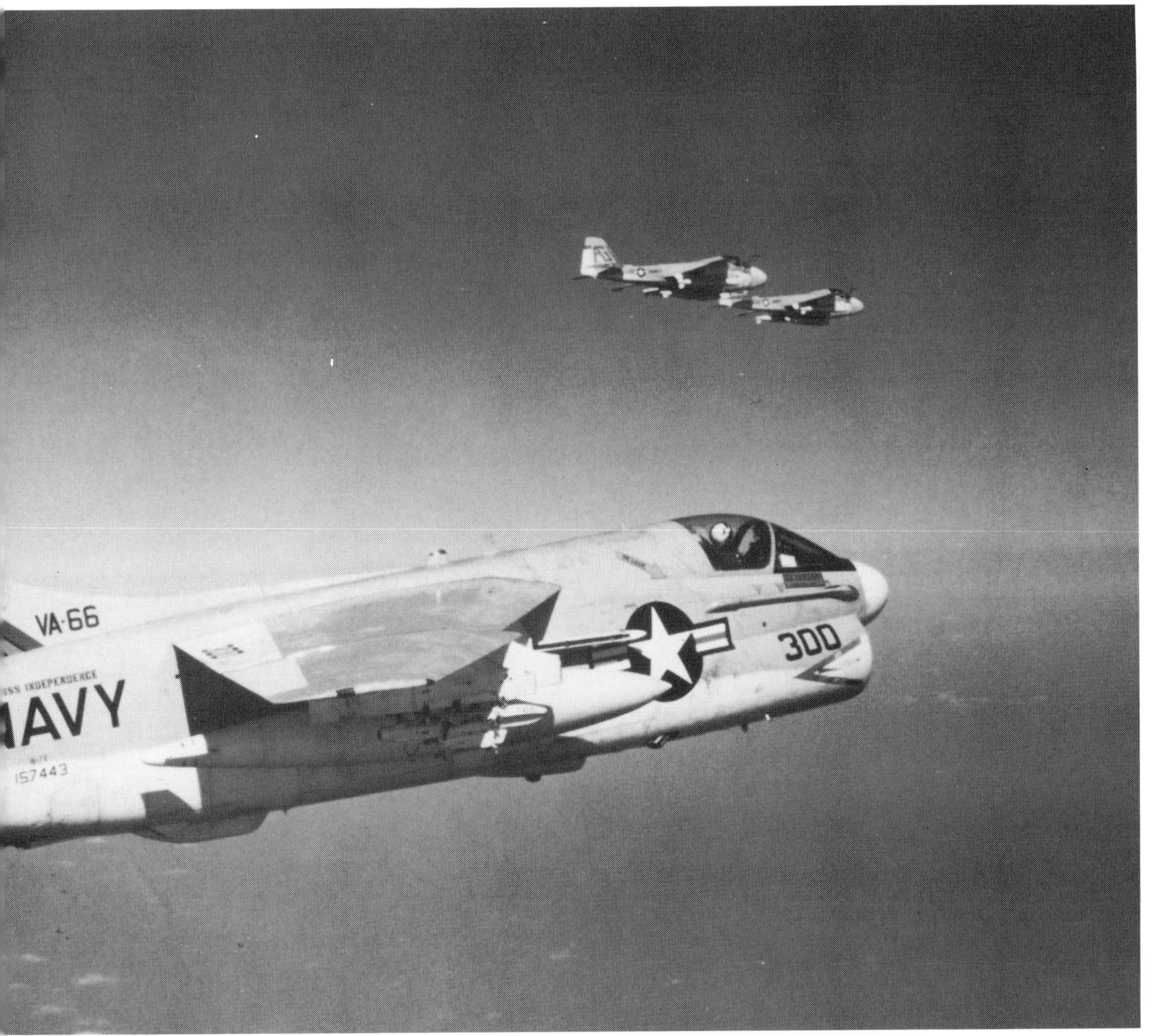

Corsair Tradition

Chance Milton Vought learned how to fly from the Wright Brothers in 1910. Vought and a handful of men threw together a company in a third-floor loft in Long Island City, New York and used resourcefulness, spit, and bailing wire to create the VE-7 biplane of 1917. Two years later, the Lewis and Vought Corporation was founded, Lewis being not an aeronaut but a financier. On 17 October 1922, a Vought VE-7SF piloted by Lt V C Griffith made the first take-off from the US Navy's first aircraft carrier, the USS *Langley* (CV-1). In 1926, planemaker Vought personally supervised the painting of an imaginative nickname on the rudder of the O2U-1 observation biplane he'd sold to the US Navy. VOUGHT CORSAIR, it said.

It was an unofficial name. On 1 January 1928, Lt Christian F Schilt of the US Marine Corps, under fire in Chipote, Nicaragua, won the highest American award for bravery, the Medal of Honor, for strapping 18 wounded troops to the wings of his O2U-1 Corsair and flying them out to safety. It was *still* an unofficial name. The first Corsair to own the name outright, the quintessential Corsair, lay one war ahead.

In 1929, the Vought firm merged with the Pratt & Whitney and Boeing airplane companies to form United Aircraft and Technology Corporation. Vought himself died in 1930 but his name would grace carrier-borne warplanes for the remainder of the century. The Vought company's offices moved to Stratford, Connecticut where a divorce from Pratt & Whitney and a shotgun marriage to a dissimilar firm made it Vought-Sikorsky (until January 1943) before resuming the Chance Vought name while remaining a division of United Aircraft (now United Technologies). The corporate offices may have been in the northeast but the principal factory was in Dallas, still a cowtown, still in the rugged West. The individualism which had won and shaped the raw American west was to show up, unmistakably, in the combat aircraft to emerge from that plant in the Dallas suburb of Grand Prairie.

On 29 May 1940, test pilot Lyman A Bullard made the maiden flight in Stratford of a machine to be manufactured in Dallas, a gull-winged naval fighter powered by a 2,000 hp (1492 kW) Pratt & Whitney R-2800 radial. At 405 mph (652 km/h), it was the first fighter in the world to be capable of speeds above 400 mph in straight and level flight. The Vought F4U Corsair fought from Guadalcanal to Tokyo, claiming

NAS Oceana, near Virginia Beach, Va., is the east coast home of the F-4s in background, but attack aircraft are strictly visitors which have their own roost farther south at NAS Cecil Field, Florida. A-7E (buno 158028) coded AA-403 of the 'Sunliners' of VA-81 aboard USS Forrestal *(CVA-59) at Oceana on 12 May 1977 has its wings partly folded, giving it an unintended resemblance to the gull-winged, prop-driven F4U Corsair (Jim Sullivan)*

VA-81
USS FORRESTAL
NAVY
A-7E
58028

Guarding its carrier USS Coral Sea *(CVA-43) on a cruise in the Indian Ocean, A-7E (buno 159970) coded NK-307 of the 'Warhawks' of VA-97 flies escort on Soviet Ilyushin Il-38* May *reconnaissance aircraft in 1979. A-7E has a strong secondary capability for air-to-air combat, but this machine is not carrying Sidewinders on its fuselage rails and would be able to use only its 20 mm M61A1 cannon*
(USN via Jim Sullivan)

2,140 Japanese aircraft destroyed with 189 losses, a victory ratio of 11.4 to 1. No fewer than 12,571 Corsairs were manufactured, making it among the half-dozen most numerous fighter types in history. F4U Corsairs fought in Korea and one shot down a MiG-15. Small wonder that almost everyone thought this was the first aircraft to bear the 'CORSAIR' name. If it were never painted on any other airframe, the name had attained immortality.

Vought's XF5U-1 'Flapjack,' a saucer-shaped STOL aircraft and its F6U-1 Pirate, an early jet, kept the company alive as a builder of Navy fighters until the F7U-1 Cutlass was unveiled in 1948. The first US jet fighter designed from the outset to use afterburners, the US Navy's first sweptwing fighter, and the first to release bombs while flying faster than the speed of sound, the F7U Cutlass enjoyed a brief and largely forgetable career with the Fleet before Vought's Crusader arrived to restore the company to the first rank of fighter manufacturers.

On 25 March 1955 at sunbaked Edwards AFB in the California desert, test pilot John Konrad lifted off in the Vought XF8U-1 Crusader (139899) and exceeded Mach 1 on the maiden flight. Powered by a

TOP RIGHT
The 'real' Corsair, to many, was the gull-winged, propeller-driven Vought F4U manufactured from April 1940 through February 1953 and credited with 64,051 combat sorties in World War II. On 24 July 1953, US Navy Reserve pilot Lt William D Clark of VF-873 stationed at NAS Oakland, California flies over the northwest side of Mount Rainier, Washington, at the controls of Vought F4U-4 Corsair (buno 96783) coded F-2. F4U Corsairs saw further action in Korea and remained in service through the late 1950s
(USN)

BOTTOM RIGHT
The Vought fighter tradition continued with the F7U Cutlass of the 1950s. Twin afterburners lit, an F7U-3 undergoing CARQUAL (carrier qualification) tests is launched from the USS Hancock *(CVA-19) in about 1953*
(Vought)

NAVY

11,150 lb (5057 kg) thrust Pratt & Whitney J57-P-12, the Crusader was to earn a reputation as a single-seat, cannon-armed, close-in gunfighter. On 21 August 1956, Cdr R W 'Duke' Windsor flew a Crusader over China Lake, California to a speed of 1,015.248 mph (1633.879 km/h), falling slightly short of the world's absolute speed record but marking the first occasion when a fully operational fighter had exceeded 1,000 mph (1609 km/h).

On 16 July 1957, Maj John Glenn flew an F8U-1P Crusader photo ship from Los Angeles to New York in 3 hours 22 minutes, the first transcontinental speed run sustained at Mach 1, averaging 723.52 mph (1164.389 km/h) despite three subsonic refuelling contacts at speeds below 300 mph (482.80 km/h). The Crusader went to sea on carrier decks. It went to the Marine Corps. It went to the French Navy. Later, pitted against an able and determined adversary, it went to Hanoi.

On 31 December 1960, having shed its United Aircraft mantle and shifted its corporate headquarters to Dallas, the manufacturer became the Chance Vought Corporation. In July 1961, entreprenneur James J Ling merged Ling-Temco Electronics with the Chance Vought Corporation to create Ling-Temco-Vought, Inc., soon to be abbreviated LTV. Several name changes have followed, each with the Vought identity being preserved in what, today, is called the LTV Aerospace and Defense Corporation.

Vought's second-generation F8U-3 Crusader lost out in a fly-off competition with a McDonnell product, the F4H-1. But the original Crusader retained enormous 'stretching' potential. While pilots raved about it, maintenance people saw its unique, high-wing configuration from a special viewpoint: virtually every access point on the aircraft could be reached without ladders or scaffolds. In a college term paper, A-7 Corsair weapons load technician Richard Stemen of Columbus, Ohio would write, 'The best feature retained from the F-8 design to the A-7 was the high wing, which allows

Swirling war clouds in Vietnam engendered the urgency which led the US Navy, in its VAL competition of 1963–64, to seek a new attack aircraft based upon a proven design. Though the A-7 Corsair II was a new airplane, it owed its heritage to the F-8 Crusader which served with the Fleet for nearly three decades. This classic portrait of Vought airframe expertise depicts F-8J Crusader (buno 150347), coded NM-202, of the 'Hellfires' of VA-194—at the time aboard USS Oriskany *(CVA-34) and in battle in Vietnam—landing at NAF Atsugi, Japan on 2 August 1972*
(Masumi Wada)

RIGHT
In 1964–65, Vought's design engineers were confronted with a challenge no less demanding than to create a replacement for the formidable Douglas A-4 Skyhawk. The Vought design was to have heavier armament and greater range than the much-loved A-4. A 'Road Runner' emblem adorns mid-fuselage of A-4C (buno 149519), coded AA-511 of attack squadron VA-36 from USS Forrestal, *at Forbes AFB, Kansas in 1970*
(Jerry Geer)

BOTTOM RIGHT
J Russell Clark, designer of the A-7 Corsair II
(LTV)

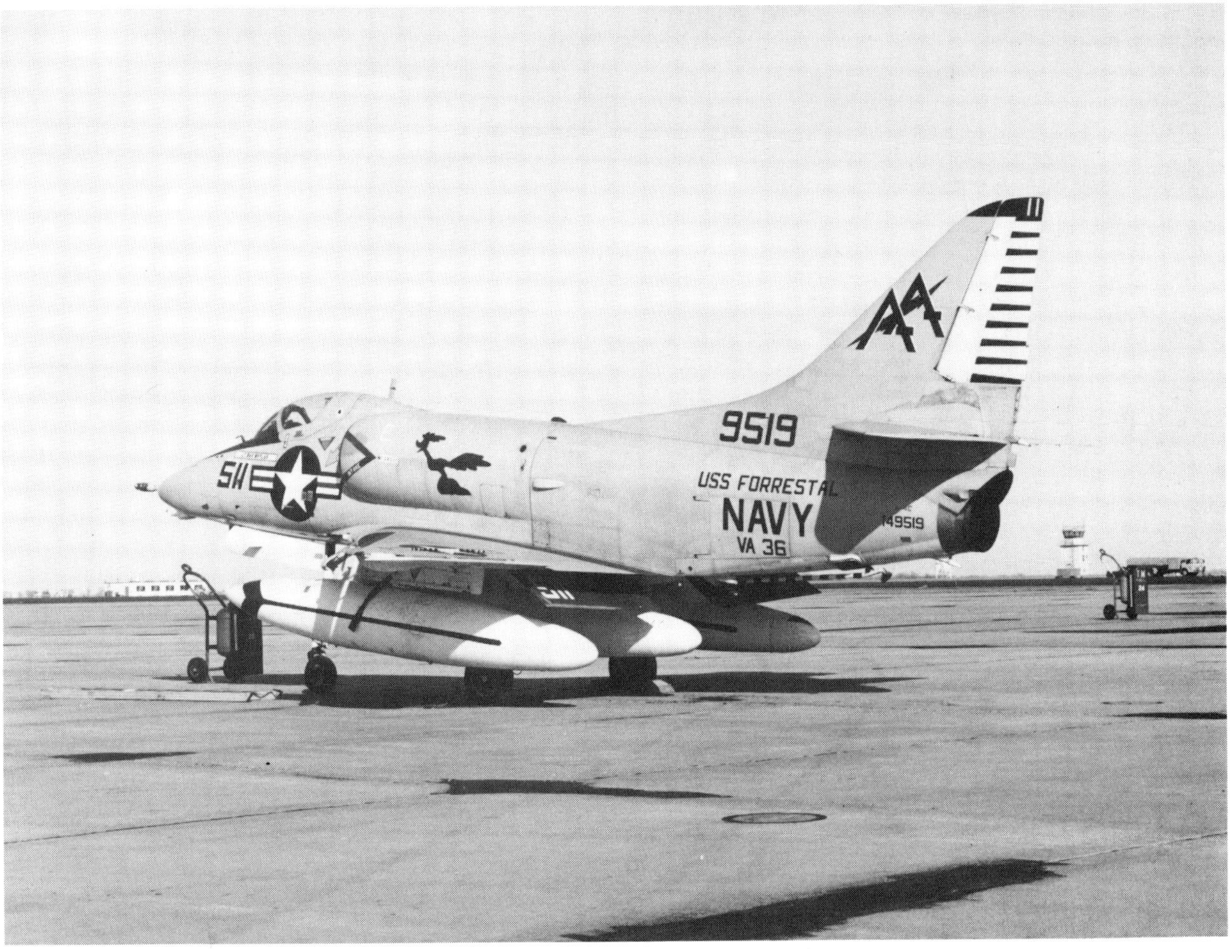

202

easier weapons loading and walk-round maintenance.' A scrunched-up Crusader it might be, but ground and deck crewmen were going to love the A-7 Corsair II.

Design and Development

On 11 February 1964, the US Navy announced that LTV Vought Aeronautics Division had won a design competition for a new single-seat carrier-based light attack aircraft to supplement and later replace the Douglas A-4 Skyhawk. *That* was no small order, for the light, nimble Skyhawk had emerged from the design genius of Douglas's Edward H Heinemann and was so loved, so respected, so needed that it would remain in production for two more decades. But an attack plane with greater payload and range was needed and Vought had earned the job. The development contract was awarded to Vought on 19 March 1964.

Behind announcement and contract lay an intense effort. First, there had been the design competition for an advanced Navy attack aircraft (VAX). The airplane which would have emerged from the 1963 competition, as was soon determined, required too much lead time and expense. It would take half a decade to develop a 100% new engine and airframe. To save time and exploit existing technology, the Navy shifted gears, abandoned VAX, and launched a new competition for a light attack aircraft (VAL). The VAL effort under project manager Capt Henry Suerstedt was a three-year project which examined virtually every aspect of the Navy's carrier-based attack aircraft needs.

Specifications called for a small low-cost machine capable of carrying immense and varied payloads over great distances. The intent was to reach a fast solution by modifying an existing aircraft design. It fell upon Vought to muster its design, sales and political forces to seek success in the VAL contest.

Vought brought together the men who had designed and developed the Crusader—Russell Clark, Sol Love, William C Schoolfield, Paul W Hare and others. Clark is the design genius, the mind behind the Crusader's unorthodox but highly successful configuration. Sol Love, later to be vice president for A-7 operations and still later the firm's chief executive, brought to the VAL exercise a combination of skills almost too formidable to believe. He was, at once, pilot, administrator, and corporate executive. Apparently, it was he who

Not yet named Corsair II, an appellation which resulted from a contest among Vought employees, the full-scale mock-up of the A-7A carries Sidewinders and bombs at the Vought plant in Dallas on 25 June 1964
(LTV)

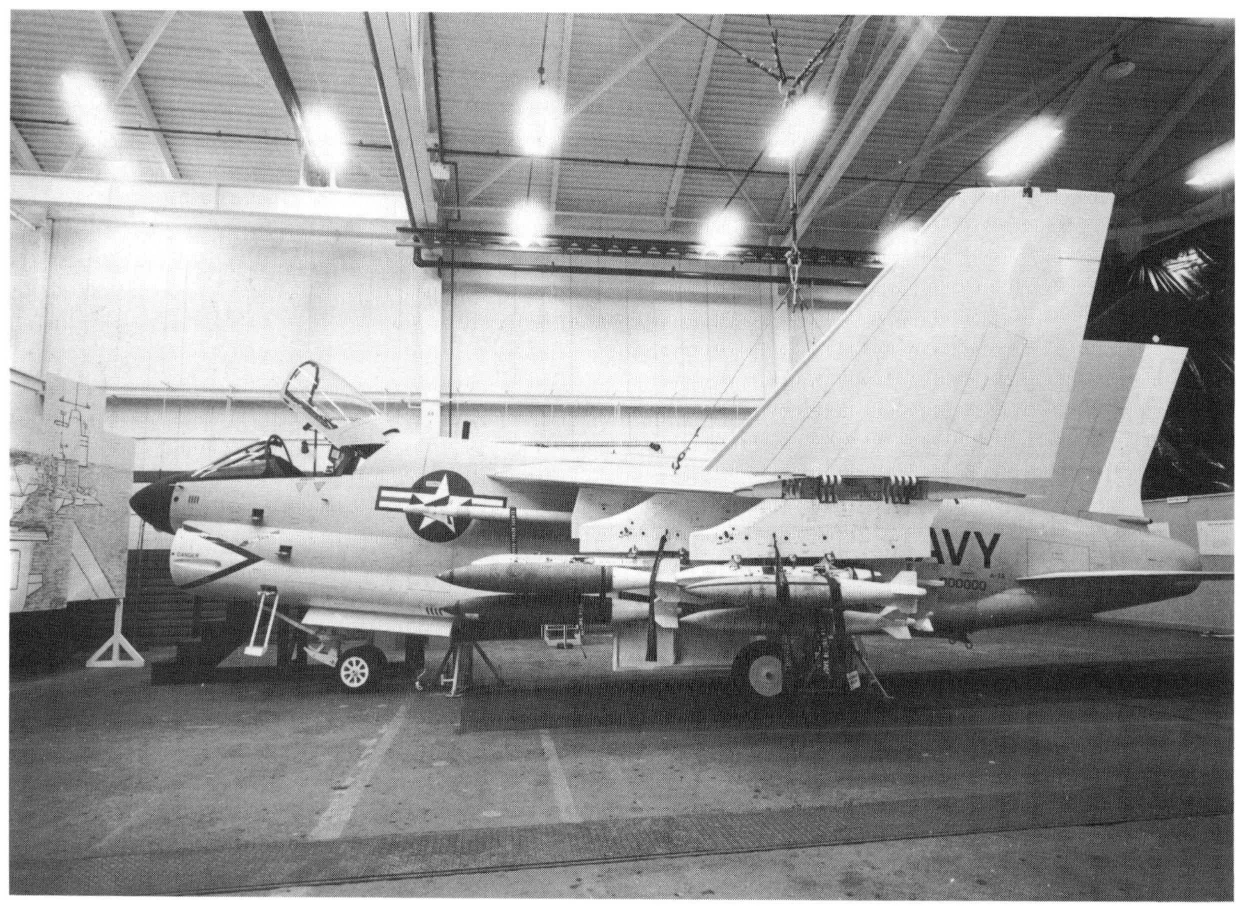

suggested that the company form two competing groups—called Red Team and Blue Team—to vy with each other in just the way Vought was vying with Douglas and Grumman. Rodger Ringham, Vought divisional chief engineer, called this the 'devil's advocate approach'. It seems to have instilled the fervour and dedication which won the VAL contract and produced the A-7A.

Russell Clark was one of that handful of distinguished American designers, like Ed Heinemann of Douglas and Lee Begin of Northrop, who have influenced the size and shape of US combat aircraft in a profound and permanent way. Clark, who is quietly retired in Texas today, created not merely the F-8 Crusader but the very promising if unsuccessful F8U-3 Crusader III. If a Russell Clark design philosophy shines forth from his airplanes, it is one of sturdiness, maintainability and effective use of load-carrying potential. Clark may also be credited, as an LTV colleague put it, with designing 'the most, best airplanes which do the job superlatively well but would never win a beauty contest.'

A company document which ticks off milestones in the design of the new attack aircraft, given the company model number V-461 and later V-463, Love is portrayed as insisting that the Crusader canopy be made to fit the new design. An office cartoon dated 4 July 1963 pokes fun at Love for requiring the V-461 design team to work on the holiday marking American independence. A few days later, the document notes that LTV Astronautics people—grabbed away from the firm's space programmes—were dragooned into the V-461 design effort to make things move faster. By 25 July 1963, the document suggests that the new attack aircraft—now the company V-463 and jokingly given the spurious Navy designation A3U-1—needed a radiation shield to protect the pilot. Like many modern warplanes, the A-7 would eventually be equipped with just such a blast shield to protect its pilot from the flash effects of a nuclear explosion but the Vought document suggests a different purpose: to save the pilot from a cloud of fumes eminating from the pipe-smoking Sol Love.

On 25 June 1964, the full-scale A-7A mockup, with bogus bureau number 000000 and very real-looking bombs, was shown to Navy officers at the Dallas plant. The mockup retained the pointed nose radome of the Crusader, blunted-off on the actual A-7 aircraft to conserve carrier deck space. The mockup also had features which would be retained by the real A-7

Not yet painted, prototype A-7A Corsair II (buno 152580) is moved out-of-doors into Dallas sunshine in about August 1965, well in advance of its formal roll-out (LTV)

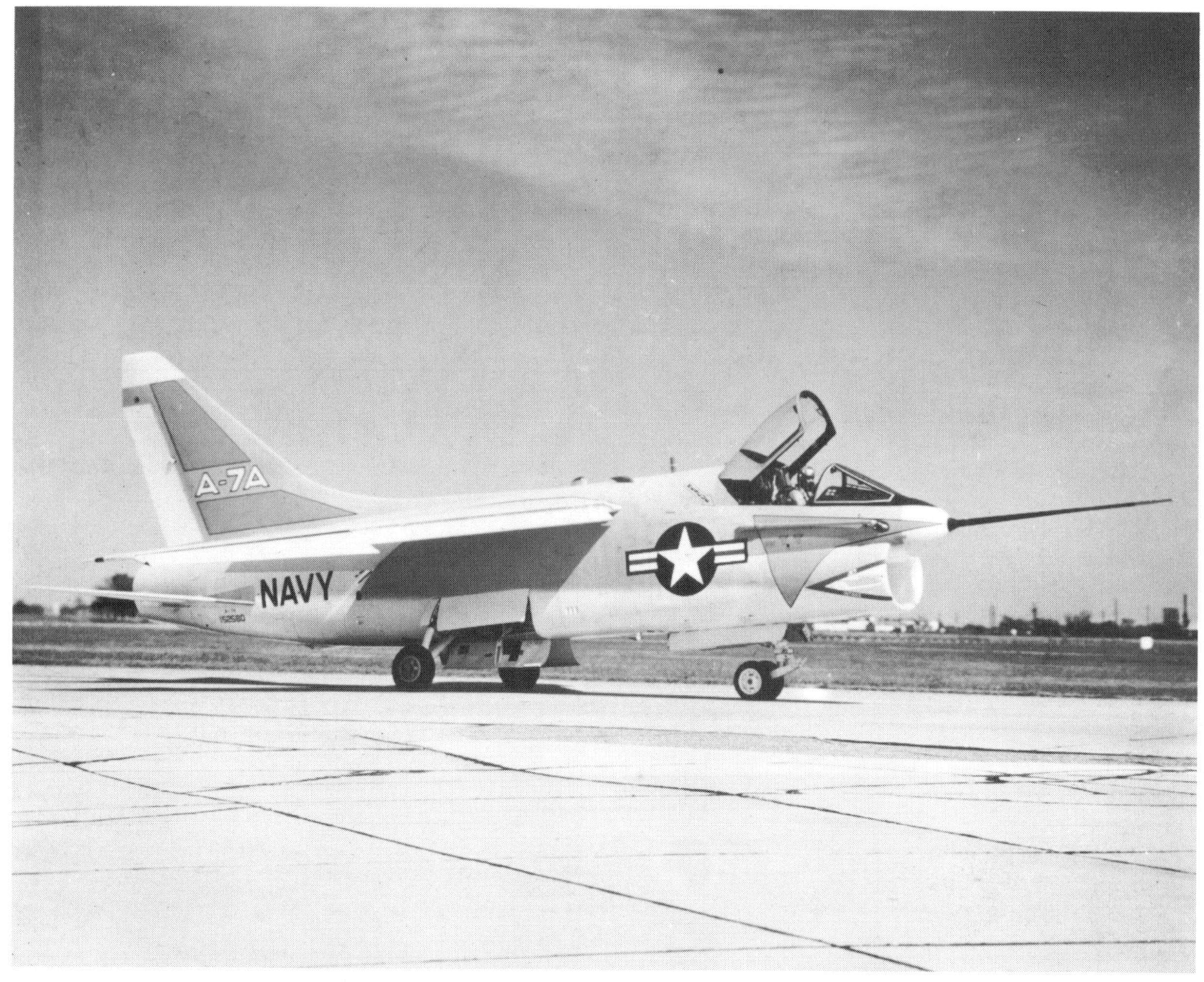

throughout its production run—widened fuselage to accommodate a generous supply of fuel and computerized navigation/delivery gear, uplifted rear fuselage to allow more deck/ground clearance on rotation, folding wings, and a chopped-off upper rear vertical fin to save carrier deck space (later negated by retrofit of a tail ECM antenna fairing). In addition to its bombload, the mockup A-7 carried twin AIM-9 Sidewinder heat-seeking air-to-air missiles on fuselage rails. The powerplant envisioned at the time, in a spirit of commonality with the Navy's ill-starred F-111B, was the Pratt & Whitney TF30 turbofan engine. Despite its Crusader lineage, the A-7 was designed from the outset to be subsonic. While 152580, the prototype A-7A, was taking shape, a company study confirmed that strike aircraft derived little benefit from supersonic speed—except when outrunning MiGs.

On 15 January 1965, engineering design of the A-7A was formally completed. There was a sense of excitement in Dallas now that models, mockup, drawings, were to become cold steel. The next step was to finish 152580 and fly it. Because of the concentrated effort, the first flight would take place 25 days ahead of schedule.

Test pilot John W Konrad at the controls, the number one A-7A (buno 152580) taxies in the Dallas sunshine at about the time of its 27 September 1965 first flight. Navy-style refuelling probe on right side of nose is clearly visible but was a non-working dummy on the prototype
(LTV)

RIGHT
John W Konrad, Vought's chief of flight test, had flown the first Crusader and did most of the early test flying in the A-7
(LTV)

The First Flight

Americans had gone into Vietnam in the early 1960s and their numbers had steadily risen. After the August 1964 Gulf of Tonkin incident, a major buildup was underway. In April 1965, President Lyndon Johnson had authorized air attacks against North Vietnam in a protracted, hard-fought campaign called Rolling Thunder. The A-4 Skyhawk was performing admirably as the principal Navy carrier-based attack plane while the campaign over the North continued in September 1965, but a machine with more fuel, ordnance and comfort was clearly needed.

First A-7A (buno 152580) in flight over Texas in 1965 (LTV)

RIGHT
A-7A prototype (buno 152580) carries twelve 350 lb (159 kg) Snakeye retarded bombs on an evaluation flight in 1965. Early ordnance-carrying tests resolved poor roll characteristics of bomb-laden prototypes. Ventral dive brake was designed to assist in manoeuvring the aircraft during low-level attack missions without noticeable trim change or buffeting (LTV)

Urgency hung over the A-7A Corsair test programme and if any shortcut could be taken to get the new aircraft into combat, it would be taken.

Says chief test pilot John W Konrad, 'The first flight and much of the subsequent testing was accomplished from NAS Dallas, adjacent to the Vought plant in Grand Prairie, Texas. Since the configuration resembled that of the F-8 and the Pratt & Whitney TF30 was being flown at the time in the F-111 aircraft, it was felt a reasonable risk to perform the first flight from the single runway at Navy Dallas instead of the more comfortable environment of the Edwards dry lake bed where other first flights have been conducted.' 152580 began taxi trials on 20 September 1965 with Konrad in the cockpit.

Two taxi tests were completed on 20 September. Konrad's recollection is that the second, conducted at high speed, included a brief lift-off—not to be confused with the equally brief and sharply curtailed first flight of a week later.

Minor difficulties with the hydraulic system were experienced and corrected. A discrepancy was also found in the pilot's ejection seat pan in that normal breathing back pressure was sufficient to cause the emergency oxygen supply to discharge when the ship's oxygen system was turned off. Ground handling characteristics were found to be satisfactory except at high idle thrust. Nose wheel steering and wheel brakes were judged outstanding.

In what Konrad called 'near perfect Texas weather' on 27 September 1965, Vought's chief test

pilot climbed aboard 152580 which, carrying a partial fuel load, grossed the scales at 22,650 lb (10,274 kg). The pilot's own report explains how he reached the cockpit to commence flight in the A-7A. 'Entry is easily accomplished by use of the manually retractable steps and hand holds provided. Ease of entry is facilitated by starting the climb to the cockpit with the right foot . . .'

Company test pilot Joseph O Engle banked overhead in the Lockheed T-33 chase plane. Konrad turned at runway's end, checking his systems. The low oil pressure warning light was not working correctly and engine idle thrust was unacceptably high.

Konrad's description of the maiden flight:

'The flight was very brief. As the aircraft accelerated following lift-off to the planned speed of 180 knots (270 km/h) a general airframe buffet occurred which increased in magnitude with increasing speed. Random control system shaking and hydraulic system oscillations were encountered which also increased with speed. The chase pilot reported that the horizontal tails were vibrating in a random manner to $2\frac{1}{2}/3\frac{1}{2}$ inch amplitude at the tip, together with random shaking of the wing trailing edge flaps. Since the driving force was unknown, a hasty 90/270 degree turn was accomplished followed by a downwind landing on the departure runway. A second flight was performed that same day, after a detailed inspection of the aircraft revealed that the flap slot tunnels were obstructed which most probably created separated air flow over the trailing edge flaps and disturbed turbulent flow over the horizontal tails.' Joe Engle in the T-33 had been mystified by the vibrations, although it was soon clear that the problem did not lie with the design of the A-7A airframe and would not impede flight testing.

Flight Testing

A second flight was undertaken immediately and Konrad found that retracting the trailing edge flaps prevented the general airframe buffeting which had cut short 152580's maiden voyage. The first flight had lasted .12 of an hour (5 minutes), the second 1.05 of an hour (1 hour, 2 minutes). In that Texas sunshine, the prototype A-7A, in standard Navy gray/white with red trim and a lengthy nose pitot probe, had begun the process of proving itself. Ahead lay proof under fire in Vietnam, Laos, Cambodia; in Grenada; in Lebanon. Ahead lay fulfillment of a promise by Secretary of the Navy Paul Nitze, who had praised this as the first aircraft since World War 2 to be developed specifically for close support of ground forces and the destruction of tactical targets in the battle area.

For now, there was a test programme to pursue.

The day after his first two flights, Konrad took 152580 aloft at a much heavier gross weight of 27,215 lb (12,344 kg), with full internal fuel for the first time. Tufts were added to the wing-flap area, horizontal tail and under-fuselage under the direction of company engineer Ray Salter. A company-owned chase/photographic aircraft was flown to provide visual and photographic observation of the tufts installed (presumably Engle in the T-33 again, although the record is not clear on this point). The third test flight lasted 1 hour 5 minutes. After completing the tuft studies with the chase aircraft giving close scrutiny, Konrad cleaned up the A-7A

Supplied by Don Wilson of LTV's air operations staff, photo was taken in the 1950s with an F8U-1 Crusader in background, but these men were key figures in the A-7 Corsair programme. Left to right:
Robert E Rostine, now deceased, who made the first flight in the A-7E model;
Stu Madison, company test pilot;
Ed Fitzgerald, company test pilot who made many early A-7 flights;
John Omvig, who ejected from the A-7A prototype (152580) on 23 March 1966 and was later killed in Vought's XC-142A aircraft;
Dick Hueholt, company test pilot and now an executive in Dallas;
John W Konrad, Vought's chief test pilot and the first man to fly an A-7
(LTV)

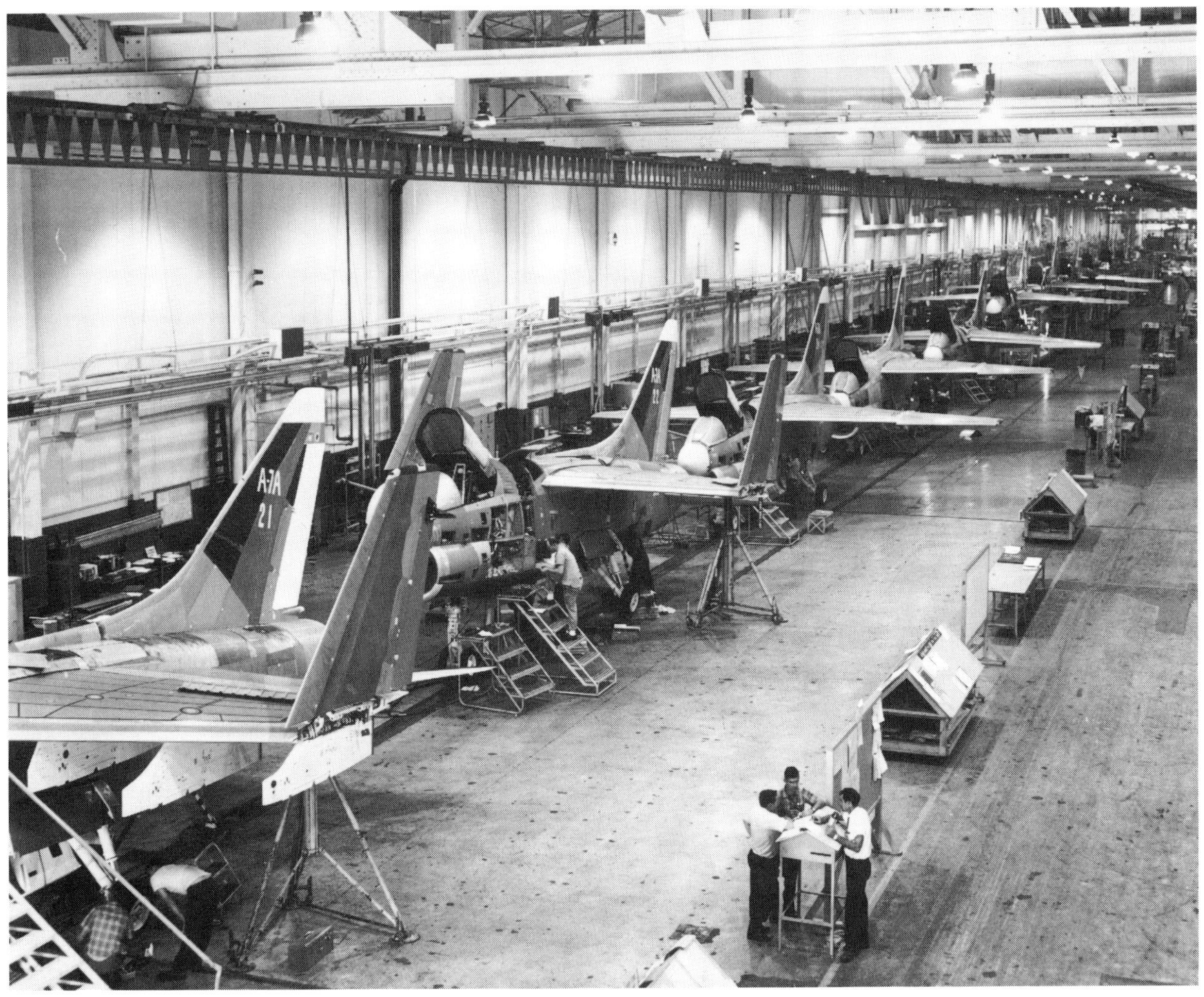

Vought production line in Dallas in 1965. Two airplanes in foreground are A-7A No 21 (buno 152664) and No 22 (buno 152665). The latter aircraft, eventually converted to A-7E standard, was observed in operation with the 'Champions' of squadron VA-56 aboard the carrier USS Midway *(CVA-41), coded NF-410, as recently as 17 January 1977 (LTV)*

and climbed up to 30,000 ft (9144 m) for stability and control investigations. His approach and landing were routine, the A-7A landing at a weight of 24,115 lb (10,938 kg) with 6,600 lb (2993 kg) of fuel aboard. Konrad had learned a great deal about the new aircraft, much of it very favourable, but he had also learned that 'engine performance appears to reduce with increasing altitude.' Konrad recommended that engine performance fuel characteristics at altitudes above 20,000 ft (6096 m) be investigated on an expedited basis. Up to now, the A-7A had demonstrated only minor teething troubles and had revealed superb promise. Up to now, the A-7A seemed clearly a winner, the machine needed halfway around the world in Southeast Asia. But flight number three had served up a strong hint that the A-7A might be underpowered.

The erstwhile prototype, 152580, flew for the fourth time under Konrad's command on 29 September. Konrad reported that 'engine parameters drooped from 94% RPM and 1095°C at 5,000 ft (1524 m) to 90% RPM and 1014°C at 30,000 ft (9144 m). The figures dropped to 88.5% RPM and 923°C at 34,000 ft (10,363 m). Konrad's recommendation at the end of the one hour 45-minute flight was that 'engine stability and droop be investigated and corrected.'

The first priority had been, and was, an accelerated test programme to get the A-7A to the Fleet in short order. Further, there were signs that the Air Force, which had adopted the F-4 Phantom II, a Navy aircraft, was taking an interest in the Navy's A-7A. If it was underpowered, 152580 also seemed to offer unprecedented weapons-carrying capability, range and endurance. The unique terms of the firm, fixed-price contact included an incentive for an unhindered and successful flight test programme. In fact, Vought would meet or exceed every requirement in the early testing and development of the aircraft—a superb

DANGER
JET
INTAKE

display of outstanding corporate performance.

Says Konrad:

'Eighteen days after its first flight, 152580 had been flown 17 times and had achieved 43,000 ft (13,106 m), a Mach number of 1.025 in a dive, and 530 knots (636 km/h) level flight speed at 5,000 ft (1524 m).' Sol Love is reported to have told a Vought colleague that the A-7A would soon 'straighten out that mess over there in Vietnam.'

Vought test pilot Robert E Rostine almost certainly was the second man to fly an A-7A. It is unclear whether Bob Rostine cut his teeth on 152580 or one of two further service-test A-7A aircraft which followed (152581/152582). Rostine was enthusiastic about the Corsair's manoeuvrability and stability. It could also be very forgiving when it 'departed' at high angles of attack. 'When that happens, the remedy is to put your hand in front of your face, count your fingers, and let the airplane straighten itself out.'

Continues Konrad:

'Thirty-four days after the first flight [2 November 1965], flight 36 was flown for a public demonstration of the A-7 Corsair. The aircraft was loaded with twelve 500 lb (227 kg) bombs on the inboard and middle pylons and six 250 lb (113.5 kg) bombs on the outer pylons. Two Sidewinders were also included on the fuselage. The demonstration consisted of low altitude high speed passes, 360-degree rolls achieving roll rates of approximately 160 degrees per second and simulated high-angle dive-bombing.' A second A-7A flown by Rostine in clean configuration also participated in this demonstration.

While Konrad and Rostine wrang out the new aircraft under careful scrutiny, ground personnel demonstrated its remarkable turnaround capabilities. A four-man LTV crew representing three Navy machinist mates and an aviation electrician tackled the 42 tasks required to remove the Pratt & Whitney TF30-P-6 engine from the airplane in an impressive 18 minutes. The Corsair configuration permits the engine to be withdrawn without breaking the fuselage and without any need to jack the aircraft to a certain attitude. The powerplant was slid onto a standard Navy engine dolly using a pair of guide rails and a special adapter cradle to cart the TF30. Other 'walk-around' maintenance tasks were demonstrated and discussed. Navy purchasing officials were reportedly impressed by the airplane's ease of access and its potential to be quickly returned to the air. Required by contract to demonstrate a maximum of no more

Second A-7A (buno 152581) in flight over Texas in early 1966 with 500 lb (227 kg) general purpose bombs and with dive brake extended. Robert E Rostine is almost certainly the pilot. This airframe was later modified for tests with the designation NA-7A and, still later, was in storage at the Military Aircraft Storage and Disposition Center (MASDC), Tucson, Arizona, before being declared Category III (struck off charge) on 28 May 1978 (LTV)

than 11.5 maintenance man-hours per flight hour during the test and development programme, Sol Love told the Press that this figure would be exceeded. The manufacturer exceeded every requirement of a contract imposing penalties for failure to meet specified goals, except that the A-7A, with its wing strengthened for carrier operations, was about 600 lb (271 kg) over design empty weight.

In November 1965, Secretary of the Navy Paul Nitze announced that the Navy would exercise its contract option by placing a fourth A-7A production order for 140 more airplanes valued at $91 million (£23 million), having purchased earlier batches of three, four, and 35 airframes. Total A-7A production, then, would reach 182 machines. The cost figure did not include the TF30 powerplant, which the Navy obtained under a separate contract.

By January 1966, the Navy Primary Evaluation (NPE) was underway. The first Navy test pilot to fly an A-7A was Cdr Lee Bausch of the NPE team from NATC Patuxent River, Maryland, who came down

Number three A-7A (buno 152582) in low flight over Dallas facility, with Carswell AFB in background, carrying 250 lb (113 kg) low-drag general purpose bombs outboard, 500 lb (227 kg) Mk 82 general purpose bombs on centre pylons, and 300 gal Aero 1-D fuel tanks inboard. Third airframe built was the last with a nose pitot tube for test instrumentation, and had been removed from inventory before 1 January 1980
(LTV)

OVERLEAF, CLOCKWISE
In 1966, A-7A number four (buno 152647) uses dummy 'buddy' refuelling pod to test coupling with A-7A number eight (buno 152651). 'Buddy' refuelling with the US Navy's probe and drogue system became an important operational capability for the Corsair II and was later used in combat operations
(LTV)

The number four A-7A (buno 152647) was used as the principal weapons test aircraft in the early development programme and served for many years with the Strike Test Directorate at NATC Patuxent River, Maryland, where it is seen on 23 April 1973. This machine later went to the Military Aircraft Storage and Disposition Center at Davis-Monthan AFB, Arizona, with storage number 6A 044. On 7 May 1980, this airframe was finally struck from US Navy inventory
(Jim Sullivan)

Early A-7A developmental aircraft stayed at the Naval Air Test Center, Patuxent River, Maryland for many years. Fitted with a 'bug screen' to prevent its ravenous engine from sucking up unwanted objects, A-7A number ten (buno 152653) is towed from a hangar at Patuxent's Strike Test Directorate on 15 November 1978
(Stephen H Miller)

A-7A number four (152647) was used in 1966 to evaluate the 'buddy' refuelling pod seen here under port wing during a test hop in the Dallas area
(LTV)

NAVY

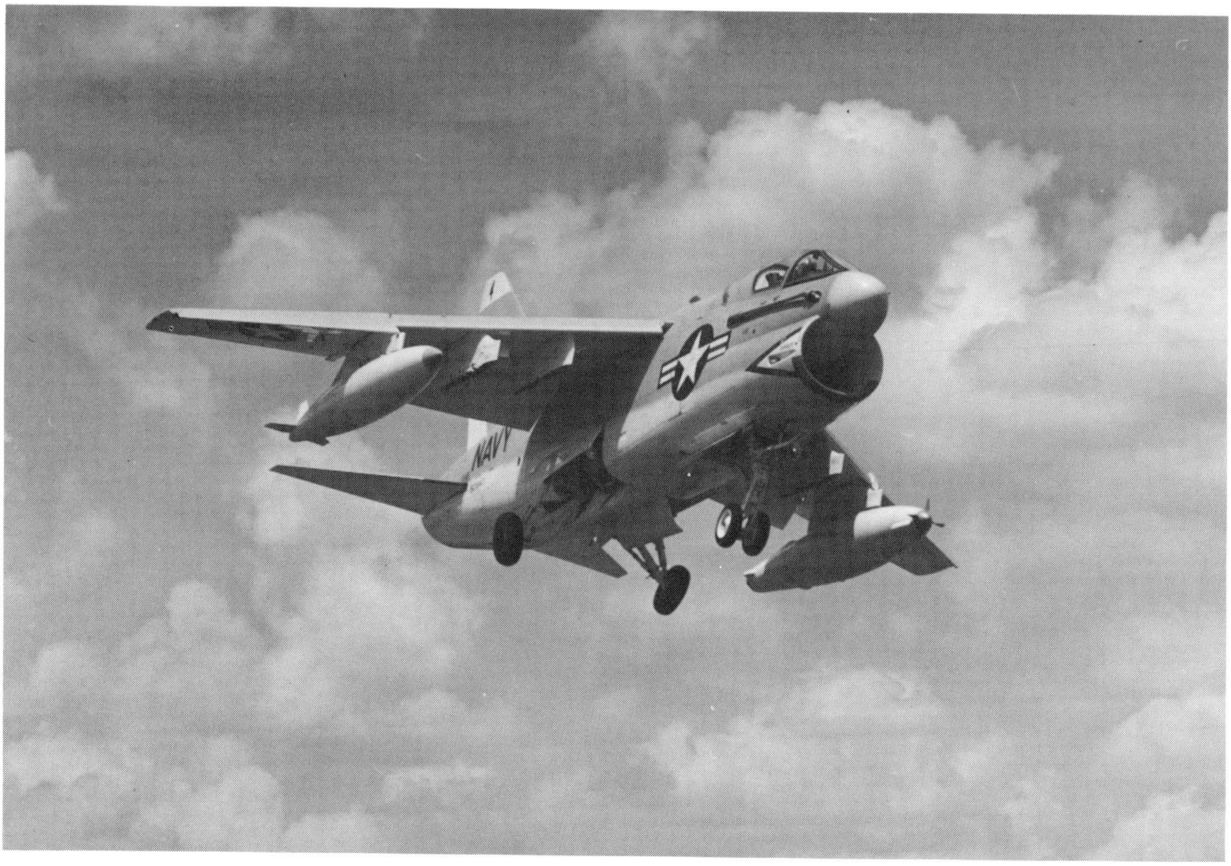
NAVY

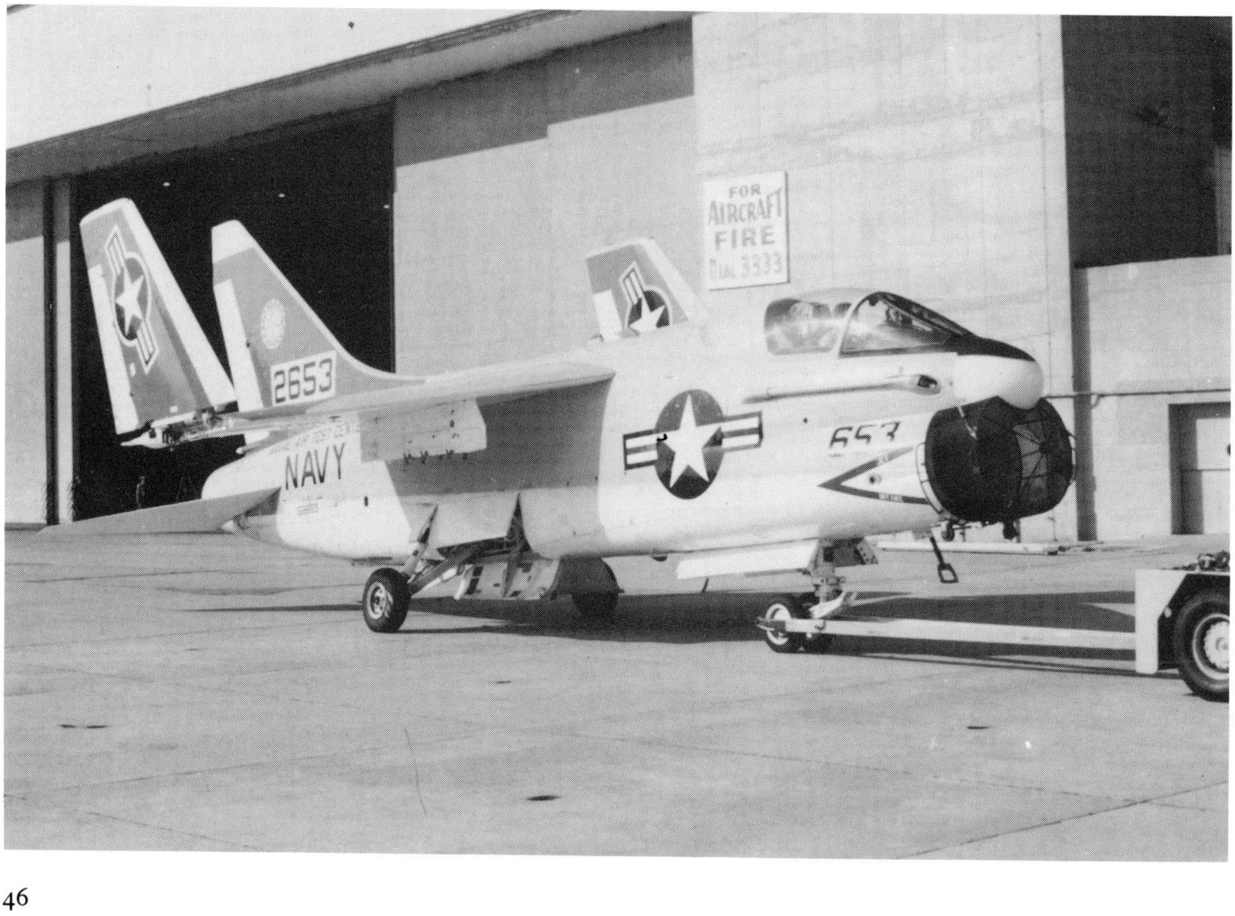
FOR
AIRCRAFT
FIRE
DIAL 3333
2653
NAVY
653

UNITED STATES ARMY
292

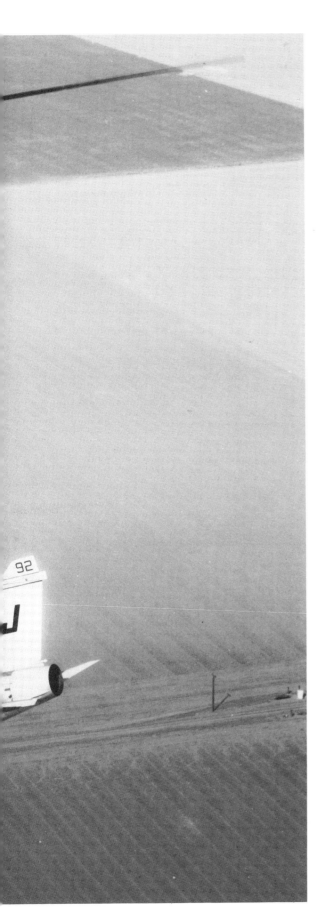

to Dallas to get his aerial initiation on 10 January 1966. It is likely, though not certain, that Bausch made his flight in the busy prototype, 152580. The purpose of the NPE was to provide a full analysis of the machine's promise and problems, its strengths and weaknesses, to prepare it for service and for combat. The NPE was undertaken in Dallas (an unusual step) and at Edwards AFB, California. Further tests were scheduled at the Naval Weapons Evaluation Center (NWEC), Kirtland AFB, New Mexico (for stores separation) and at Patuxent. The final prelude to all-important carrier qualifications, the board of inspections and standards (BIS) tests would be conducted at Patuxent.

It was an active, energetic programme. At every point the new Vought attack aircraft seemed to perform admirably. Its computerized navigation system was a giant step forward in 1966 and pilots found that even in a single-seat warplane they could adjust easily to the elaborate array of 'black boxes.' By 22 June 1966, eight A-7As had completed 750 flight hours and 500 flights.

There were, of course, the inevitable losses which occur in any test programme.

The prototype began it all. 152580 was shifted to Edwards. On 23 March 1966, Vought test pilot John D Omvig was airborne near China Lake when power difficulties led to an abrupt emergency. As historian Arthur L Schoeni relates it, 'Omvig bailed out at extremely low altitude at China Lake. He made one swing in his parachute before he hit the ground.' Had Omvig waited a split-second longer before ejecting, he would have made it impossible for Schoeni to add, 'Nobody was killed in early A-7 [crashes].' Omvig later lost his life in a crash of the XC-142A V/STOL aircraft built by Vought.

The A-7A test programme moved ahead now on all fronts, in Dallas, at Edwards, at Kirtland. Less than ten months after Konrad's first flight, on 27 July 1966, the 1,000th flight hour and 681st test flight were achieved. There were fits and starts, high points and low points, the stuff inevitable in a frenetic test programme carried out with wartime urgency. The second loss of an aircraft occurred on 18 August 1966 near Cleburne, Texas. The fact that it *was* the second rather than the first was, in itself, evidence of the wisdom of undertaking the programme in Texas. In the number three A-7A (152582), Lt Richard Birtwhistle, another member of the NPE team, had a compressor stall and ejected. Recalls Schoeni: 'The

History has left no record of why A-7A (buno 153151), coded NJ-292 of the 'Flying Eagles' of VA-122 was carted by CH-47C Chinook (58-16001) from NAS Lemoore to NAS Alameda, California on 23 October 1969. Later, this machine was held at the Military Aircraft Storage and Disposition Center (MASDC), Davis-Monthan AFB, Arizona, with storage number 6A 066 before being converted into an A-7P for Portugal (USN, via Jim Sullivan)

plane flew along fine and made a beautiful wheels-up belly landing in a wide farmer's field near Cleburne, south of Dallas. It was scarcely damaged and made a flat furrow for several hundred yards, headed right for some farmhouse. Birtwhistle had parachuted [nearby]. The plane was in such good shape it was used as a mockup at the plant after it was retrieved.'

On 2 August 1966, Cdr James C Hill became the first Fleet pilot (as distinguished from a test pilot) to fly the A-7A. Hill pronounced the A-7A 'just what we are looking for.' He had travelled to Dallas from NAS Cecil Field, Florida, home of east-coast carrier attack aviation and soon to be home for the 'Hell-razors' of VA-174 under Cdr Don Ross, the Atlantic Fleet's A-7 replacement air group, or RAG. To operate from land in preparing men to take the A-7 to sea, the west coast's home for the naval attack community, NAS Lemoore, California, would soon host a similar RAG, the 'Flying Eagles' or 'Corsair College' of VA-122. It was a time when a leapfrogging process was taking place. No one had proved that the A-7 could operate from a carrier yet, let alone fight, yet RAG squadrons were already being planned and operational, carrier-borne squadrons would come next. Cdr Hill's destiny lay to the west, first in the baked flatland of that central California vastness around Lemoore and, later, still farther west—for Hill was to be handpicked for a great and frightful responsibility.

Not all the men testing Corsairs in mid-1966 wore the starched whites of the American naval officer. A few were attired in shade 84 blue, the dress of the United States Air Force. The A-7 Corsair was about to be selected by the USAF as its first subsonic attack craft in a generation.

On 13 September 1966, test pilot Cdr Charles W

Inside the one-time dirigible hangar at NATF Lakehurst, New Jersey, derelict naval aircraft are launched from a mock carrier deck to train catapult crews. Outdoors, they are burned to train firefighters. History has left no explanation of why the number eighteen A-7A (buno 152661) bears the name US Naval Sea Cadets, this being an apparent reference to midshipmen at the Naval Academy, Annapolis and the name of USS Eisenhower *(CVN-69), from which it never flew. This airframe had already been struck off charge for nearly three years when seen at Lakehurst on 15 July 1978 (Robert F Dorr)*

Fritz formally accepted the first A-7A for delivery to the Navy and flew it to Patuxent River for BIS trials. That same day, Maj David W Morrill of the US Marine Corps delivered an A-7A formally accepted by the Navy to NWEC Kirtland. Further deliveries took place on 15 September. Patuxent, in the Maryland tidewater on the scenic Chesapeake Bay, was the Navy's best-known experimental flight establishment and Kirtland, in the green-brown western desert outside Albuquerque, was the ideal spot to practice dive-bombing. The Corsair was spreading its wings.

BIS trials and carrier qualifications lay ahead. There remained much to learn about how the new machine would adjust to carrier decks. These tests can take months, even years. Some aircraft get this far and still end up not having the right stuff for production orders or squadron service. But it was already the end of the beginning. In September 1966, Cdr James C Hill received a phone call asking him to start planning to lead the first A-7 Corsair squadron into battle.

Chapter 3
Rolling Thunder in Vietnam
Introducing the A-7 to Combat

'How many rounds of twenty mike-mike you carrying?'

At the lead of four A-4C Skyhawks of the 'Flying Ubangis' of VA-12, Lt James J McBride was heading back to the carrier USS *Shangri-la* (CVA-38) after a routine mission when the voice of the forward air controller (FAC) boomed in his ears. The FAC had discovered a Viet Cong supply barge in one of the narrow inland waterways of South Vietnam. Air strikes in the south were controlled by FAC to prevent bombing of civilians and now the controller, in a Cessna O-1 Bird Dog, was preparing to choose which flight of fighter-bombers to bring in. McBride readied himself to get the call. Before choosing a flight from among several in the air in his region, it was routine for the FAC to ask about the state of your fuel, ordnance, and 20 mm cannon rounds.

'Uh, be advised that we have around four hundred rounds of unused twenty mike-mike,' uttered McBride.

'Thank you, sir,' McBride was ready for directions to the target when the FAC added, 'We won't need you today.'

The Skyhawk pilot couldn't believe his ears. Why *wasn't* his combat-ready, four-plane division of Skyhawks needed? In moments, the answer came. The leader of another four-plane attack flight from another carrier told the FAC that he had a couple of *thousand* rounds of 20 mm which could be brought on the target.

It was a letdown. It was also McBride's introduction to the A-7 Corsair.

The numbers were impressive. A single A-4C carried two 20 mm cannons with a total of 200 rounds, so a four-ship Skyhawk division with no ammo expended would possess, altogether, 800 rounds. The A-7E variant of the Corsair carries one 20 mm M61A1 Gatling-type cannon with 1,000 rounds, so a division with nothing expended would possess 4,000 rounds—*five times* the strafing capacity. The Corsair also gave its pilot, for the first time, a capability to select rates of fire over a range from four to six thousand rounds per minute.

The McBride incident occurred at a later date, with a later Corsair, the A-7E. But Skyhawk pilots were seeing the shape of things to come as early as December 1967 when the A-7A was already in combat. (The A-7A carried two 20 mm Mark 12 cannons with 680 rounds). Skyhawk pilots were impressed, right up front, by the new airplane but felt it would have to be proven. There were those who wondered whether getting the 'Argonauts' of VA-147 under Cdr James C Hill into combat by 1967 wasn't rushing things a bit much. Development, testing and production of the A-7 was moving relentlessly ahead and, in general, moving very favourably but there were going to be some glitches which would suggest that maybe the programme was moving too fast.

The two RAGs received their first airplanes within weeks of each other. On 14 October 1966, the first A-7A arrived at NAS Cecil Field, Florida for pilot training with Cdr Donald S Ross, skipper of VA-174, delivering the east coast RAG's first machine. On 10 December, Cdr Scott Smith of VA-122, the west coast RAG, delivered the first A-7A to NAS Lemoore, with Lt Cdr Lou Taylor following from the factory the next day with the squadron's second machine. The 'Hell-razors' of VA-174 and the 'Flying Eagles' of VA-122, the latter to become known as 'Corsair College', would spend a generation introducing naval aviators to the A-7 and qualifying them to join operational squadrons at sea. Off the Florida coast near Cecil, over the sunbaked central California valley surrounding Lemoore, men would learn the peculiarities and potential of the aircraft type. Men are still doing this today.

Till now concentrated at Dallas and Edwards, and spreading to the RAGs at Cecil and Lemoore, the test

An early A-7A (buno 153167), coded AD-204, of the 'Hell Razors' of VA-174, the east coast replacement air group (RAG) and the first unit to operate Corsairs, stationed at NAS Cecil Field, Florida. Aircraft carries twelve 250 lb (113 kg) inert bombs on its four outer pylons and two 2,000 lb (907 kg) bombs on the inboard mounts, as well as fuselage-mounted AIM-9 Sidewinders (LTV)

TOP RIGHT
The West coast replacement air group (RAG), the 'Flying Eagles' of VA-122 at NAS Lemoore, California, received the A-7A Corsair II immediately after its east coast counterpart, in 1966. Better known as 'Corsair College' for its role in training Pacific Fleet pilots, VA-122 began operations with the twenty-first A-7A (buno 152664), coded NJ-201. This machine had been removed from US Navy inventory by 1 January 1980 (Robert Esposito)

RIGHT
Most Corsairs at NATC Patuxent River, Maryland were employed by the Strike Test Directorate. But the twelfth machine (buno 152655) was being used by Patuxent's Test Pilot School (TPS) in April 1974. This machine later went to MASDC with storage number 6A 040, and finally was turned over to Portugal for spare parts in the A-7P programme (Jim Sullivan)

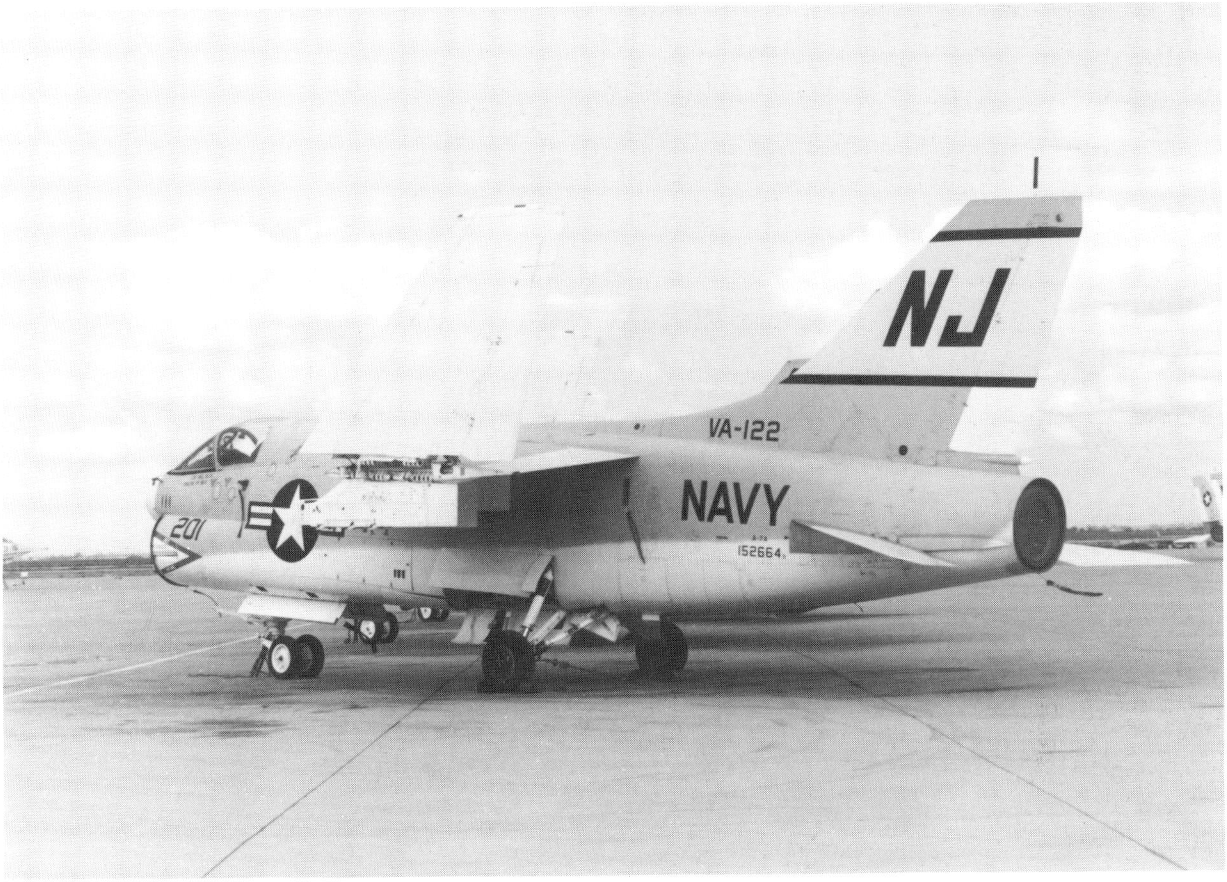
NJ
VA-122
NAVY
201
152664

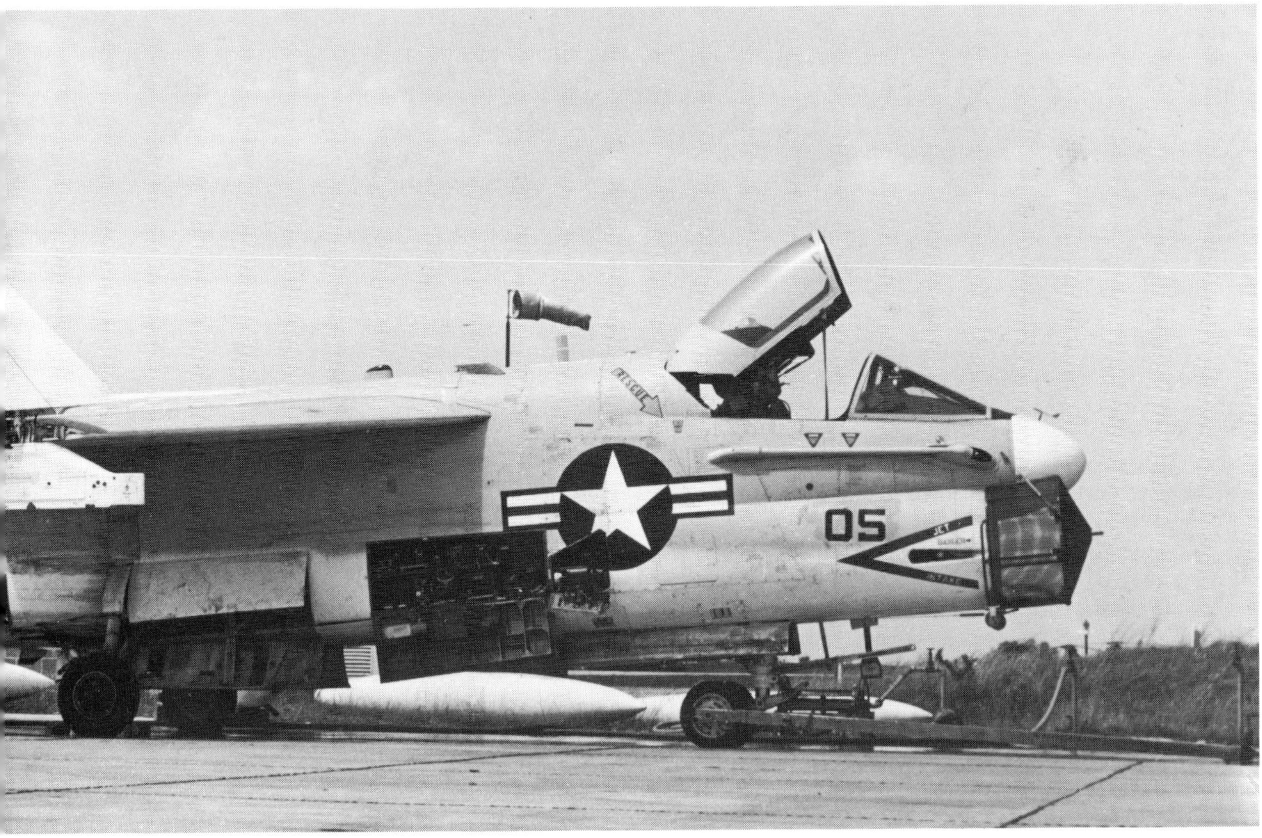
RESCUE
05

programme shifted to the scenic Maryland tidewater at NATC Patuxent River where test pilots put the machine through its paces. BIS trials were followed by operational evaluation. It was time now to go to sea.

Corsair on the Boat

Carrier qualification trials (carquals) were scheduled aboard the 80,800 ton USS *America* (CVA-66), cruising in the Atlantic near its home port at Norfolk. On 15 November 1966, records show, Lt Cdr Fred Hueber of NATC Flight Test won the distinction of making the first Corsair shipboard landing, touching down on *America*'s angled deck in machine number seven (152650). Photographic evidence suggests that the first carrier landing may actually have occurred on 14 November or earlier. During that week, the two A-7A airframes made 75 catapult launches, 73 landings and 79 touch-and-goes. The other carqual airplane was A-7A number fifteen (152658). Though the carquals were conducted without ordnance or realistic fuel loads, aviators and shipboard personnel were pleased with the Corsair's performance.

Not 100% pleased, however.

During catapult launches on the ground at Patuxent and again aboard *America*, it was found that ingestion of steam from the catapult could cause compressor stall. The intake on the aircraft for its 10,000 lb (4534 kg) thrust Pratt & Whitney TF30-P-6 turbofan was located just behind the shuttle connecting the A-7A to the catapult during launch. On other aircraft types, the shuttle is located farther to the rear. As a consequence, an above-normal amount of steam was being sucked into the intake at launch.

There were fixes for the problem. One solution was for the pilot to pay painstaking attention to compressor bleed-air ducts controlled by a cockpit switch, it having been discovered that if the engine's 12th-stage compressor was opened for bleed air at launch, there was little or no ingestion. Another

solution was for the Navy to coat its carrier-catapult systems with new sealant to inhibit the amount of steam escaping from below deck. But the steam-ingestion problem was to tarnish the Corsair's reputation until arrival of the A-7B model with a slightly more powerful TF30-P-8. And it would cause the Navy to limit maximum take-off weight of the A-7A during combat operations to 38,000 lb (17,236 kg) rather than the design 41,500 lb (18,824 kg). The weight restriction would mean that the A-7A would go into battle with only about 8,000 lb (3629 kg) of bombs, only a 1,000 lb (454 kg) improvement over the A-4E Skyhawk. At design maximum take-off weight the A-7A would have toted 2,200 lb (997 kg) more bombs than the A-4E.

Showing It Off

A few years earlier, the US Navy had drawn its new F-4 Phantom into the public limelight with a spectacular series of speed and altitude records. The

LEFT
Tailhook lowered, the seventh A-7A Corsair (152650) crosses the angled deck of USS America *(CVA-66) on 14 November 1966 with Lt Cdr Fred Hueber at the controls. The 7th and 15th Corsairs performed carrier qualifications for the aircraft type. The black cross painted on the side of the aircraft, and repeated on the front of its radome (not visible), warns the landing signal officer (LSO) to distinguish this machine from the similar-looking F-8 Crusader, which he guides to a deck landing at a different speed and sink rate*
(USN)

Fred Hueber in number seven (152650) taxies gingerly toward America's *steam catapult in tossing Atlantic seas on 15 November 1966 for the first carrier launch of an A-7A Corsair*
(Roger F Besecker)

A-7 Corsair wasn't designed to push back the parameters of the envelope. It was merely heavily-armed and highly accurate, not faster or higher. It would have to be paraded before the public in a different way. In early 1967, it was impossible to think about showing off a new airplane without thinking, too, that the Paris Air Show was coming up.

Meanwhile, the first coast-to-coast flight was launched from Cecil Field on 3 January 1967. Cdr Donald S Ross of VA-174 and another pilot, carrying external fuel tanks, flew two A-7As from Florida to Yuma, Arizona. They orbited overhead but poor weather prevented a landing so they flew on to San Diego and orbited again. San Diego was also socked in, so Ross and his wingman flew back to Yuma and landed barely below the maximum gas load allowable for landing. The flight had lasted 5 hours, 18 minutes.

On 1 February 1967, attack squadron VA-147 was commissioned at Lemoore. Cdr James C Hill, who'd been the first Fleet pilot to fly the A-7A, would lead the 'Argonauts' into the fight. His exec was Cdr W Scott Gray. Their squadron was to have several Air Force officers assigned on exchange tours, in anticipation of the Air Force receiving its own variant of the A-7.

On 14 February, the first A-7 carrier operations with realistic loadings began aboard USS *Independence* (CVA-62) near Norfolk. A-7As were loaded with four 300 gal (1350 lit) tanks holding 8,000 lb

Fred Hueber in number seven (152650) has nose arrester gear chocked and horizontal tailplane canted for engine runup on America*'s flight deck 15 November 1966, preparing for the first-ever launch of an A-7A from a flat top*
(Arthur L Schoeni)

RIGHT
In 1972, an RA-5C Vigilante was forced down virtually intact on a river sand-bar in North Vietnam and, to keep it out of Hanoi's hands, had to be bombed by A-7 Corsairs. In November 1966, A-7A number seven (152650) was the first Corsair to operate from a ship at sea and appeared ungainly in contrast to the sleek RA-5C Vigilante (148925), coded GJ-209, of heavy attack squadron RVAH-3 on USS America (CVA-66)
(Arthur L Schoeni)

(3629 kg) of fuel. Added to 9,000 lb (4082 kg) internal fuel and a basic aircraft weight of 19,600 lb (8890 kg), this meant that the A-7A grossed 36,600 lb (16,601 kg), again considerably less than its design combat weight. The A-7A made six catapult shots with this fuel load plus 22 to test further its steam-ingestion problems, a total of 28 launches. Pilots were Lt Cdr Fred Hueber, Cdr Don Lyman, and Capt James E Isles, USMC.

The Paris Air Show was scheduled for 3–4 June 1967. On 19 May, Cdr Charles Fritz and Capt Alec Gillespie, USMC, launched from Patuxent for the nonstop flight to the French capital. They were to traverse the 3,600 miles (5794 km) to Evreaux airfield

in just seven hours, one minute. Commodore Gary F Wheatley, who was at Paris with another aircraft, remembers that Fritz and Gillespie had a far from routine trip:

'The planes were fully loaded with both internal and maximum [four] external fuel tanks. The flight plan required that the external tanks be jettisoned as they emptied in order to decrease drag and permit accomplishment of this long range flight.

'Due to a maintenance oversight, the bomb rack jettison cartridges had been omitted from one of the two aircraft, and it was not until the planes had been committed far at sea and they attempted to jettison tanks that the error was discovered. The decision was made to press on, and the aircraft which could not jettison its tanks made it nonetheless. However, it landed perilously low on fuel. The A-7 went on to be one of the hits of the '67 Air Show.' Wheatley, who spent much of his career in the Grumman Intruder, did not fly the A-7 on a regular basis until he became a CAG ten years later. 'What impressed me most about the aircraft was the amazing accuracy of the head-up display and the visual weapons bombing system.'

Argonauts Into Action

Cdr Hill's VA-147 was the first operational squadron to 'break off' from the RAG, VA-122, at Lemoore. (Proud east coast fliers claim they were ahead of Hill: 'VA-86 [at Cecil Field] chopped off of the RAG prior

Second aircraft in the November 1966 carrier qualifications aboard America *in the Atlantic was A-7A number fifteen (152658)*
(USN)

RIGHT
The same airplane (152658) on the launch bar aboard America *while number seven (152650) waits in background during the first carquals in November 1966*
(Arthur L Schoeni)

to VA-147, so if you go by who got out of the RAG first, VA-86 would be the first [operational] A-7 squadron.') Jim Hill found, in VA-147, a Navy squadron which had four Air Force pilots and 21 airmen under Maj Charles W McClarren, assigned to learn flying and maintenance techniques. To an extent, Hill was in friendly competition with the Navy's *second* operational A-7A squadron, the 'Sidewinders' of VA-86, working up at Cecil Field. But by July 1967 when he took VA-147 aboard USS *Ranger* (CVA-61) for its carquals, Hill could not have worried much about being upstaged by a mere *east coast* squadron. The war lay to the west.

Even while they logged 315 catapult shots and landings, many of them at night, Hill's men were tidying up their affairs, consoling their women, packing their sea bags. Since before the initial flight of the A-7A, carrier aviators had been pitted against North Vietnam. Some were prisoners now in downtown Hanoi and they would not be abandoned. Jim Hill's *west* coast VA-147 would set forth to sea and sky to press the fight closer to Hanoi.

On 28 August 1967, Hill sent a team under Capt Nicholas Jones, USAF, to Dallas to pick up deployment-ready A-7As fresh from the factory. The squadron was trading in its first airplanes for others with minor improvements based on test experience. Meanwhile, Hill took an A-7A team to NAAS Fallon Nevada for realistic navigation and ordnance delivery exercises, logging 508 missions in three weeks. On 27

September, second anniversary of the first flight of the A-7A, airplane, men, squadron and ship all came together on the Pacific coast off California. VA-147 went aboard *Ranger* not for carquals but for its combat cruise. Hill assembled his pilots. 'We're going,' he said.

The Navy had picked a real leader to take the Corsair into the crucible. James C Hill had begun his Navy career as an enlisted sailor in 1948 before transferring into the aviation cadet training programme. His first tour of duty was with an anti-submarine squadron and he served as an instructor pilot between shipboard cruises, first on USS *Leyte* (CVS-32), later with an A-4 squadron, VA-172, on USS *Franklin D Roosevelt* (CVA-42). After attending the staff and command course at the Naval War College in Newport, Rhode Island, he became attack training officer at Fleet headquarters, Norfolk. After helping to introduce the A-7A in 1966, Hill was named skipper of VA-147. The chief Argonaut was lanky and soft-spoken and could grin readily, but he also had a way of inspiring those around him.

Combat deployment of Hill's squadron was announced on 8 November 1967 by Vice Admiral Thomas F Connolly, Deputy Chief of Naval Operations (Air). Said Connolly, 'The A-7A is a very fine light attack aircraft. We have confidence in it.' By now, 30,000 flight hours had been logged in A-7As. Connolly's enthusiasm was genuine. Two days earlier, *Ranger* had cast its lines and steamed under the Golden Gate. Hill's men must have been thinking about steam ingestion and compressor stalls, about the Triple-A and missiles and MiGs that lurked in wait in the region around Hanoi known as Route Package Six.

VA-147 was aboard the ship as part of Air Wing Two (CVW-2) also with F-4B, A-4, A-6 and KA-3 squadrons. On 4 December, Hill's pilots flew the first Corsair combat strikes, using 5 inch (127 mm) Zuni rockets to assault bridge and highway targets around

'Combat operations against North Vietnam . . .' In Dallas sunshine, September 1967, A-7A Corsairs belonging to the 'Argonauts' of Cdr James C Hill's VA-147 prepare to go in harm's way aboard USS Ranger *(CVA-61). VA-147 was the third Corsair squadron, after the two RAGs. In distant background is A-7A (153239), coded NE-313, which became the first Corsair lost in battle on 22 December 1967 and the only machine lost by Hill's squadron on its cruise. In foreground is A-7A (153242), coded NE-317, eventually lost in a crash on 15 September 1977 while with the reservist 'Blue Dolphins' of VA-203 at NAS Jacksonville, Florida (LTV)*

RIGHT
A rattlesnake poised on the rudder. For two decades, this has symbolized the 'Sidewinders' of VA-86, the fourth squadron to operate the Corsair, following the two RAGs and VA-147. The 'Sidewinders' acquired A-7A Corsairs in June 1967 at NAS Cecil Field, Florida under Cdr Charles R Long and became the first operational east coast squadron. TF30-powered variant known initially as the A-7C (later A-7E) 156738, coded AJ-413, embarked on USS America *(CVA-66) sits beside a squadron mate at Cecil Field on 9 October 1973 (Duane A Kasulka)*

Vinh in the narrow 'neck' of North Vietnam just above the 17th Parallel. On 17 December, A-4s, A-6s and A-7s from *Ranger* attacked the Hai Duong rail and highway bridge complex between Haiphong and Hanoi. MiGs were scrambled against them. Hill was narrowly missed by a SAM. He spotted MiGs in the distance. 'I got a really good shot at a flak site and I'm sure it hasn't fired at anybody since then. I launched a missile at a SAM site shortly after we got in and both my wingman and the strike leader confirmed my shot as a direct hit.' Perhaps mindful that Sidewinders gave the A-7A air-to-air capability, the MiGs did not engage.

On 22 December 1967, in a grim prelude to Christmas, an A-7A (153239), side number NE-313, was hit by ground fire and became the first Corsair lost in combat. It was to be some consolation to Hill and his shipmates that this was the *only* Corsair lost during the cruise.

The A-7A flew from carrier decks against North

NAVY
A-7C
156738
413

To fly and fight. Ordnance gone, except for Sidewinders, Cdr James C Hill returns to Ranger *from North Vietnam at the controls of A-7A (153219), coded NE-315. Note lowered tailhook and multiple ejector racks on centre wing pylon. By January 1968 when US Navy photographer PH1 Donald F Grantham caught the essence of speed in this grainy shot, Hill's 'Argonauts' of VA-147 had been in combat for a month*
(USN)

Vietnam in every manner of mission. The Alpha Strike, pitting the resources of a carrier air wing against a simple target, was the biggest. A typical Alpha Strike combined F-4B Phantoms, A-4 Skyhawks, A-6 Intruders and A-7 Corsairs, with supporting ECM, tanker and reconnaissance aircraft—from 24 to 48 airplanes in all—with a coordinated attack on a single target or closely-clustered series of targets, such as the Hai Duong railway marshalling complex near Hanoi. The carrier air wing commander, or CAG (the term dates to the carrier air *groups* of the 1950s) used the varying performance capabilities of different aircraft with varying ordnance to outguess and overcome North Vietnamese defences. Some A-7s flew 'Iron Hand' missions against SAM sites with Shrike anti-radiation missiles while other A-7s brought their ordnance, such as 500 lb (227 kg) Mk 82 bombs against the prime target. The A-7 fitted smoothly into the team effort that went into an Alpha Strike. The pilot, apart from dodging SAMs and Triple-A, had little opportunity to show his individual mettle—but the airplane was ideal for the mission.

At the other extreme were roving, armed 'road recce' strikes handled by small numbers of aircraft—a division of four, or a section of two A-7As. The A-7A could spend hours flying road recce searching for targets of opportunity. Pilots enjoyed prowling the highways, rivers and countryside of North Vietnam looking for something that would ignite and explode when hit. In the A-7, they could also prowl North Vietnam at night.

Before the end of 1967, Jim Hill's pilots in VA-147 attacked the Nui Long tunnel complex north of Thanh Hoa using 500 lb (227 kg), 1,000 lb (454 kg) and 2,000 lb (907 kg) bombs. Their bombs sealed off entrances and produced secondary explosions from North Vietnamese ammunition dumps. Hill's Corsairs also flew repeated strikes against bridges and waterborne logistics craft, barges, railroad equipment, roads, supply dumps, POL concentrations and vehicle convoys. The A-7A proved itself relatively free of maintenance problems and pilots were impressed by the comfort they felt in its roomy cockpit while dodging everything the enemy could throw at them.

The scene shifted. In January 1968, *Ranger* was in

Scorch marks evident around the muzzle of its port 20 mm cannon, A-7A Corsair (153222) coded NE-305 taxies past Phantoms and Skyhawks aboard Ranger *after returning from targets in North Vietnam, January 1968. This machine survived the first combat cruise by the plucky 'Argonauts' of VA-147 but was lost in combat in Southeast Asia on 12 April 1969 (USN)*

the Gulf of Tonkin when the US intelligence ship *Pueblo* was seized by North Korea, three thousand miles to the north.

Ranger departed the combat zone and cruised north, arriving in the Sea of Japan off the east coast of Korea on about 1 February. The situation was tense. 82 American crewmen from *Pueblo* were being held prisoner, a team of North Korean commandos had gotten into downtown Seoul in an attempt to assassinate South Korea's President Park, and it seemed as if a second Asian war could erupt at any moment. Cdr Hill and his VA-147 pilots suddenly had the unexpected opportunity—if it could be called that—to evaluate the A-7 under torturous winter conditions, with temperatures far below freezing and icy winds washing over *Ranger*'s deck. For 60 days, *Ranger*'s air wing operated at heightened readiness off the Korean coast. The situation was to remain tense, but when *Enterprise* (CVN-65) arrived, *Ranger* was relieved to take Hill's Argonauts back to the Gulf of Tonkin.

New Squadrons In Combat

On 10 April 1968, two new A-7A squadrons were deployed aboard USS *America* (CVA-66) on the east coast. The ship's crew had expected a routine Mediterranean voyage and A-7A pilot Ben Short's wife, Jef, had already purchased a ticket to Athens—but it was not to be. As had been customary for several years, Atlantic Fleet carriers and east coast squadrons periodically changed oceans so that the combat burden could be shared, standing in for Pacific Fleet flat-tops in the Gulf of Tonkin. The 'Marauders' of VA-82 under Cdr John E Jones and the 'Sidewinders' of VA-86 under Cdr Jack E Russ were on board when *America* sailed around the Cape of Good Hope, traversed the Indian Ocean, and began launching strikes against North Vietnam on 31 May 1968. The arrival of *America* finally provided relief to *Ranger*, which had returned from Korean waters, and after a long and eventful cruise, Jim Hill and the men of VA-147 went home.

Lt Ken W Fields of VA-82, at the controls of an A-7A (153255) was hit by ground fire on the first day's strikes near the DMZ. Fields ejected. He came down in thickly vegetated terrain swarming with North

Vietnamese regular troops. Fields retained the use of his personal radio and was able to talk with shipmates while wending his way between troop concentrations and struggling toward a safer area. A massive rescue operation was mounted and a 'Jolly Green' helicopter piloted by Maj Lewis Yuhas eventually reached Fields and plucked him out, after 39 hours on the ground. During the rescue, or RESCAP, operation another A-7A from Ken's squadron (153258) suffered fuel starvation and its pilot ejected safely near the carrier.

That same day, Ben Short of VA-86 wrote into his journal:

'5-31-68. Launched on a close air support hop in the DMZ area with terrible weather, large build-ups. I ended up flying a large semi-circle from the DMZ to Cape Mui Ron trying to find the FAC. Ended up by dropping on a revetted storage area just north of Dong Hoi. [I carried] six Mk 117 [bombs].'

Two decades later, Short, now a retired Navy captain, reflected on the *America* cruise and the four line periods spent off the enemy coast:

'We lost one pilot during the first line period, Randy Ford. [In an A-7A Corsair (153265) of VA-86 on 10 June 1968], he was out on an early morning flight (0200-0400) and suddenly ejected. While on the ground [using his survival radio] he never said what happened. We surmise he was captured just about sunup. I launched just before dawn and talked to him a couple of times. He went down just south of Ha Tinh, and we learned many years later that he died shortly after he was taken prisoner in Ha Tinh. He never made it to Hanoi.

'During this period we were only bombing North Vietnam up to the 19th parallel, so the entire cruise was spent working over the real estate between 18 and 19 degrees north except when the weather was bad and they would send us south to work with Air Force FACs. The Air Force had the territory between the DMZ and the 18th Parallel. There were one or two SAM sites around the gunnery school at Vinh Son, and they managed to pick off a couple of aircraft from

Bomb-laden, guided toward Ranger*'s launch catapult by gesturing Cat officer, a pilot of VA-147 prepares to confront anti-aircraft, missiles and MiGs in a flight from Yankee Station in the Gulf of Tonkin, January 1968 (LTV)*

OVERLEAF
Until selected in 1985 for the F/A-18A Hornet, attack squadron VA-147 had a two-decade association with the A-7 Corsair. First operational A-7 squadron, first in combat, the 'Argonauts' began with the A-7A variant and took it to Hanoi during 1965–68 Rolling Thunder operations. But the squadron later operated the TF41-powered A-7E variant, exemplified by 158013, coded NG-413, nick-named 'CITY OF TULARE', flown by the squadron aboard USS Constellation *(CVA-64) in 1974. Tulare is a small town in California, perhaps the pilot's home town, and 158013 is but one of many 'CITY' nicknamed aircraft*
(LTV)

NE
312

13
NG
VA-147
USS CONSTELLATION
158013

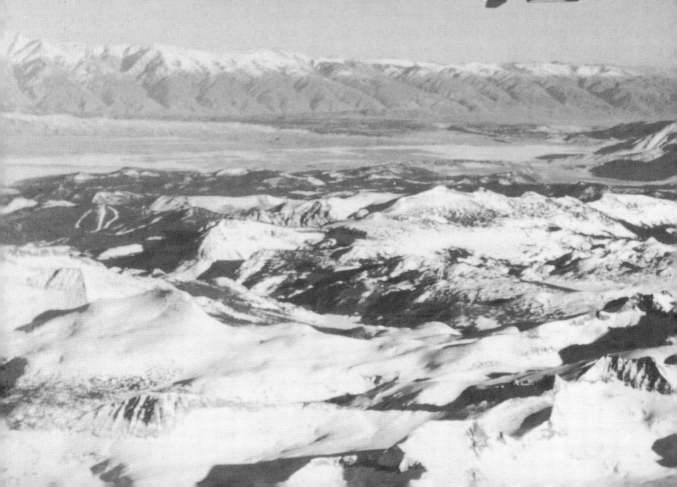

CITY of TULARE
413

CDR. VAL VAILLANCOURT
202
JET
DANGER
INTAKE
AD
NAVY

One of the last squadrons to operate the A-7A model, and long a familiar sight in Asian climes, the 'Champions' of VA-56 operate from USS Midway *(CVA-41), home-ported in Yokosuka, Japan. A-7A bureau number 153248, with modex number NF-404, approaches NAF Atsugi, near Tokyo, in September 1975*
(Hideki Nagakubo)

LEFT
'From some angles, downright pretty . . .' No one seriously accuses the A-7 Corsair of ravishing beauty, but in bright sunshine 152660, the seventeenth A-7A, serving as AD-202 with the east coast RAG reveals some attractive lines. After duty with VA-174, this A-7A subsequently went to the Naval Weapons Evaluation Facility (NWEF) at Kirtland AFB, New Mexico
(USN via M J Kasiuba)

BELOW
A-7A Corsair II during evaluations in 1966 carries an unusually diverse ordnance load of (outwards) AIM-9 Sidewinder, AGM-12B Bullpup B, Walleye TV-guided glide bomb and AGM-45 Shrike anti-radiation missile (LTV)

606
VA-27
NAVY

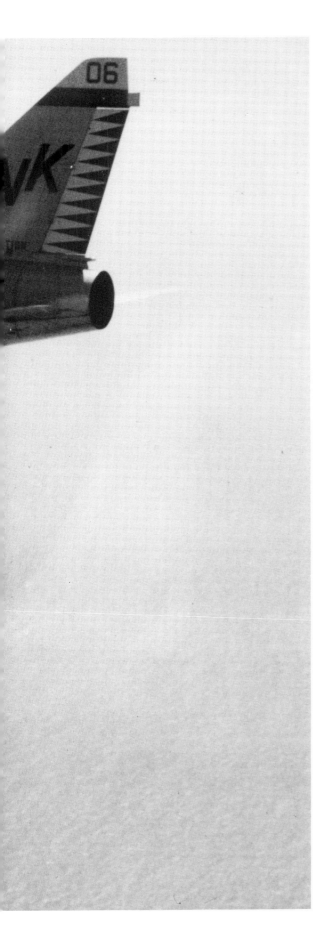

the Air Wing [not A-7s] during the course of the cruise.

'The normal operations were twelve hours on, noon to midnight, or mid to noon, then twelve off. Every six to ten days we would stand down for 24 hours and change the cycle. This played hell with my biological clock. If I had a 0300 hop, I would just get up at that hour. Initially we were carrying 12 Mk 81s on MERS [multiple ejector racks] on stations one and eight. I was out with a load of twelve 81s when I picked up a concrete bridge on Route 1 (probably 300–400 ft long) and being new to the game decided to dump the entire load on the bridge. I made a pretty good run cutting across the bridge at a slight angle putting eight or nine of the bombs on the bridge. As I pulled off, I rolled up on a wing tip after getting my nose well above the horizon to observe the hits. There was a lot of smoke and fire but after the smoke flew away there was no apparent damage to the bridge.' North Vietnamese bridges were to prove formidable targets indeed, and *America* quickly replaced the 250 lb (113 kg) Mk 81 bomb with the 500 lb (227 kg) Mk 82 bomb on standard A-7A operations.

Continues Short, 'One night I spotted a small brush fire going on the ground near a canal. Since the road recce hadn't proven very effective that night, I decided to drop a couple of bombs on the fire. My hit was a little bit long, but I got one helluva secondary explosion and got a good fire going. My wingman and I dropped the rest of our ordnance on the fire and got some additional secondaries. In jest I have always said some North Vietnamese barge driver let his rice-cooking fire get away from him, and I came along and spoiled his whole evening. The fire was still burning when the next cycle (an hour and a half later) got over the beach. They dropped on it, got some additional secondaries and spread the fire even further.' The Corsair pilots of VA-82 and VA-86 were shot at repeatedly by all sorts of guns in North Vietnam and Short recalls that, during an Independence Day breather on 4 July 1968, when *America* had temporarily retired to Subic Bay, Philippines, the pilots did not derive the usual enjoyment from the holiday's fireworks display.

By July 1968, USS *Constellation* (CVA-64) arrived at Yankee Station with the fourth and fifth operational A-7A squadrons, the 'Royal Maces' of VA-27 under Cdr George Pappas and the 'Warhawks' of VA-97 under Cdr Richard P Vaillancourt. For the rest of the year, the four A-7A squadrons on *America* and *Constellation* were available for Rolling

1,000 lb (454 kg) Mk 83 bombs fall from an A-7A Corsair II of the 'Royal Maces' of attack squadron VA-27, flying from the carrier USS Constellation *(CVA-64). This was one of the early units to introduce the A-7A to combat in Southeast Asia. This machine (153232), side number NK-606, survived two combat cruises without being damaged (USN, via M J Kasiuba)*

06
AE
GOLDEN WARRIORS
VA-87
USS ROOSEVELT
NAVY
154412
406

04
NE
404

11
AB
VA-72
USS
JOHN F KENNEDY
NAVY
411
154371
NAVY

TOP
The A-7B model was delayed getting into service but, once in action, was an improvement over the A model. This A-7B (154412), side number AE-406 of the 'Golden Warriors' of VA-87 operating from USS Franklin R Roosevelt *(CVA-42) is seen at NAS Cecil Field, Florida on 15 June 1973. This airframe was later converted to a two-seat TA-7C*
(via Norman Taylor)

MIDDLE
The A-7B model of the Corsair continued to serve into the latter stages of the Vietnam war. An A-7B (154535), side number NE-404 of attack squadron VA-56 lands on USS Ranger *(CVA-61) in the Gulf of Tonkin in 1970. This aircraft was still serving with Reserve Squadron VA-305 in 1985*
(M J Behrend via Jim Sullivan)

BOTTOM
A-7B Corsair (154371), side number AB-411, of attack squadron VA-72 aboard USS John F Kennedy *(CV-67), at NAS Miramar, California on 28 February 1976. This longtime veteran airframe later joined Reserve squadron VA-203*
(Bruce Trombecky)

Thunder missions against North Vietnam and Steel Tiger operations in Laos.

In late 1968, times were changing fast. The Navy A-7B model was entering squadron service, the Air Force's A-7D was in production and the Navy A-7E would not be far behind. The entire air war over North Vietnam petered into a bombing halt in October 1968 as Lyndon Johnson sought to grease negotiations by letting up the pressure. It didn't work. Americans elected a new president the following month, Rolling Thunder became history, and a second round of fighting over North Vietnam lay ahead before Hanoi would be brought to a settlement, not with a bombing halt but by force of arms.

The A-7A Corsair had been through its baptism of fire and had won high marks from tough-minded men who did not bestow favour easily. The Corsair's steam-ingestion problems, by now publicized more than they needed to be, were eventually resolved. Although the A-7A was widely understood to be under-powered, Cdr Hill of VA-147 saw as its 'most desirable advantage' the low fuel consumption of the first operational turbofan jet engine in a tactical aircraft. Hill noted that the Pratt & Whitney TF30-P-6 offered 'almost unbelievable fuel specifics in terms of previous jet engine performance.' Jim Hill and other pilots had praise for many other features of the Corsair which was just beginning to show its stretching potential. Vice Admiral William F Bringle, commander of the 7th Fleet, told the Press that every Navy carrier would have two A-7 squadrons by mid-1969.

The second round over North Vietnam would not come until 1972. Meanwhile, there would be long and heavy fighting in the south where the A-7 would be used effectively. When the rematch with the North did come, the Air Force would join the Navy in using the A-7 to take the war 'downtown'—to Hanoi.

Chapter 4
Structural Changes at Patuxent
A-7 Corsair Variants

Few songs, no poetry, and not much praise has begifted the valiant SLUF in its combat career, but the A-7 Corsair enjoyed a respectable production run and a solid pattern of growth. 1,545 airframes rolled from the Dallas production line and many came back later to be modified, upgraded, rebuilt. Of the 65 two-seat Corsairs for the US Navy which came along late in the type's career, all but five were converted from existing single-seaters. Portuguese A-7Ps were converted from earlier marks. Almost no 'odd' or unusual modifications of the Corsair have appeared, and development has followed an undramatic, logical progression, albeit with some shuffling of designations of the naval two-seat variants.

In Dallas, LTV people identify an individual airframe by its US Navy bureau number (these being assigned, too, to Greek and Portuguese machines) or its US Air Force serial, freeing the historian from serious purpose in pondering the 'constructor's number,' or c/n, applied at the plant. For the armchair purist who must know, LTV constructor's numbers follow no pattern that can be conveniently deciphered, the first A-7A being c/n A-1 while the first two-seater converted from an existing single-seat airframe is c/n TE-3. Some material on this subject appears in the Appendix. It is of little interest to

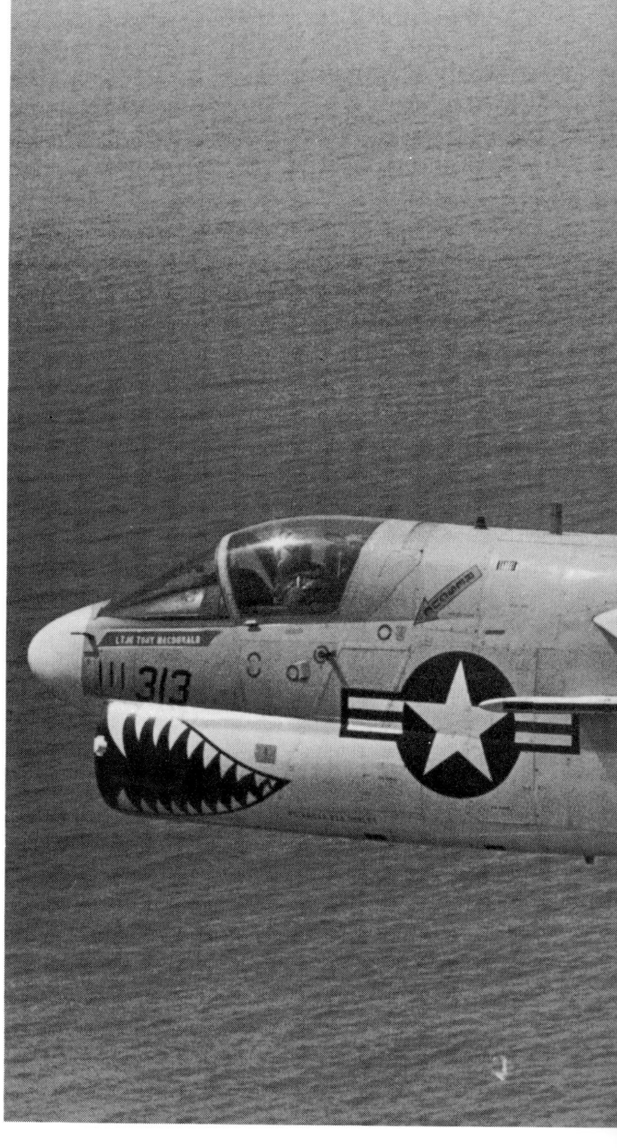

TOP RIGHT
The A-7A. Sharkteeth jutting open, laden down with fuel and buddy refuelling pod (far wing), A-7A 153228 wearing 'side' number NK-313 settles in at NAF Atsugi, Japan in May 1976. Operating from USS Midway *(CVA-41), the 'Ravens' of VA-93 were among the last Fleet squadrons to operate the A model Corsair (Hideki Nagakubo)*

The A-7A. Same aircraft, different load. 153228, bearing Modex code NF-313 of squadron VA-93 on Midway *is the same brightly coloured Corsair depicted above but now carries iron bombs instead of buddy refuelling pack (USN via M J Kasiuba)*

NF
313
NAVY
153228

13
NF
VA-93
NAVY
USS MIDWAY
153228
313

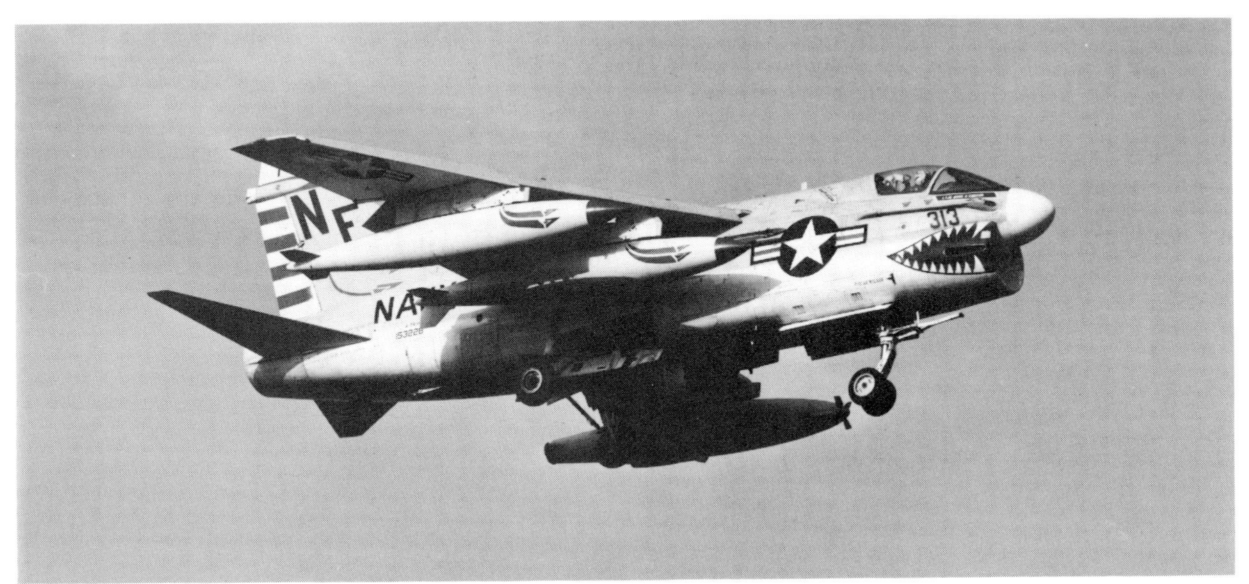

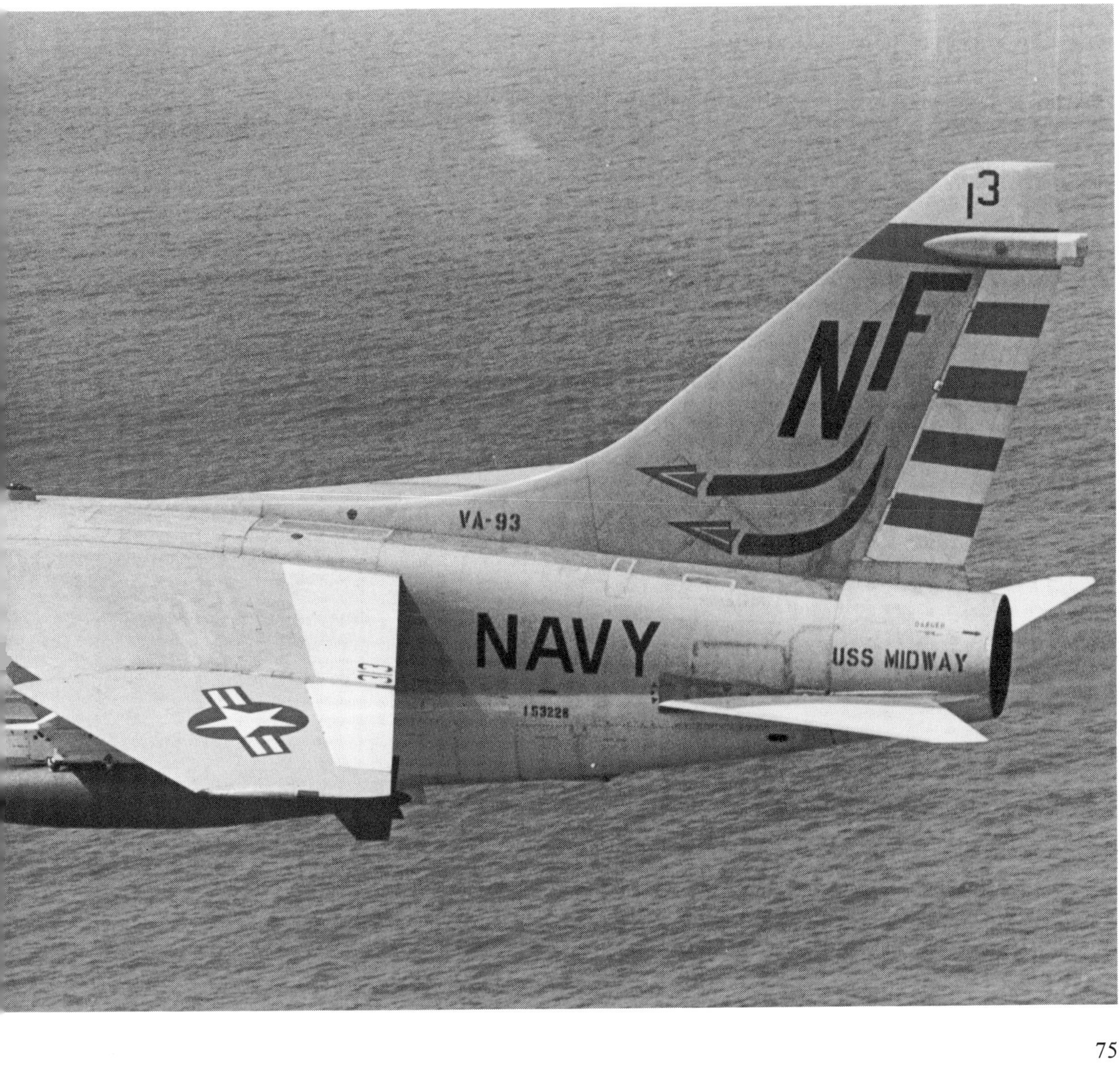

The A-7B. Differing from its predecessor with only a minor engine change, A-7B buno 154468, a colourful CAG aircraft of the 'Barn Owls' of Cdr Jim Crummer's VA-215 basks at NAS Miramar, California, just after the cessation of hostilities in 1974. The two zeroes, or 'double nuts' in the aircraft side number, AE-400, indicate that it is assigned to the carrier air wing commander aboard USS Franklin D Roosevelt *(CVA-42)*
(Duane A Kasulka)

pilots. Indeed, naval aviators often refer to an individual machine by its Modex or 'side' number, this being a temporary three-digit numeral on the nose which places the machine in sequence within a particular carrier air wing.

The A-7 offers little joy to recognition buffs. Except for minor differences in detail, one Corsair looks like another Corsair. A-7 pilots over North Vietnam feared that higher-flying, faster F-4 Phantom jocks would mistake them visually for MiG-17s.

The following is a summary of key differences among variants of A-7, produced or proposed. Given the potential of the A-7 for development and upgrading, it is unlikely that this is the final word in a story which will continue into the 1990s.

A-7A

The maiden flight on 27 September 1965 of the first A-7A (152580), carried out in Dallas by John W Konrad, has been recounted. The A-7A was powered by the Pratt & Whitney TF30-P-6 turbofan engine rated at 11,350 lb (5148 kg) thrust under sea-level static conditions. The US Navy contract specified an empty weight of 15,037 lb (6820 kg) and an ordnance capacity of 15,000 lb (6803 kg).

Like all Navy Corsairs, the A-7A had an in-flight refuelling probe on the forward right fuselage which swung out to take on fuel from a drogue trailing behind a tanker. A-7A flaps could be lowered to one position only, while subsequent Corsairs had variable flaps.

This narrative has reached 1967–68 when the A-7A variant joined the fray in Southeast Asia, and has introduced Cdr George T Pappas, skipper of VA-27, the squadron nickname 'Royal Maces.' On 14 September 1968, Pappas led a flight of three A-7As from the decks of *Constellation* to assault the Linh Cam ferry crossing near the 17th Parallel. Pappas had rolled towards the target and was beginning his run-in at the controls of his A-7A (154344), side number NK-610, when a sudden crunching sound rended his ears and he felt the impact of anti-aircraft shells mangling his starboard wing.

Pappas knew immediately that the damage was serious. To his surprise, the A-7A was still manoeuvring perfectly, so he pressed home his attack and laid his ordnance on target. Then, with a wingman confirming that fuel was streaming from the burning wing, Pappas sought to recover at Da Nang.

The fire became more intense. At low level over the clustered ships in Da Nang harbour, where a crash would surely cause loss of life, Pappas experienced control difficulties. He continued to descend, landed on the runway, and—when all directional control was lost—ejected.

Flames engulfed the A-7A as he punched out. The plane swerved off the runway and came to rest near a hangar. Although cut and bruised, Pappas was able to

rejoin his squadron the following day and later received a Distinguished Flying Cross for his efforts to save the airplane and human life. Pappas believes that the toughness of the A-7A airframe was a major factor in his safe return from what might have been, otherwise, an ejection over enemy territory. Naval officers will never forget that it was the A-7A version, brought into combat earlier and more effectively than anyone could have hoped, which began the Corsair's war story.

The first three A model airframes (152580/152582) are called service-test YA-7A in some literature but this designation seems unofficial. At least one machine in the series was converted to NA-7A (next page). No fewer than 72 were employed in the first

BELOW
A-7B (buno 154492), coded AE-300, of the 'Valions' of attack squadron VA-15 drops 2,000 lb (907 kg) bombs at the practice range near Fallon, Nevada in 1975. This aircraft was assigned to the carrier air wing commander (CAG). This machine was lost at sea on 25 May 1975 while VA-15 was deployed aboard the since-retired USS Franklin D Roosevelt *(CVA-42)*
(USN via Jim Sullivan)

phase of the Portuguese programme, 44 being converted to A-7P, six to TA-7P, and 22 retained as spares. 199 examples of the A-7A were manufactured in Dallas from 1965. The operational and combat career of this variant continued well into the following decade, but as early as 1967 the A-7A had been replaced on Vought's production line by later models.

NA-7A

At least one A-7A, possibly the eighth built (152651) was given the NA-7A designation in evaluations at NATC Patuxent River, Maryland.

The 'N' prefix has been much-misused in recent years. It ostensibly signifies 'special test, permanent,' and is supposed to mean, in the Pentagon's own words, that the airplane's configuration is so drastically changed that return to its original configuration is 'beyond practicable or economic limits.' An aircraft modified only temporarily, and later restored to original shape, is supposed to bear a 'J' prefix and, in this illustration, would be JA-7A. But the latter has fallen into disuse while the actual modifications to the NA-7A are so insignificant as to be anticlimactic. It is understood that the NA-7A was simply a standard A model rewired to test an item of ordnance not originally compatible with the variant, such as the second-generation version of the Walleye TV-guided bomb.

A-7B

First flight of the A-7B was accomplished at Dallas on 6 February 1958 by LTV's Joe Engle, who was flying the number three airframe in the A-7B series (154363). The A-7B was powered by a higher-thrust Pratt & Whitney TF30-P-8 turbofan rated at 12,200 lb (5534 kg) thrust. The A-7B introduced variable flaps but was otherwise little different from the A model which preceded it. Both the A-7A and A-7B have a retractable stirrup-type footstep for boarding, not found on later versions. The A-7B was delivered to NATC Patuxent River, Maryland for BIS trials on 25 April 1968 and was expected to quickly replace earlier Corsairs in Fleet service.

Turbine problems with the TF30 powerplant resulted in the US Navy refusing to accept the first three months' production—some 50 aircraft—in the A-7B series. Pratt & Whitney reported that the problem was associated with the second stage of the TF30-P-8. An engine tested by the maker with

The A-7C. Sixty-seven aircraft were produced which were identical to the A-7E except that they were powered by the TF30 rather than the TF41 engine. This one, with a non-standard nose pitot probe, is 156754, coded 7T-402, in the livery of the Strike Test Directorate, NATC Patuxent River, Maryland, in August 1983
(Don Linn)

7T
NAVY

modifications designed to clear the problem failed. By April 1968, it looked like the chances for early introduction of the B model into the Southeast Asia conflict were rapidly diminshing.

The glitch with the engine was resolved. The west coast's 'Blue Diamonds' of VA-146 under Cdr Ford Schultz and 'Barn Owls' of VA-215 under Cdr Georges E Le Blanc, Jr took the A-7B variant into the fight. It was an especially difficult period. While en route near Hawaii in January 1969, a disastrous fire broke out on the deck of USS *Enterprise* (CVAN-65), taking 28 lives, causing a hundred injuries, and destroying a dozen or more aircraft, including Corsairs from both A-7B squadrons. This caused a two and a half month delay at port in Pearl Harbor before *Enterprise* reached Yankee Station in April 1969. With a bombing halt in effect only a few highly specialized missions were being flown over North Vietnam, but operations continued over the south and against targets in Laos. Operations on the line were normal until 15 April when another development in Korea infringed upon the Vietnam war.

MiG-17s of North Korea's 2nd Air Division shot down an unarmed Lockheed EC-121M reconnaissance aircraft (135749) over international waters, killing all 31 men aboard and bringing about a bizarre situation in which Soviet units assisted in unsuccessful rescue operations near North Korean waters. As *Ranger* had done the previous year, *Enterprise* steamed into the Korean region for a show of force. The North Koreans took no further hostile action and the carrier returned briefly to the shooting war. By the time *Enterprise* came home in July, its men had

The TA-7C. Flying over Dallas, the first of sixty two-seat TA-7C trainer conversions is bureau number 154477, modified in 1975 from the airframe of the 117th A-7B (LTV)

endured the catastrophic fire, fought in Southeast Asia, and come close to fighting again in the north of the same continent. The A-7B was a veteran.

The A-7B was eventually replaced with the active-duty Fleet but is scheduled to remain in service with the US Naval Reserve until 1992. 24 were converted to two-seat TA-7C trainers. An unspecified number were slated for conversion or parts for the Portuguese A-7P programme. A total of 196 airframes were built in the A-7B version, the last (154556) being delivered in Dallas on 7 May 1969.

A-7C

To keep production moving, the first 67 machines in the A-7E series were powered by TF30-P-8 turbofans. To distinguish these from later E models powered by the Allison TF41, this batch was designated A-7C by the Navy. For a time, the 'Sidewinders' of VA-86 were the only operational A-

The TA-7C, with friend. Belonging to the west coast replenishment squadron or RAG, the 'Flying Eagles' of VA-122, two-seat TA-7C keeps company with A-7E near NAS Lemoore, California in 1978. Aircraft in foreground is 154412, with side number NJ-206, and was converted 25 August 1976 from the airframe of the 52nd A-7B Corsair (LTV)

7C squadron in the Fleet.

Ben Short, whose first combat cruise with VA-86 is described on pages 63–65, returned in 1972 for a second combat cruise in the A-7C model. Short's squadron experienced one of the most painful incidents of the war:

'Early in the cruise [on 17 July 1972], the skipper was out on a night mission in South Vietnam with an Air Force F-4 leading on a LORAN drop [F-4D 66-8772]. The skipper used electric and mechanical fuzing for a straight and level drop from 16,000 ft [4877 m], and one of the electric fuzes went off at the

USAF 14582

The A-7D. US Air Force photographer TSGT Frank Garzelnick caught A-7D 70-955, coded EL, from the 23rd TFW, England AFB, Louisiana, dropping Mk 82 retarded bombs. Bomb drop took place at the Tyndall AFB, Florida range in May 1980. 23rd TFW was commanded in the mid-1970s by Col Charles McClarren who, as a major, accompanied the Navy's first combat deployment in the A-7A. Bulge beneath the chin of 70-955 is a Pave Penny laser target identification sensor, being retrofitted to Air Force/Air National Guard A-7Ds and A-7Ks
(USAF)

RIGHT
The A-7D. In 1969, C-5A Galaxy and A-7D number eight (68-8222) are subjected to Arctic and tropical extremes in the climate test hangar at Eglin AFB, Florida. 68-8222 is fitted with Navy style refuelling probe on right forward fuselage, found on the first sixteen A-7Ds only
(LTV via M J Kasiuba)

PRECEDING PAGE
The YA-7D. The service-test YA-7D appellation went to the first five airframes completed for the US Air Force. It is believed that the first two YA-7Ds only were completed with TF30 engines rather than the TF41, the first of these (67-14582), shown here, being flown at Dallas by John W Konrad on 6 April 1968
(LTV via M J Kasiuba)

The A-7E. Heading home to USS Constellation *on 10 April 1972 following a combat sortie against North Vietnam, A-7E bureau number 157438 wears side code NG-310 with the 'Blue Diamonds' of VA-146. Ordnance has been expended, but 157438 carries multiple ejector rack (MER) on outboard pylons*
(USN via Jim Sullivan)

TOP RIGHT
The NA-7E. Buno 156754, coded 7T-402 at NATC Patuxent River, Maryland on 3 October 1983, is one of several Corsairs modified for developmental work with the 'N' prefix. A non-standard nose pitot tube seems to be part of the modification
(Joseph G Handelman, DDS)

RIGHT
The A-7E, with friend. Strategic Air Command Boeing KC-135A (60-317) pumps fuel into A-7E 157549 of the 'Hell Razors' of VA-174, the east coast RAG, while another Corsair (157489) loiters in foreground. Air Force tankers have long carried a device enabling them to couple with the Navy's probe and drogue refuelling system
(LTV)

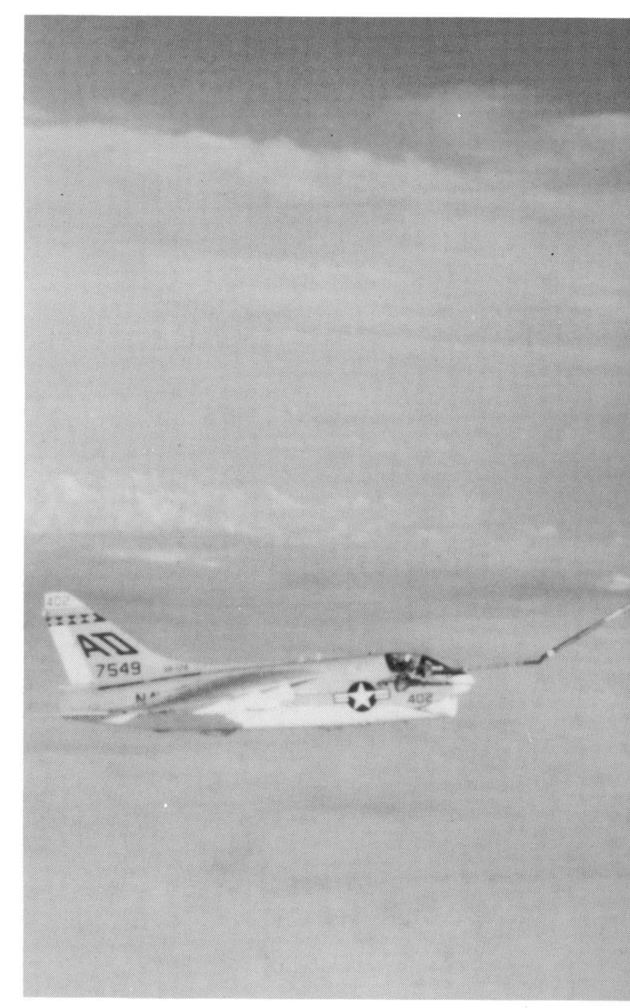

end of safe separation time. It blew the skipper's aircraft [156771] and the F-4 out of the sky almost instantly. One of the other A-7Cs [156792] was so badly holed he ran out of gas over the Gulf heading for Da Nang, and the third A-7C survived. We picked up the skipper the next morning, and also got the pilot out of the Gulf. The two F-4 types were captured, but only one came back when the POWs were released.'

Apart from powerplant, the A-7C was in all other respects identical to the A-7E, with a single M61A1 Vulcan 20 mm cannon with 1,000 rounds rather than two Mk 12 20 mm guns with 680 rounds. 36 of these machines were later converted to two-seat TA-7Cs.

AIR TEST CENTER
NAVY

00317
U.S. AIR FORCE
401
AD
7489
VA-174
401

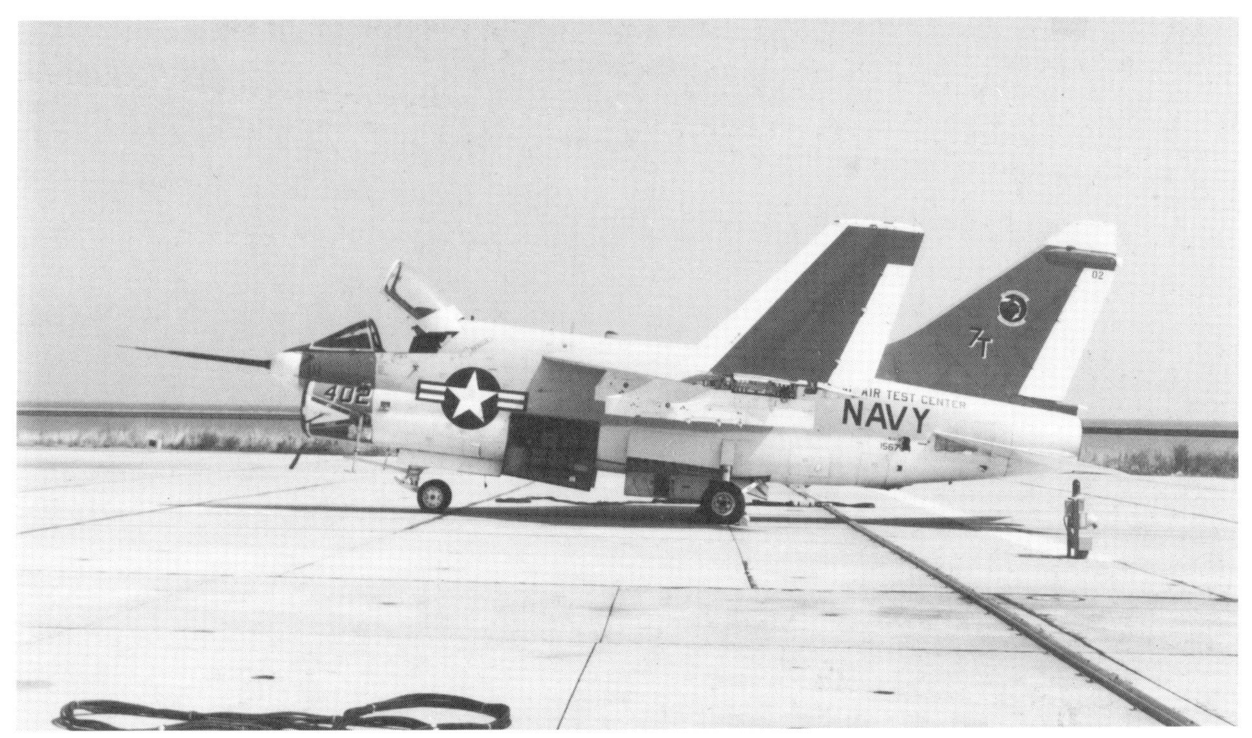

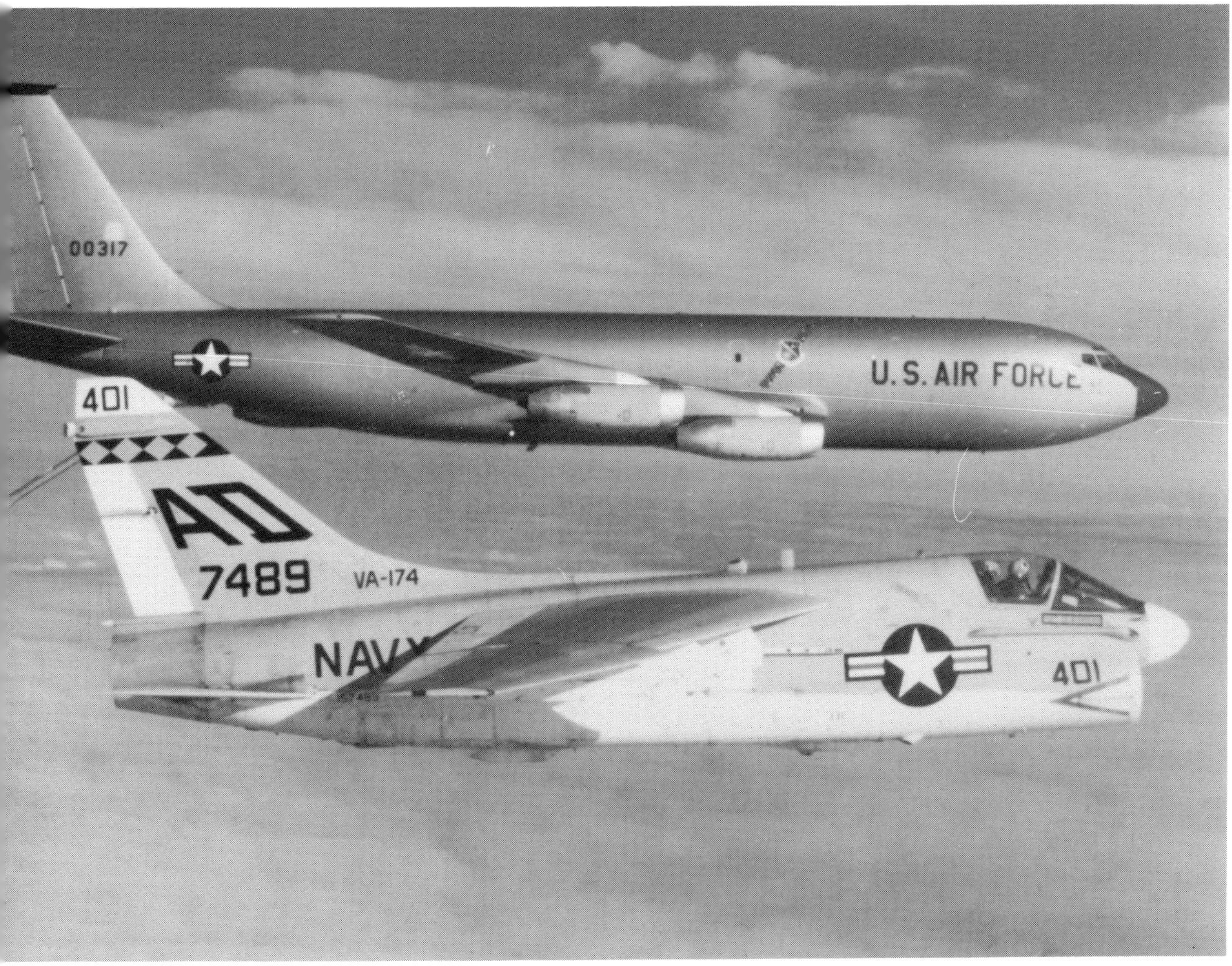

NA-7C

As with the A model earlier, structural changes at Patuxent resulted in the 'N' prefix for at least one aircraft in the A-7C series.

TA-7C

The first TA-7C (154477) made its first flight in mid-1975. It had been converted beginning 28 February 1975 from the 117th A-7B. TA-7C is the current designation for the US Navy two-seat Corsair trainer, used by the RAGs for pilot familiarization. The designation was decided upon only after conversion of one A-7E single-seater to a two-seat YA-7H, and after the designation YA-7E, too, was briefly used for this two-man variant. The TA-7C was initially delivered with the TF30 engine.

The conversion to TA-7C called for addition of a 16 inch spacer aft of the cockpit with an additional 18 inch added behind the wing. In a fairing directly over the exhaust tailpipe, the TA-7C carried a drag chute not found on other variants. Although equipped with a new cockpit and longer fuselage, the front-seat pilot could note no difference in the cockpit arrangement from single-seat variants.

60 TA-7C aircraft were converted in Dallas, 24 from former A-7Bs and 36 from former A-7Cs, the final example (156791) being modified beginning 20 June 1978. On 21 November 1979, a TA-7C (156748), side number XE-08 with evaluation squadron VX-5 (the 'Vampires') crashed on a high-speed run over the desert at China Lake, California. On 2 October 1979, another TA-7C (154536), side number NJ-207, of VA-122, the west coast RAG, crashed at NAS (the 'auxiliary' in NAAS by now removed) Fallon, Nevada. In May 1982, it was reported that the TA-7C inventory comprised 57 surviving airframes, 36 active, 19 in storage, and two non-flyable. In March 1983, six were assigned to VAQ-34 for the electronic warfare role and were redesignated EA-7L.

On 29 January 1985, the Navy took delivery of the first of 49 re-engined and upgraded TA-7C airplanes, rebuilt by LTV to receive TF41 engines in place of TF30s, new Stencel ejection seats, automatic manoeuvring flaps (AMF), and an engine monitoring system. An unspecified number of these TA-7Cs will also be equipped with forward-looking infrared receivers (FLIR). The programme to upgrade the TA-7C was scheduled to continue through 1986.

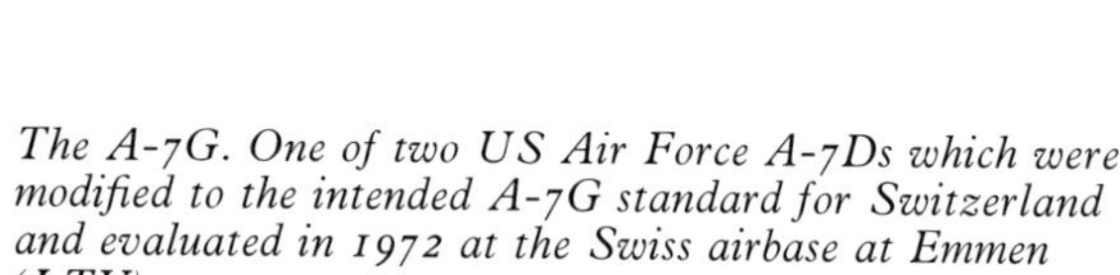

The A-7G. One of two US Air Force A-7Ds which were modified to the intended A-7G standard for Switzerland and evaluated in 1972 at the Swiss airbase at Emmen (LTV)

The YA-7H. Continuing his long career as Vought's chief of flight test operations, John Konrad looks down from the YA-7H, US Navy prototype two-seater in Dallas in 1972. Clearly visible are the retractable pilot's ladder, footholds for the rear seater, and nose-gear catapult harness (LTV)

YA-7D

The YA-7D designation was assigned to the initial batch of five aircraft (67-14582/586) delivered to the US Air Force, the first two of which were completed with TF30-P-6 engines, the first (67-14582) being flown at Dallas on 6 April 1968 by John W Konrad. The 'Y' prefix signified the service-test evaluation function.

The Air Force's decision to purchase the Vought aircraft dates to 1965. Maj Donald M Sorlie became the first USAF pilot to fly a Corsair on 18 February 1966 at the controls of the number two A-7A (152581) and Maj Gen Gordon Graham took the same aircraft aloft from Dallas on 3 March 1966, becoming the first general officer to pilot the type.

The Air Force's choice of a tactical jet designed for Navy shipboard use—the same decision it had reached with the F-4 Phantom with some swallowing of pride—marked a dramatic change in thinking about attack and close-support aviation. The A-7D would replace the F-100D Super Sabre which, more than a decade earlier, had dazzled the world as the first tactical jet capable of sustained, level supersonic

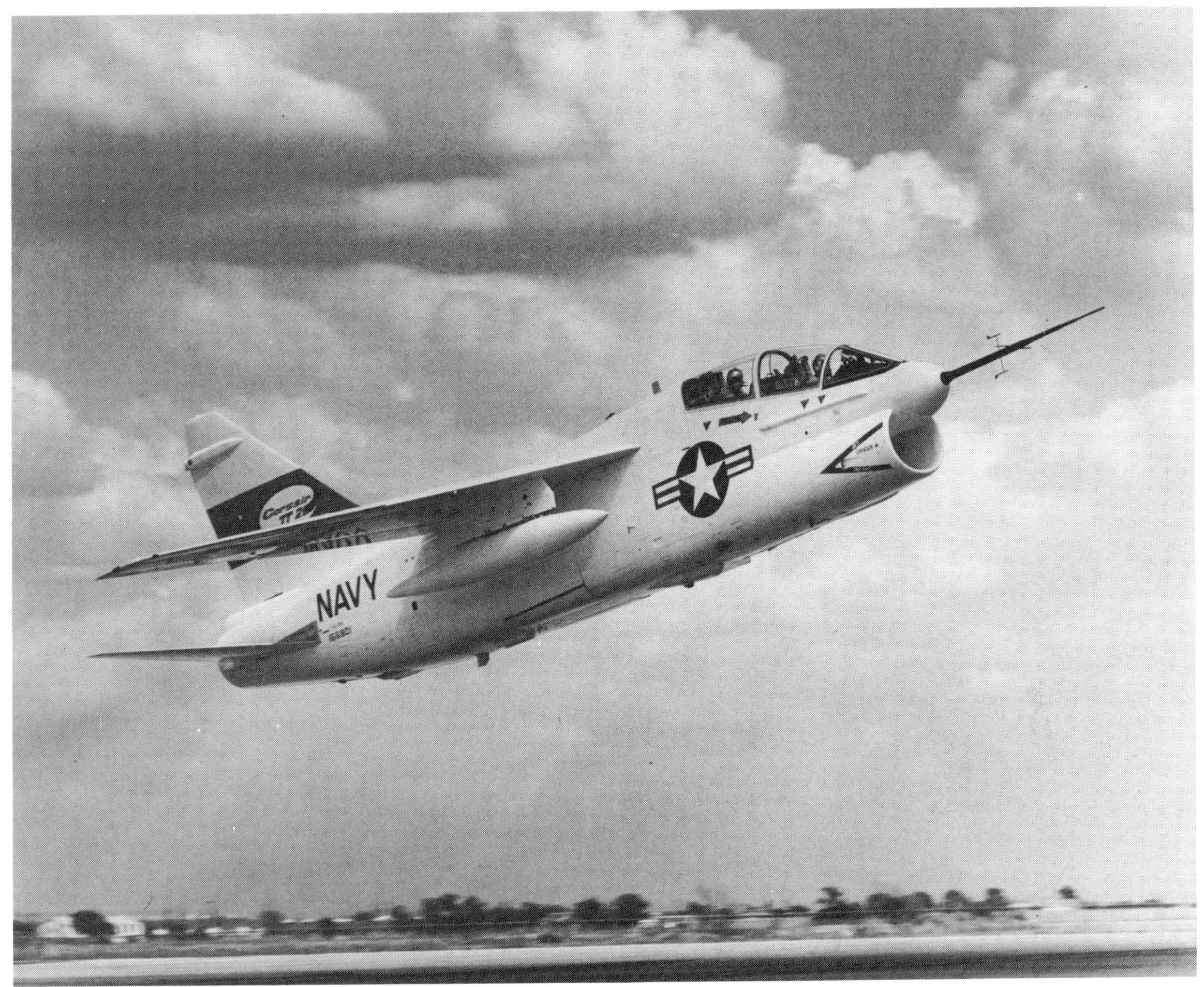

flight. Forced in this later era to resurrect prop-driven A-1 Skyraiders for the Vietnam conflict because of their load-carrying and loitering capacity, as well as their ability to absorb punishment, the USAF had finally realized that 'faster' was not 'better' and that an unglamorous, subsonic airframe could handle the job very well. Powered by the Allison TF41-A-2 turbofan generating 14,500 lb (6577 kg) thrust, an engine developed jointly by the American maker and Rolls-Royce Limited from the RB.168-62 Spey 25, and introducing the M61A1 gun and head-up display (HUD), the Air Force YA-7D was identical to the first A-7D (68-8220) and almost identical to the Navy A-7E to follow. Several of the first five airframes are still flying today, albeit with the 'Y' prefix removed.

A-7D

First flight of the A-7D took place on 26 September 1968 when LTV's Robert E Rostine went aloft from Edwards AFB, California for 1 hour 50 minutes in the third machine, still with a 'Y' prefix (67-14584). This was also the first flight with the TF41-A-2

The YA-7H. Taken by Arthur L Schoeni, who was Vought's principal photographer for many years, 5 September 1972 photo records the first flight of the two-seat YA-7H with two men on board
(LTV)

engine. A speed of Mach 0.94 at 20,000 ft (6096 m) was attained. The aircraft had been transported from Dallas to Edwards on 14 September in a Super Guppy with only its outer wing panels removed.

The first 16 A-7Ds were delivered with US Navy-style refuelling probe while the remaining D models had a 'flying boom' fuel receptacle on the dorsal spine of the aircraft. The A-7D had 35 access panels, 90 per cent of which could be reached without an aircraft stand, continuing the tradition of 'walk-around' maintenance. Officially the Air Force never adopted the Corsair II nickname for its variant, which employed the TF41 engine and M61A1 cannon, although no one seemed to notice.

OVERLEAF
The YA-7H. Vought's two-seat prototype, buno 156801, which led to the operational TA-7C, in flight over cloud cover in 1974 without instrumentation probe
(LTV)

3
RESCUE
JET
DANGER
INTAKE

Corsair
II 2
NAVY
156801

The A-7H. In Great Britain for a visit to RAF Coltishall in 1984, A-7H of Greece's Hellenic Air Force wears its US Navy bureau number 159938 (John Dunnell)

The first flyaway delivery occurred 30 June 1969 when Capt Robert Lilac took the eighth A-7D (68-8222) to Eglin AFB, Florida for climatic tests in the temperature chamber in 1969. The A-7D withstood conditions typical of the frozen Arctic (minus 65°F) and sweltering tropics (165°F). This machine later went to Panama, Alaska and Yuma, Arizona for tropical, Arctic and desert evaluation. The seventh A-7D (68-2221) was assigned to Edwards AFB, California in 1969 for armament tests. The first production batch of A-7Ds was delivered on 1 December 1969 to Detachment 1 of the 4525th Fighter Weapons Wing at Luke AFB, Arizona under Maj Charles W McClarren, veteran of the initial Navy combat deployment with Jim Hill's VA-147.

One A-7D (67-14583) was modified with a 'Digitac' system for fly-by-wire operation and partially equipped with fiber optic bundles in place of conventional wire bundles.

As Air Force A-7D squadrons began to proliferate, the service turned to Col Evan W Rosencrans to assemble the first A-7D wing and ready it for combat. Rosencrans became the first commander of the 354th Tactical Fighter Wing at Myrtle Beach AFB, South

Carolina. Meanwhile, the overseas deployment capability of the A-7D was confirmed during Category II testing at Edwards AFB when two aircraft flew a nonstop unrefuelled mission of 3,052 miles (4912 km) which terminated at Homestead AFB, Florida after a dog-leg over the Gulf of Mexico which represented a California–Hawaii flight. The two aircraft landed with 2,500 lb (1134 kg) of fuel remaining.

459 A-7D aircraft were produced. One (73-1008) was converted to become the first two-seat A-7K. By the mid-1980s, the type had been replaced in front-line USAF units (prematurely, some said) by the Fairchild A-10A Thunderbolt II. The A-7D continued with Air National Guard squadrons. But the only regular Air Force A-7Ds were at Edwards AFB as safety chase planes for F16, F-15 and A-10 testing, and with the 4450th Tactical Training Group (LV tailcode) at Nellis AFB, Nevada. The first two YA-7Ds have long since been retrofitted with TF41 engines. These and other survivors among the first 16 A-7D airframes have been retrofitted with Air Force-style refuelling receptacles.

BELOW
The TA-7H. Five two-seat trainers from new production went to Greece's Hellenic Air Force, the final example being bureau number 161222, seen during a visit to RAF Coltishall in 1984
(John Dunnell)

GA-7D

The GA-7D, 'G' for 'ground' has been applied to several non-flying A-7D airframes used for training of mechanics and technical personnel. In 1984, this included six airframes at Chanute AFB, Illinois (68-8220, 8223, 8226, 8230; 69-6190, 5193), one at Lowry Field, Colorado (69-6188), and four at Sheppard AFB, Texas (68-8225, 8228, 8229, 69-6192).

YA-7E

The YA-7E designation was applied briefly to the two-seat US Navy trainer which began life as the YA-7H and serves today as the TA-7C.

A-7E

First flight of the A-7E was made at Dallas by LTV's Robert E Rostine on 25 November 1969, apparently in the first airframe in the series (156801). The flight lasted 33 minutes. Acceptance and fleet trials of the Navy's 'ultimate' Corsair variant proceeded simultaneously.

The A-7E employed the TF41-A-2 turbofan and introduced improved automatic throttles. The M61A1 gun and head-up display (HUD) were fitted. Both A-7D and A-7E models had a retractable, two-step ladder for pilot entry different in shape from the stirrup-type step of the A-7A and B. Like all Navy Corsairs, the A-7E also had folding wings for carrier stowage, a feature, interestingly, not found on the A-4 Skyhawk it replaced. The bombing system on the A-7E introduced automatic wind compensation for improved accuracy; where pilots had had to set wind parameters on earlier models, the A-7E's computerized bombing system kept track of the wind on a real-time basis. Also new to the A-7E were brazed

The A-7K. Two-seat trainer 80-291 (OH) of the 112th Tactical Fighter Squadron, Ohio Air National Guard, during a rare visit to England in 1984
(John Dunnell)

LEFT
The A-7K. Sharp contrast and fine detail mark the work of Norman Taylor, whose photography has aided aviation history over the years. The only Corsair variant never to serve with active-duty forces, A-7K 80-295 (OK) is the 24th two-seater built for the Air National Guard and belongs to the 125th Tactical Fighter Squadron, Oklahoma ANG, at Tulsa in October 1984
(Norman Taylor)

joints and redesigned fittings aimed at reducing hydraulic leaks. The A-7E also had anti-skid brakes. These were in fact an Air Force-sponsored item also found on the A-7D model and were intended to correct a tendency of the airplane to hydroplane on wet runways. The risk of hydroplaning with the A-7 is understood to have been greatly exaggerated in pilot's locker-room banter and the new brakes, if they were every needed at all, had the drawback of significantly increasing tyre wear.

The first operational A-7E reached Lemoore on 8 October 1969. By February 1970, the west coast RAG, VA-122, had fully switched to the A-7E and the veteran 'Argonauts' of VA-147, together with the 'Blue Diamonds' of VA-146, were readying to become operational and to take the A-7E into combat in Southeast Asia.

535 A-7E airplanes were built. At least one was converted to NA-7E for tests. The first machine (156801) was converted to two-seat configuration and became the YA-7H in 1972.

NA-7E

As had occurred with the A model, at least one A-7E Corsair was given structural changes which warranted an 'N' prefix for tests at NATC Patuxent River, Maryland. With an extended nose pitot tube

Old Corsairs never die, they just go to Portugal. Seen in storage at the Military Aircraft Storage and Disposition Center (MASDC) at Davis-Monthan AFB, Arizona, A-7A 153171, coded ND-400 of squadron VA-304, with the storage number 6A081 and nickname 'Pegasus', was returned to duty in the late 1970s as an A-7P for Portugal (Philip D Chinnery)

TOP LEFT
The EA-7L. A TA-7C converted for the electronic warfare role with squadron VAQ-34, airplane 156761, coded GD-205, was redesignated EA-7L in 1984. Aircraft is seen in low viz gray on a visit to Andrews AFB, Maryland on 14 January 1984 (Joseph G Handelman, DDS)

BOTTOM LEFT
The A-7P. Portuguese Corsair, a rebuild of an earlier variant, on a visit to England in 1984 (John Dunnell)

and the side number 7T-402, the NA-7E (156754) was active at 'Pax' as recently as October 1983.

KA-7F

The KA-7F appellation was assigned to a proposed tanker development of the Corsair, never built, which would have replaced the Douglas KA-3B Skywarrior on carrier decks. Other Corsairs routinely carried 'buddy' refuelling packs but, because they did not require structural conversion or degradation of their attack function—as did the Grumman KA-6D Intruder—they never warranted a 'K' prefix for the tanker role.

A-7G

The A-7G nomer was applied to the version of the Corsair intended for the Swiss Air Force. Two US Air Force A-7Ds were temporarily modified to meet Swiss requirements and were evaluated for a few weeks beginning 11 April 1972 at the Swiss airbase at Emmen. Apart from wiring changes, no other modifications are known to have been decided upon. In the end, Switzerland decided not to obtain the A-7 at all, and the A-7G was never built.

YA-7H

First flight of the two-seat YA-7H (156801), a converted A-7E, took place at Dallas on 29 August 1972 with John W Konrad doing the flying. Early flights in the YA-7H two-seater were also made by Cdr James J McBride, who went from carrier-borne Skyhawk and Corsair duties to an interesting tour as 'Navpro', the US Navy representative at the Vought plant. The two-seater was adopted by the Navy but the 'H' suffix was pre-empted by the *H*ellenic Air Force—so the Navy two-seater became the TA-7C and the Greek single-seat aircraft became the A-7H.

A-7H

First flight of the Greek A-7H aircraft (159662) took place on 6 May 1975, with Vought pilot Jim Read at the controls. The Greek A-7H, powered by 15,000 lb (6803 kg) thrust TF41-A-400 engine, was delivered under a programme which began in 1974 and ended with the last of the 60 single-place Greek aircraft arriving in Athens in 1977.

The Greek Air Force, or *Hellinki Aeroporia*, was the first export customer for the A-7 following Switzerland's decision not to purchase. (Later, after the Carter administration killed a sale to Pakistan, Portugal became the second and only other export buyer). It is understood that Greece operates three squadrons of A-7Hs. The 345th *mira* (squadron) of the 110th *pterigha* (wing) is based at Larissa in Thessalia in northeast Greece. The 338th and 340th *mire* (squadrons) of the 115th *pterigha* are based at Soudha Bay near Iraklion in Crete.

TA-7H

The first Greek two-seat TA-7H (161218) took to the air on 4 March 1980 at Dallas with Jim Read in the front seat and Bob Dewey in back. The Greek purchase of two-seat aircraft, funded under grant aid, was initiated in 1978 with all deliveries taking place in 1980. Greece obtained six two-seat TA-7H machines, five of them from new production and one through conversion. Greece divided these machines so that two served with each A-7H *mira*.

A-7K

The first two-seat A-7K (73-1008), an A-7D conversion, came along so late in the SLUF's career that it was never operated by the active-duty US Air Force. The second and subsequent A-7Ks came from new production and one was scheduled for eventual delivery to each Air National Guard squadron operating the A-7D (14 of the latter being assigned to each squadron) with the remainder being operated by the 152nd Tactical Fighter Group, Arizona Air National Guard, at Tucson. The final A-7 aircraft built was A-7K number 31 (81-77), officially delivered in September 1984 without ceremony, partly because the aircraft had been completed and on-station in Dallas awaiting forward-looking infrared receiver (FLIR) retrofit before delivery. LTV records list the final airplane as number 1,545, although a count of serial numbers (Appendix) adds up to 1,551.

EA-7L

On 1 March 1983, squadron VAQ-34 was formed at NAS Point Mugu, California for the electronic warfare role with EA-7L aircraft. Modified from TA-7C trainers, the EA-7L is equipped to carry five different ECM pods or a drone to simulate other aircraft, missiles, and radar of potential enemies. The A-7 airframe was chosen for this role because of a shortage of A-4 Skyhawks to be converted to EA-4F standard. It is understood that six EA-7Ls were converted in all, and that they are included among the 49 two seaters (page 88) scheduled for update with the TF41 engine.

A-7P

The A-7P single-seat airplanes for Portugal retain the two 20 mm Mark 12 cannons and TF30 engines of the A-7A and B models, whilst incorporating the electronics suite, head-up display (HUD), and navigation fit of the A-7D and E. The TF30-P-408 variant of the engine is installed. The A-7P programme includes 50 aircraft, spares, and support equipment.

Vought refurbished and modernized 20 stored A-7A airframes under a $112 million (£100 million) contract signed in 1982. Deliveries of the first batch of 20 machines actually began in late 1981 and were finished by mid-1982. Deliveries of the second batch of 30 A-7Ps were begun 10 October 1984 in ceremonies in Portugal. The operational site for the A-7P is Air Base 5, near the town of Monte Real in central Portugal. The aircraft belong to *Escuadra* 302 of *Grupo Operacional* 51, a former F-86 Sabre squadron. Maintenance not available on base is provided by the *Forca Aerea Portuguesa* (FAP) overhaul facility, OGMA, at Alversa, a suburb of Lisbon.

TA-7P

The final variant of the A-7 Corsair is the two-seat TA-7P trainer for Portugal's FAP, six of which were converted from earlier single-seat A-7A airframes.

Looking to the future, Vought has proposed to make advanced Corsair aircraft available to potential buyers. These would come from conversion of the large number of stored, existing airframes. The company has no plans to re-open the production line to manufacture new airplanes. In fact, the LTV Aerospace and Defense Company, bearer of the time-honoured Vought name, no longer builds any airplanes at all.

Chapter 5
The Longest Mission
The Air Force and the A-7D

In hot, muggy darkness at 0425 hours, 18 November 1972, Maj Colin A 'Arnie' Clarke strapped into an A-7D at Korat, Thailand and taxied out for one of the longest combat missions ever flown by a single-seat warplane. With the final Linebacker campaign now being pressed against the heartland of North Vietnam, Clarke's 354th Tactical Fighter Wing had taken over the 'Sandy,' or Rescap, mission previously carried out by the A-1 Skyraider. Clarke was heading for enemy airspace not to assault new targets but to cover men who were down and get them rescued. It was tradition: no matter the cost, you did not leave your men behind.

Two days earlier, 16 November 1972, a Republic F-105G Wild Weasel (63-8359), callsign BOBBIN 1, of the 561st TFS, Korat, had been on an Iron Hand or SAM suppression flight in support of a B-52 Arc Light strike in the Route Package 3 area. SAM sites engaged the F-105G and shot it down. It was the last F-105G to be lost in Southeast Asia. The two-man crew ejected.

Enter Arnie Clarke.

Clarke's callsign, SANDY 1, identified him as flight leader in a massive rescue force of no fewer than 60 aircraft, including Jolly Green (HH-53C) helicopters, an HC-130P Kingbird (mission coordinator), tankers, F-4D Phantom MiGCAP cover, and F-105G Wild Weasels for SAM suppression. As he lifted out from Korat and headed for rendezvous with the Jolly Greens along the Laos-Vietnam border, Arnie Clarke could only ponder the hostile environment he was heading into.

The two downed airmen from the F-105G were hacking through dense underbrush near Thanh Hoa in a valley surrounded by AAA and SAM sites and close to a MiG base. The men had already been down for two days, a remarkable time for Americans to go uncaptured in densely-populated North Vietnam. Spotted by A-7Ds yesterday, the men were still in voice contact via hand-held radios, but their voices seemed increasingly filled with doubt and despair.

Clarke understood. He'd been shot down on an earlier tour in F-100Ds. As he drove toward them, Clarke saw that the treacherous hills and valleys of North Vietnam were socked-in under a heavy, oppressive overcast. . .

Working Up: Myrtle Beach

Arnie Clarke's 354th TFW was the principal combat user of the A-7D. But the Air Force's operational A-7D story had begun two years earlier. Tactical fighter training in the SLUF began during the fall of 1970 with the 310th Tactical Fighter Training Squadron at Luke AFB, Arizona under Lt Col Robert M Bond.

The 310th TFTS operated the A-7D for months before experiencing its first major loss at the Gila Bend Gunnery Range on 25 November 1970. The pilot was practicing a precautionary landing when the A-7D (69-6211) 'departed' at low altitude, turned over, and crashed. The accident board concluded that the loss was due to pilot error but a rebuttal was submitted and the final determination is not known. This is understood to have been the first operational loss of an A-7D.

Lt Col Bond went on to be one of the major figures in the A-7D community, in stateside operations and in Asia. Bobby Bond was wearing the three stars of a lieutenant general when he was tragically killed in 1984 in the crash at Nellis AFB, Nevada of an aircraft widely reported to be a captured MiG-23.

Once the Air Force A-7D reached Col Evan W Rosencrans' 354 TFW at Myrtle Beach, South Carolina, it was inevitable that men would take it into combat. Myrtle Beach is a summer tourist town on the Atlantic beach front, half a world removed from the karst ridgelines and SAM sites of North Vietnam. 'Rosie' Rosencrans, gravel-haired at 45, at times bespectacled, was mild-mannered, persevering and thorough, the antithesis of the tyre-kicking, devil-may-care fighter jock. The Air Force had got it right.

Rosie came from the long gray line at West Point. In Korea, he'd flown 133 combat missions in the F-80 Shooting Star and—no easy task in that aircraft—had shot down a MiG-15. In Vietnam in 1968, he'd flown 132 combat missions in the F-100 Super Sabre. He had made his first flight in an A-7D on 25 September 1970 with Bobby Bond's crowd at Luke and had been amazed at the stability of the A-7, at how difficult it was to get the airplane into a spin ('you had to work at it') and at 'how beautifully it handled.' Later to be another wearer of lieutenant general's stars, Col Rosencrans took command of the 354th TFW in May 1970. His first task was to oversee the wing's transition from F-100D to A-7D. He began to get the new airplanes on 17 September 1970 when Lt Col William F Lloyd delivered the first A-7D straight from Dallas.

Rosencrans established a diligent, disciplined approach to working up with the new airplane, working closely with his three squadron commanders and with the wing's Vought representative, retired colonel Erv Ethell. On 29 January 1971, Rosie became the first Air Force colonel to be rated as combat-qualified in the A-7D.

Ethell recalls those early days at Myrtle Beach as an exciting time. It was unusual for a company rep, but he attended Rosencrans' staff meetings every day. 'I never talked to any pilot who disliked the A-7.' The knowledge of the war was ever-present and though there was still a bombing halt in 1971 the men seemed to know that there lay ahead another round of fighting near Hanoi. Rosencrans' rich combat experience was invaluable and his practical, business like approach to preparing the wing achieved results. While the 354th TFW was still building up, two Air Force captains, James Read and Robert Dewey, took two A-7Ds to the Paris Air Show on 21 May 1971 in a journey which went routinely, unlike the Navy's earlier Corsair expedition to Paris. (These were the same two pilots who later demonstrated the would-be A-7G to the Swiss). Two months later, Rosencrans' wing at Myrtle Beach was fully equipped with three operational A-7D squadrons as of 1 July 1971.

The 354th TFW would go to war without Rosie. Col Thomas Knoles assumed command before deployment to Southeast Asia. Though they would not proceed to the combat zone, two other wings were to follow in equipping with the A-7D, the 355th TFW at Davis-Monthan AFB, Arizona under Col John F Barnes and the 23rd TFW at England AFB,

Into the crucible. American pilots were not supposed to fly over the beautiful Anghor Wat temple in tortured Cambodia, but at times it was unavoidable. A-7Ds of the 354 TFW from Korat (70-957 and 71-354) demonstrate the effectiveness of Air Force camouflage against Asian rain forest in this low-level sweep
(LTV)

MB

LEFT
Colonel Evan W Rosencrans, a Korean War MiG killer, became the first commander of an Air Force A-7D wing when his 354 TFW at Myrtle Beach AFB, South Carolina began receiving the Vought attack aircraft in September 1970
(USAF)

At Korat AB Thailand on 18 October 1972, just as the wing was becoming fully operational in combat, A-7D (70-956), coded MB, of the 354th Tactical Fighter Wing is ready for action, without Sidewinders but with eight Mk 82 500 lb (227 kg) bombs
(USAF)

Louisiana under Col Louis W Weber, activated on 1 July 1971 and 1 July 1972 respectively.

While A-7Ds readied for Southeast Asia, they also were called up for Exercise Gallant Hand 72, the largest stateside military manoeuvres since the Vietnam war buildup of 1965. Col Barnes' 355th TFW was slated for a major role. At Davis-Monthan AFB near Tucson on 16 March 1972, Sgt David L Perry and 41 other armament technicians were handed orders and hustled to D-M's building 1246, the Red Horse hangar, for C-141 transport to Bergstrom AFB near Austin, Texas. Bergstrom isn't normally an A-7 base but the forested region around the Texas capital and nearby Fort Hood provides space for men to practice at war. Perry was to arm one of the 355th TFW A-7Ds committed to the exercise. 23,000 Army, Air Force Reserve, and Air National Guard personnel were to participate. Secretary of Defense Melvin Laird would observe. That month, the same month as the Watergate break-in, neither Perry nor Laird knew that while Americans mimicked battle in the Lone Star State, the North Vietnamese were girding up for a full-scale invasion of South Vietnam.

Eighteen A-7Ds from Perry's wing deployed to Bergstrom. On 19 March, Perry and his mates bombed-up the A-7Ds for sorties in the war games. A few missions were flown, carefully coordinated with Army armour units in an assault exercise which demonstrated the Corsair's potential for close air support. But the A-7D was to be denied stardom in Gallant Hand 72. On 20 March, half a country away, one of the Myrtle Beach birds with the 354th TFW became disabled. The pilot ejected. The A-7D impacted in a wooded area 16 miles (25.8 km) northwest of Myrtle Beach AFB. The Air Force thought the problem 'had something to do with the engine', as Perry recalls. An earlier crash near Tucson of a 355th TFW A-7D on 20 July 1971 had been caused by mechanical problems while the pilot was setting up for a landing. The pilot ejected safely while his plane smashed into a railroad spur about a mile west of Tucson's Wilmot Road. *This* time, with the Myrtle Beach crash, the Air Force reacted dramatically. Amid its largest war games and only days away from the spring invasion which would send US

warplanes back into North Vietnam, the Air Force grounded its entire A-7D fleet. Dave Perry and his fellow ground crewmen peered through the Texas heat at hamstrung airplanes, shook their heads, and reflected that the A-7D had a long way to go.

The Longest Mission

An hour into the mission, Maj Arnie Clarke in SANDY 1 piloted his A-7D on a north-northeast heading, at the lower extremity of North Vietnam, still comfortable outside the enemy's AAA and SAM envelope. It was 0530 hours.

The thick, clawing overcast went all the way north to the tricky ridges and valleys at Thanh Hoa, location of a strategic bridge nicknamed the 'Dragon's Jaw', where the downed F-105G crew struggled to evade capture. The overcast topped at 8,500 ft (2591 m), obscuring mountain peaks which could transform any rescue aircraft into smouldering junk. While Clarke's Rescap force remained at marshal south of the SAM envelope, Clarke pondered the possibilities for a rescue, including the risk of further losses, and concluded that the situation was grim. Maj Clarke wanted to lead a couple of A-7Ds and a Jolly Green HH-53C into one of those shrouded valleys. He wanted to use SANDY Flight to cover a helicopter on a low-level run-in, down in the trees, hugging the earth to remain below SAM parameters until the critical moments following a pick-up. But Clarke's earphones kept crackling with bad news. 'We can't get in,' a helicopter pilot radioed. Clarke held SANDY 1 in a gentle orbit above the soup, looked down, and seethed with frustration. 'We can't find our way down into that stuff,' reiterated the pilot of the other chopper, the one to be used in reserve. The two HH-53Cs from the 3rd AARS at Nakhon Phanom, Thailand circled within distant eyesight of Clarke's A-7D, looking like great thrashing insects—helpless.

At his pre-mission briefing held not long after midnight and before the full consequences of the weather were known, Clarke had hoped a rescue could be achieved early in the daylight hours. Each new moment as the day progressed significantly increased the chances of the North Vietnamese capturing the downed duo. Clarke kept searching for a way in, but the morning began to drag on and visibility did not improve. He took full advantage of the A-7D's manoeuvrability, descending again and again into the clouds looking for a valley wide enough to follow toward the intended pick-up point.

In an earlier Sandy aircraft like the Skyraider, Arnie Clarke's relentless butting-up against the North Vietnamese weather would have been impossible. Clarke was making full use of the A-7D's projected map display and radar altimeter. It was tricky: he kept descending until his radar altimeter began jumping around or until the soup enclosed him in darkness. On several instances, he broke beneath the overcast only to find himself in a valley too narrow for manoeuvrability or for assembling the A-7D/HH-53C team for a final run-in. Remaining in constant contact with the choppers and support aircraft, the persistent Clarke—leaving his wingman behind—kept attempting to penetrate the overcast, searching for a way in. His voice conveyed frustration as he sent home his pair of HH-53C Jolly Green helicopters when they reached bingo fuel and called up another pair. Those HH-53C crews were unsung heroes, every-ready to risk a let-down anywhere in the enemy's homeland if there existed a reasonable chance of saving a fellow airman, but today it remained unclear whether they would have the chance. As the morning continued to progress, the two F-105G crewmen remained in voice contact via

LEFT
Myrtle Beach's 354th Tactical Fighter Wing retained its MB tail-code while in action in Southeast Asia. On 25 October 1972 at Korat, an A-7D (71-331) loaded with CBU-58 cluster bombs taxies out for a mission against North Vietnam. This aircraft survived the war but, on 25 July 1978, while serving with the 32nd TFW at England AFB, La., collided with an F-106A interceptor at Nellis AFB, Nev. and was lost
(USAF)

It isn't a Corsair, it's a SLUF. A-7D (70-971), coded MB, of the 354 TFW, lands at Korat with ordnance expended
(USAF)

A-7D (70-953), coded MB, of the 354 TFW loaded with Mk 82 bombs taxies out at Korat for take-off on 25 October 1972 (USAF)

RIGHT
On 28 June 1969, Capt Colin A 'Arnie' Clarke receives a Silver Star award at Phan Rang AB, South Vietnam, for actions as an F-100D 'Misty FAC' pilot. In 1972, Major Clarke received the Air Force Cross, the second highest award for valour, for another FAC mission in an A-7D 'Sandy' aircraft, to become the highest-decorated A-7 pilot of the war (USAF)

their survival radios, while scrambling to evade capture and running low on hope. The endurance of the A-7D was all-important now, but equally important was Clarke's own stamina. The helicopters could be relieved and replaced, but there was no one to fit in Clarke's shoes.

A radio report from RED CROWN, the surveillance ship off the coast, seemed to indicate that the best hope was to change the scenario and attempt to marshal the A-7D/HH-53C force for a run-in from the shoreline. The only alternative seemed to be an abort, scrubbing everything for the day, while the downed airmen's voices continued to boom in Clarke's ears with remarkable clarity. To test the proposed shift in plan, Clarke swang out over the Gulf of Tonkin, reversed course, and flew directly over the downed airmen—purposely risking engagement with SAM sites surrounding Thanh Hoa—noting the men's exact position on his projected map display. He learned from this experience that the proposed change was a mistake. If anything, the weather was even trickier from the east. . .

You do not leave your men behind. . .

Clarke made a second pass over the downed airmen. Suddenly, all hell broke loose. Explosions burst around him. The coastal ridgelines were covered with AAA gun positions and every one of those guns seemed to be locked-in on SANDY 1. Clarke accelerated to 400 knots (681 km/h) and began pulling 2Gs, manoeuvring sharply at a scant altitude of 2,000 ft (610 m) with vertical terrain all around him. He struggled to keep the AAA fire behind him and outside his turn radius while searching, still, for an opening to bring in a chopper. The situation was deteriorating relentlessly and the alternate plan to bring the Jolly Greens in from the Gulf was further scotched by the unexpected ferocity of the AAA barrage.

Everything was wrong. Clarke couldn't get his A-7Ds in through the soup to assault those AAA emplacements, the choppers couldn't navigate below the murk, and the weather was getting worse—2,500 ft (762 m) ceiling with broken clouds and three miles (4.82 km) visibility.

Two F-4D Phantoms supporting Clarke's force were vectored to the west of Hanoi to intercept MiGs reported in the area. The report turned out to be inaccurate.

It was 1100 hours. Arnie Clarke had been in his A-7D cockpit for six and one-half hours.

'*Anybody* see a break in this stuff?' Clarke asked.

MB
207
MB
323

Bomb-carrying A-7Ds of the 57th Fighter Weapons Wing, Nellis AFB, Nevada (71-297, in foreground) in flight over the south-western US following cessation of Vietnam hostilities in 1974
(LTV)

LEFT
Returning from a 'Sandy' combat search and rescue mission over North Vietnam, two A-7Ds (69-6207; 71-323) wearing the MB tail-code of the 354th TFW escort a Pave Nail North American OV-10 Bronco. The Bronco was especially useful on night missions to assist A-7D pilots in pinpointing targets on the ground
(LTV)

'We're negative on that', reported an HH-53C pilot.

'Negative', added another A-7D pilot.

'This stuff can burn off', somebody opined. 'If we can wait—'

'We've got to do it *now*!' Clarke thought out loud. He refused to give up on the hope that he could bring his wingman down into the soup with him to identify and attack the AAA positions. But 'now' had become a relative term. First, he would have to top off from a tanker. With everybody shooting at his aircraft and exhaustion racking him, Clarke told himself that it *could* be done, *would* be done. The fury raged inside him. He'd come to this place to fly and fight, not to be stymied by weather, bingo fuel and triple-A. 'Those guys on the ground can't *wait* for better weather,' Clarke thought out loud. '*The rescue has to be now or never. . .*'

Working Up: First Blood

After an exhaustive review, the US Air Force decided that the March 1972 crash of an A-7D, and grounding of the A-7D fleet, did not mean any mechanical or structural flaw in the airplane and need not delay its introduction to combat. The grounding of all A-7Ds turned out to be a brief interlude. Events resumed their momentum.

The 354th TFW ferried its airplanes from Myrtle Beach to Korat. The mere feat of moving an entire fighter wing halfway around the world was, itself, no small accomplishment. Capt Michael P Curphey was one of the last 354th TFW A-7D pilots to make the long journey and to emerge from his cockpit in the bright, dry heat of the Thai airbase. 'We began getting A-7Ds in there much earlier but it wasn't until 16 October 1972 that the last airplane arrived to put the wing on a fully operational basis. By then, of course, it was a free-for-all in both North and South Vietnam. In April the North Vietnamese had followed up on years of subversion and infiltration with their full-scale invasion, turning loose the elite regular divisions they'd held in reserve, using tanks for the first time, coming down the pike with everything they had. In May, we mined Haiphong harbour—it was *Navy* A-7s that did most of *that*—and began the Linebacker campaign, hitting previously off-limits targets in the North. By October, it was a real punch-out. We were building up to the final air actions which would pressure North Vietnam towards a settlement.

'At this point, you might think there was nothing new the A-7D could contribute. But there was. The A-7D went to Korat to fly interdiction and close-support. It provided night escort for AC-130 gunships working the Ho Chi Minh Trail. It also did combat search and rescue—the Sandy function. And of course, just ahead was the Christmas bombing when the A-7D became a "straight" bomber for attacks on industrial targets in North Vietnam.' By the end of its first ten weeks in combat, the A-7D had logged 16,819 hours flying 6,568 sorties with an average of 62 sorties per day.

Baptism of fire for the 354th TFW came in the infantry war in South Vietnam. On 16 October 1972, the 320th Division of the North Vietnamese Army (NVA) had surrounded South Vietnamese troops and their American advisors in a beseiged encampment at My Thach in the central highlands near Pleiku. The defenders, who had been in constant action for many months, were fading fast under incessant bombardment from mortars, recoilless rifles, rockets and small-arms. At mid-day, it appeared My Thach was about to be overrun. US Army AH-1G Cobra gunships struggled valiantly to pick out and assault the NVA positions, but more firepower was needed.

For the next six hours, Col Knoles' A-7Ds pounded the NVA with 500 lb (227 kg) bombs, CBU-58 clustered ordnance, and 20 mm fire. Joined part of the time by US Navy close support aircraft from USS *Saratoga* (CVA-60)—including A-7Es of the 'Bulls' of squadron VA-37—the 354th TFW aircraft broke the seige.

Over the next 48 hours the A-7Ds returned to clear out the NVA and send them scurrying in such a total reversal that the fleeing enemy left behind an arsenal of weapons, making a renewed attack on My Thach impossible.

A-7D (69-6205) of the 58th Tactical Fighter Training Wing, Luke AFB, Arizona, flying over mountains in 1974 (LTV)

Aboard USS Saratoga *(CV-60) in the Mediterranean, a ready pilot checks the cockpit of his Corsair, side number AJ-404. With air intake covered, maintenance door open and no Sidewinder installed, he is unlikely to take off soon (Jean-Pierre Montbazet)*

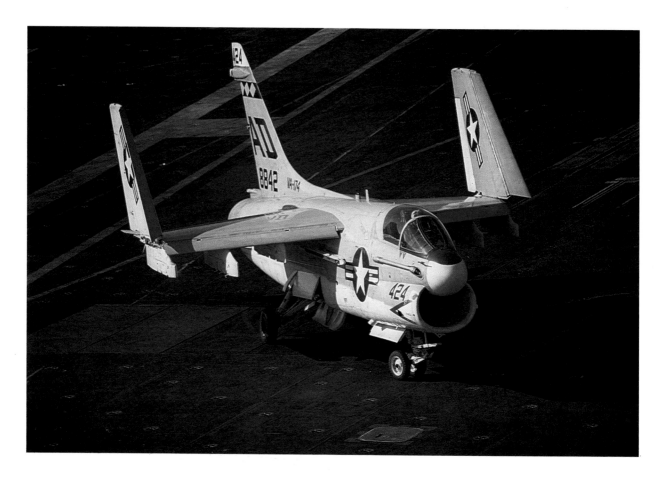

Wings folded, A-7E Corsair II (158842), side number AD-424 of the east coast replacement squadron, the 'Hell-razors' of VA-174, taxies aboard USS Lexington *(CVT-16) in the Atlantic*
(Don Spering)

TOP RIGHT
Corsair on carrier in low visibility paint scheme
(Jean-Pierre Montbazet)

***A-7P** Corsair II of the Portuguese Air Force (No 5511) is* ***a rebuilt** A-7A*
*(**Milslides**)*

RIGHT
A-7E in low visibility gray landing on USS Saratoga *(CV-60) during a Mediterranean cruise in August 1984 (Jean-Pierre Montbazet)*

BOTTOM RIGHT
Corsair nose. The wide, low-slung air intake demands caution on the part of the deck crews. Weathering like this is a feature of the current low-viz scheme (Jean-Pierre Montbazet)

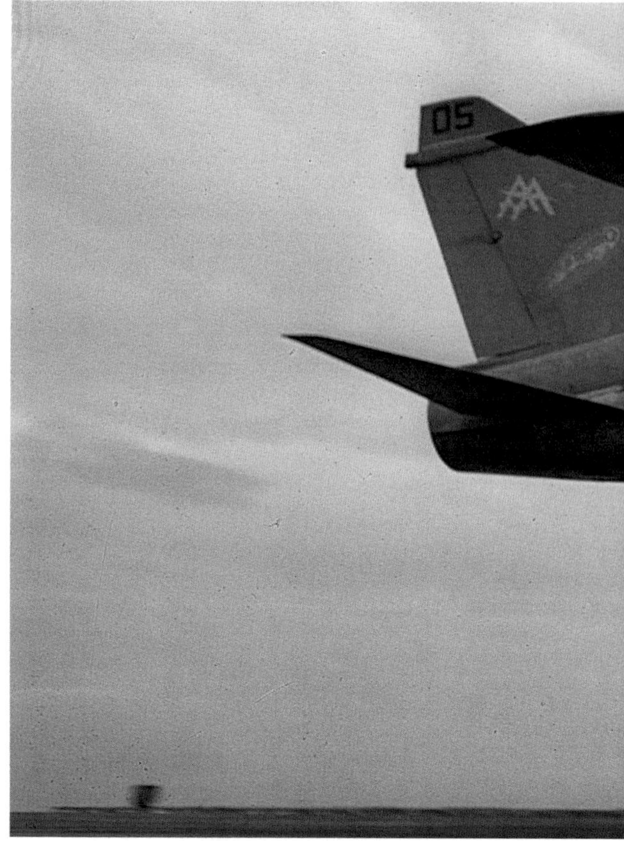

BELOW
Pausing at NATC Patuxent River, Maryland en route to Greece on 31 March 1977, A-7H (159962) of the Greek Air Force still wears US ferry markings (Robert F Dorr)

305
LCDR SLICK LEHMAN 
306
305

A-7D (72-243), coded CO, of the Colorado Air National Guard's 120th TFS, refuelling from a KC-135 tanker (Don Spering)

BELOW
A pair of A-7Ds (71-295; 71-353) of the 132nd TFW, Iowa Air National Guard, pictured in July 1982 (Don Spering)

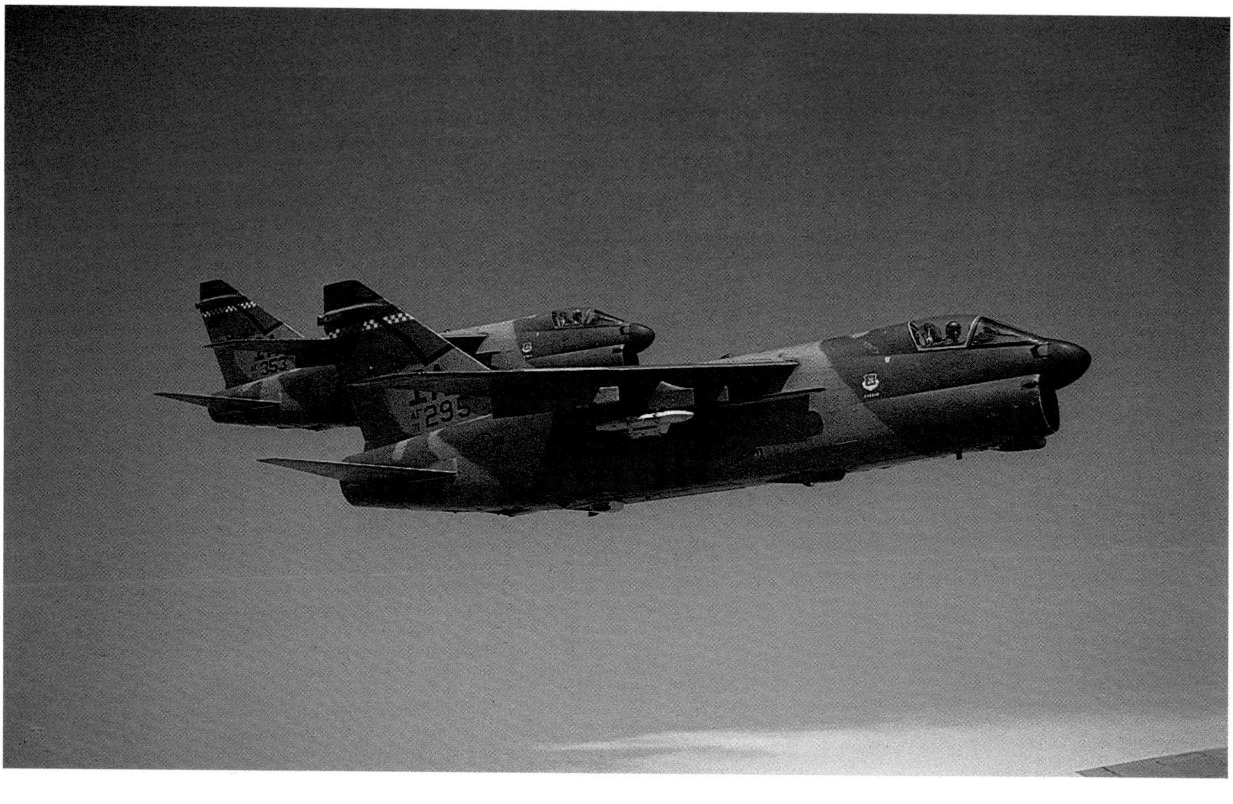

Brightly decorated for the 200th anniversary of American independence, Spirit of 1976, *the New Mexico Air National Guard's bicentennial A-7D (70-1048) is accompanied by another A-7D (73-992) in standard camouflage. Both belong to the 150th TFG*
(Jim Wallace)

BELOW
Toting live bombload on a training mission, A-7E Corsair II (156813), side number NG-413 of the 'Dam Busters' of VA-195 flies over snow-covered terrain in the western US in 1983
(HM2 Martye Dixon)

THIS PAGE
A-7E Corsair II of VA-86 recovering aboard USS Nimitz *(CVN-68) during a Mediterranean cruise in 1983. F-14 Tomcats of VF-41 'Black Aces' in background painted in high and low visibility markings (Jean-Pierre Montbazet)*

TOP RIGHT
Pathfinder mission. A General Dynamics F-111A aircraft with long-range navigation gear leads two Vought A-7Ds of the 354th TFW into North Vietnam for a high-altitude bomb drop using precision aiming. The A-7Ds appear to be carrying Mk 82 500 lb (227 kg) bombs and electronic countermeasures (ECM)
(LTV)

BOTTOM RIGHT
Still wearing its stateside Tactical Air Command badge on the tail but with shark teeth added in the combat zone, squadron commander's A-7D (71-354) of the 354th TFW heads aloft from Korat for a combat mission in Southeast Asia
(LTV)

The 3rd Tactical Fighter Squqdron (JH tailcode) was formed to give PACAF its own operational A-7D unit in the combat theatre. 3rd TFS aircraft like this A-7D (73-315), seen at Korat in July 1975, were the first American warplanes to wear black tailcodes instead of white. They participated in the evacuation of Saigon in April 1975 and the rescue of the crew of the merchant vessel Mayaguez *in May*
(George Bracken)

RIGHT
A-7D aircraft (71-311, in foreground) of the 3rd TFS stationed at Korat, Thailand in 1974. When the Vietnam conflict ended in a settlement, these aircraft remained in Southeast Asia after the 354th TFW returned to Myrtle Beach with its A-7Ds
(LTV, via M J Kasiuba)

The Longest Mission

Maj Arnie Clarke decided to make one more attempt to pull off the rescue before either heading for a tanker or giving up. Clarke instructed an A-7D wingman to stay with him. It was 1125 hours. Time was critical now.

Clarke plunged into the murk. By mistake, he swung into the wrong valley with SANDY 2 close behind. The two A-7Ds flew straight across the Thanh Hoa Bridge, the notorious 'Dragon's Jaw' which was one of the most heavily-defended targets in North Vietnam. Tracers and 57 mm shells swirled around them.

JH
JH
AF 70 983
JH
AF 71 311

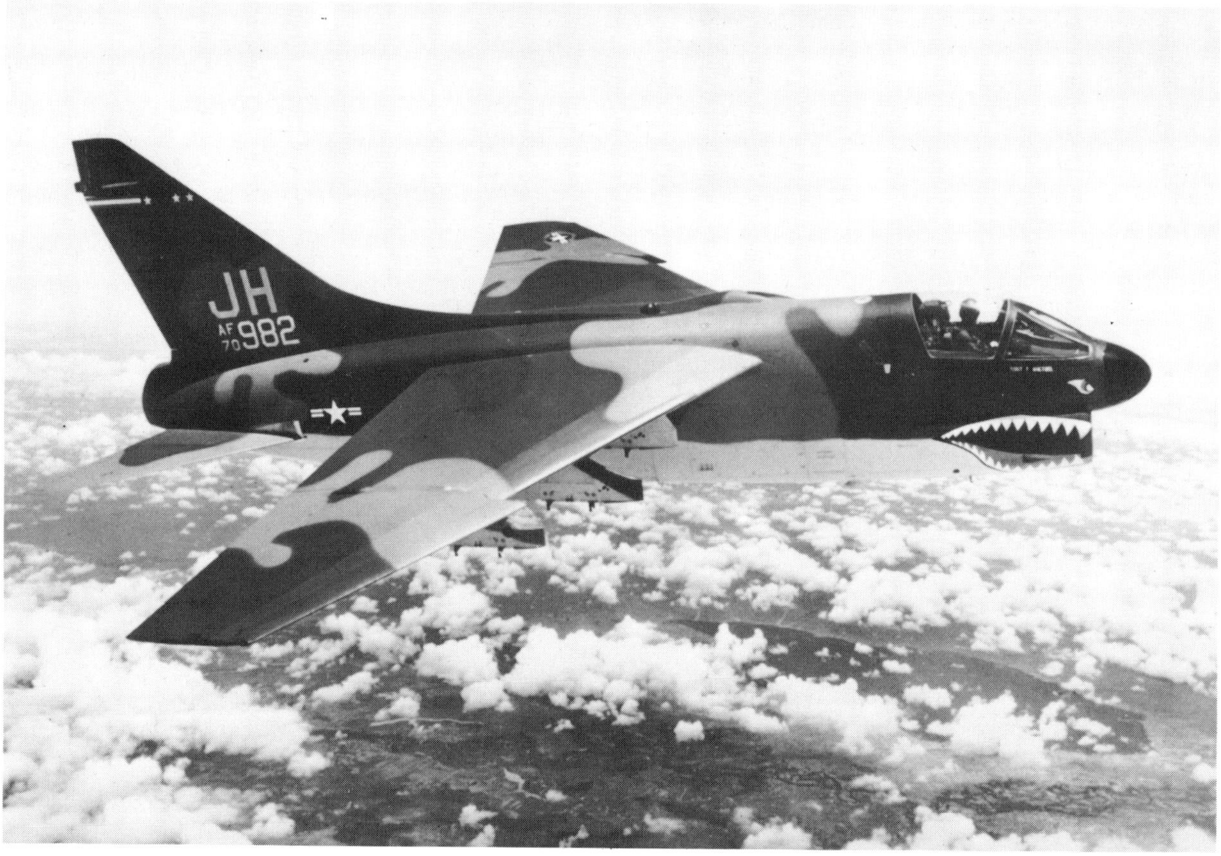
JH
AF
70 982

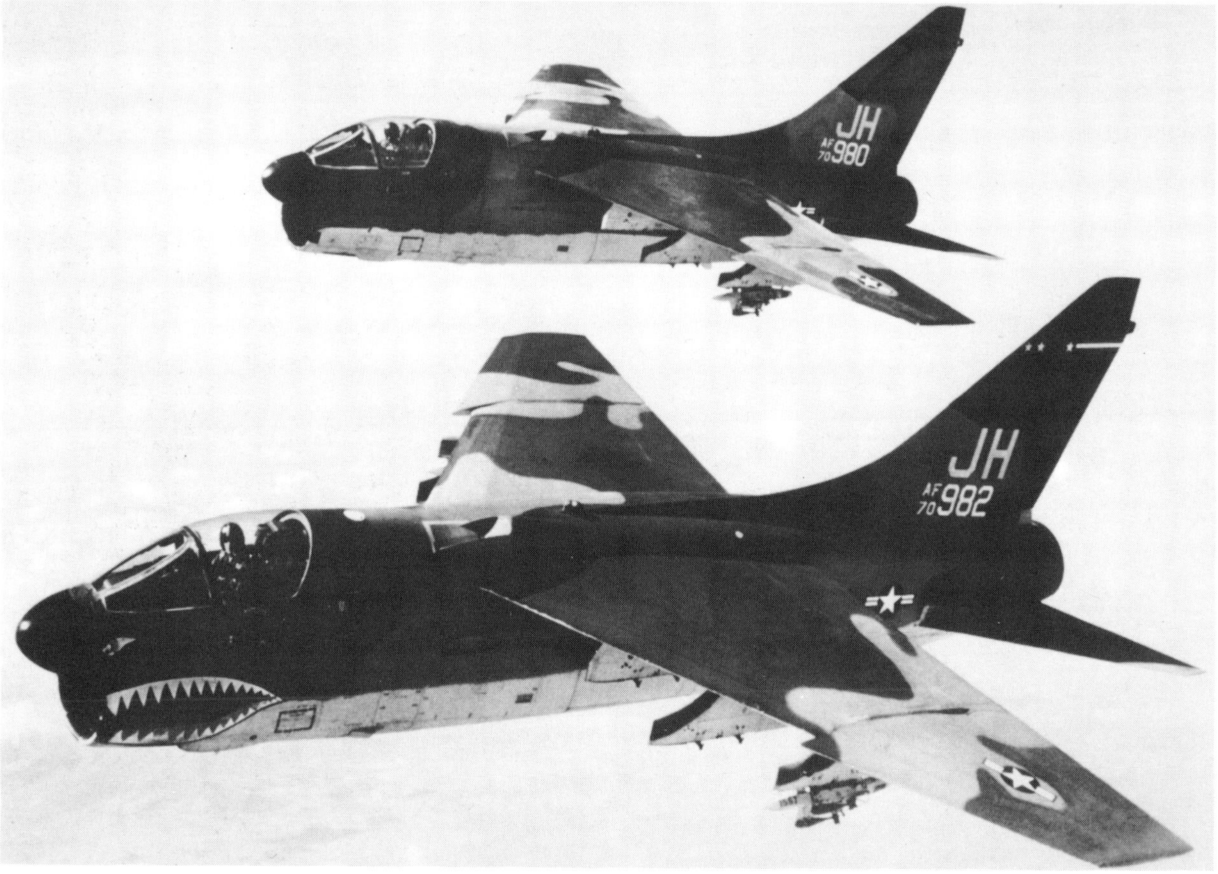
JH
AF
70 980
JH
AF
70 982

'Now or never', Clarke had said. He peered down at the puffy black explosions from large-calibre shells. Fatigued and cramped, with the enemy coming closer and closer to swatting him out of the sky, Clarke knew he'd reached the end-game. Everybody was running out of everything—himself out of stamina, the Jolly Greens out of fuel, the men on the ground out of luck. Within minutes his second pair of HH-53Cs would have to turn back.

At what had to be the very last moment, an HH-53C penetrated the overcast, found a valley large enough to manoeuvre in, and informed Clarke. Having spent the entire day trying to get in ahead of a chopper, Clarke now followed one. He took SANDY 1 down through the soup to attempt a link-up. For long moments, HH-53C and A-7D groped toward each other while jockeying into position for a run-in on the downed airmen.

'We're at bingo', the chopper pilot announced. His voice was forlorn with apology.

TOP LEFT
A-7D (70-982) of the 3rd TFS, Korat, on a flight over Southeast Asia. Shape of the aircraft is altered somewhat by wide-angle camera lens
(USAF)

BOTTOM LEFT
A-7Ds (70-982, 70-980) of the 3rd TFS, Korat, in flight over Southeast Asia
(USAF)

The helicopter was beyond fuel limits. If they went in now, they wouldn't come out.

Clarke authorized the chopper to pull away and head for home. He pulled out of the valley at the edge of the SAM envelope, came up on the radio to the Kingbird coordinator, and ordered the original pair of HH-53Cs back in for a new sortie. He wondered how to tell the men on the ground that the mission would have to be abandoned. True, the new pair of helicopters was approaching, but even the long-legged A-7D could not fly forever, and. . .

Maj Clarke simply could not accept the end-game culminating in his defeat.

BELOW
No details are available regarding this experimental paint scheme which long pre-dates US plans for desert operations in the Middle East. A-7D (73-993), coded DM, of the 355th Tactical Fighter Wing at Davis-Monthan AFB, Arizona on 11 September 1974. A more recent desert paint scheme for the US Rapid Deployment Force is depicted on page 185
(Don Spering)

OVERLEAF
The only aircraft ever shot down by an A-7 was . . . this A-7. In May 1975, while USS Midway *(CVA-41) was completing the evacuation of Saigon, Cdr Mike Boston, skipper of the 'Champions' of VA-56 ran into mechanical problems in this A-7A (152685), side number NF-413. Boston ejected and was rescued by helicopter, but his stubborn Corsair continued flying. Other A-7As from the squadron had to shoot the aircraft down*
(Norman Taylor)

13
NF
VA-56
USS-MIDWAY
NAV
152685

413

'We're not going home. We're going to cycle on the tanker'. It was 1145 hours. The new pair of Jolly Greens was manoeuvring into position. Clarke banked, climbed, and took SANDY Flight away from the shrouded valleys—heading not for his base at Korat but for KC-135s circling over the Gulf. . .

Clarke was a man of incredible perseverence. His aircraft, with an uncommonly roomy, 'man-efficient' cockpit, may have been the only single-seater in which a man could continue for so long with so many people trying to kill him.

Clarke led SANDY Flight out to the Gulf where KC-135s were holding in a racetrack pattern. They were brave men, these tanker crews who routinely ventured perilously close to the enemy coast. They obligingly topped-off his tanks.

Still getting voice communication from the downed airmen near Thanh Hoa, Clarke returned, briefed his new pair of incoming Jolly Greens, and led an HH-53C down through the soup. For long moments, a gap in the overcast remained open to them. Clarke broke through and levelled off at about 800 ft (244 m) above the ground.

He found just enough working space to pull a 1½G continuous turn and remain in the valley. The helicopter had gotten in with him! For the first time, SANDY 1's intrepid pilot was leading a chopper with sufficient fuel toward the rescue site.

Because the HH-53C could do only 150 knots (241 km/h), Clarke had to continuously fly 360° turns in front of the chopper as they worked their way toward the intended rescue site. Heavy AA fire boomed up at them. After establishing a planned pick-up and alerting the men on the ground that it wasn't over yet, Clarke got the first of several readings of a SAM site radar locking-in on his aircraft.

The signal faded. But Triple-A fire grew heavier as Clarke 'talked down' the remainder of his A-7Ds and finally brought his force directly over the downed airmen at low altitude.

'Time to start hitting 'em back.' Clarke set up a daisy chain with three A-7Ds and began continuous strafing of AAA gun positions on a slope just above the downed airmen. Amid much noise and confusion,

Protruding tailpipe illustrates how easily walk-around maintenance can be performed on the SLUF. A-7D (69-6191), coded DM, of the 355th TFW at Davis-Monthan AFB, Arizona on 11 September 1974 (Don Spering)

the Jolly Green crew, unaware of the gun position, swooped in and touched down. In a few remarkable seconds, the helicopter picked up both F-105G fliers, sprang aloft, and headed west.

It was anticlimax. But there was more. Pulling away from a strafing attack, Arnie Clarke felt a sudden jolt and heard a clattering sound, like tin pans banging together. It was the noise and concussion associated with a direct hit by 57 mm AAA fire. At the same time, his warning receiver told him that a SAM site was locking-on again.

Smoke gushed from his starboard wing. 'I'm hit!—' In the soup now, Clarke lost all instruments! He was blind, with no reference to his own altitude, with ridgelines all around him. And a SAM was locked-on, ready to fire. . .

Working Up: Korat

The decision to employ the A-7D for combat search and rescue was made in August 1972 at Seventh Air Force headquarters in Saigon when a six-month plan was devised to replace the A-1 Skyraider, the latter being badly needed for transfer to the South Vietnamese Air Force under President Nixon's 'Vietnamization' programme. At the same time, plans were made for a distinct squadron to perform this role, the 3rd TFS, although the 354th TFW would handle the job until A-7Ds could be made available for the new squadron.

As noted earlier, the 354th TFW was up to strength in the combat zone by 16 October. Early in November, A-7Ds began working with Jolly Greens in practice missions, with a Skyraider pilot observing from the helicopter to comment on the A-7D's performance.

Because of their greater speed, the A-7Ds could not fly alongside the helicopters. In flying racetrack patterns around the choppers, the A-7D pilots faced unique problems of navigation, flight discipline and preparedness for enemy defences, solved only through effective real-time communication. But if the A-7D's speed was not always an asset—except when racing toward men in trouble, or evading under fire—its computerized navigation system could mark and store the exact coordinates of a downed airman's position.

On 7 November, Skyraiders flew their last Sandy mission. Arnie Clarke's 18 November 1972 rescue marathon was the first of 22 combat 'saves' by the 354th TFW.

On a typical Sandy mission, the first three A-7Ds in a flight carried two CBU-38 cluster bombs, two LAU-3 launcher pods with 2.75 inch high-explosive rockets, and two more LAU-3s with white phosphorus rockets. The fourth airplane carried two CBU-38s and two CBU-12 cluster smoke bombs, used to screen a rescue LZ (helicopter landing zone) from approaching enemy troops. All A-7Ds carried a full load of 20 mm ammunition and two external fuel tanks. On some missions, A-7Ds were accompanied by North American OV-10 Broncos carrying the Pave Nail night observation system which could find, track and designate targets for laser-guided weapons and the bore-sighted laser range designator called Pave Spot which could beam a laser to mark the slant range and heading of a target, thus pinpointing its location. A little-known fact is that one Sandy A-7D in a flight usually carried riot control gas—in gas or powder form—in a CBU cannister. This was used only a few times but was very effective if conditions were right.

Capt Don Cornell of the 354th TFW noted that the A-7D, unrefuelled, could reach any target in Laos, Cambodia and North Vietnam except for the

Barely visible to the eye, directly beneath the pilot, two red stars representing MiG kills are painted on this A-7D (71-355), coded DM, wing commander's aircraft at the 355th TFW, Davis-Monthan AFB, Arizona—the only A-7 ever to wear MiG kills. Col (now Major General) Fred Haeffner, CO of the wing in 1973, is credited with one MiG kill and one 'probable' while flying a different type of aircraft, the F-4 Phantom (USAF)

RIGHT
A-7Ds (69-6201, 69-6200) of Lt Col Robert Bond's 310th TFTS, part of the 58th TFTW at Luke AFB, Arizona, in flight over southwest American desert in about 1970 (USAF)

uppermost extremity of North Vietnam. Cornell uttered eloquent praise for the A-7D typical of the affection felt by men who love the airplane. Said he, 'I guess about the only thing I'd do would be to make it a little prettier. . .'

The Longest Mission

The best thing that ever happened to Arnie Clarke was that the SAM site, whose *Fan Song* radar was locked-on his smoking, crippled A-7D, didn't fire. The next-best thing: the hit he'd believed to be a 57 mm shell was actually a 7.62 mm round which had inflicted less than mortal damage to his starboard external fuel tank and wing.

Clarke diverted to Da Nang, without instruments, where two A-7D wingmen talked him in to an IFR landing. At just after 1330 hours, nine hours into his longest mission, Clarke's tyres screeched on concrete.

The 23rd Tactical Fighter Wing, England AFB, Louisiana, was the final USAF wing to receive the A-7D. This machine (71-352), with the wing's EL code, is on a 1976 flight
(via M J Kasiuba)

He was awarded the second highest American decoration for valour, the Air Force Cross.

On 18 October, Henry Kissinger announced that 'peace is at hand'—referring to his negotiations with North Vietnam's Le Duc Tho in Paris—and on 19 December 1972 it was decided that, after all, peace wasn't. To bring Hanoi's diplomats in Paris to the final settlement, US forces launched Linebacker II, the massive Christmas bombing campaign. 354th TFW A-7Ds assaulted rail yards, radio communication sites and supply depots in downtown Hanoi. It ended in January 1973 when a negotiated agreement finally permitted the American pullout.

Pacific Air Forces (PACAF), which managed air operations in Southeast Asia, wanted its own A-7D squadron. The 354th TFW, after all, belonged to the stateside Tactical Air Command (TAC) and was officially only in the combat theatre for a temporary stay. The war in Vietnam may have ended in January 1973, but there seemed an incredible number of loose ends lying around. Combat missions over Cambodia were to continue until August 1973. For two years after that, the US would continue to prop up the regime in Saigon. There would be a continuing need for the 3rd Tactical Fighter Squadron, under Lt Col 'Moose' Skowron.

An Air Force officer recalls the mood of the times: 'Because there were so few A-7D pilots in the Air Force at the time, a TDY [temporary duty] rotation was started, bringing in both 354th and 355th TFW crews [the latter from Davis-Monthan AFB, Arizona]. At one time in August 1973, I counted over 75 A-7Ds on the ramp at Korat, both JH and MB tail codes [3rd TFS and 354th TFW]. At any given time, five to eight of them were without engines as the TF41 was having blade problems and was in short supply. In early 1973, PACAF wanted a PCS [permanent change of station] A-7D unit. There were some problems with all those TDY A-7D types—they flew by TAC rules, not PACAF. Also, every 90 days a new group came in and had to learn the ropes all over again—ROE [rules of engagement], area familiarization, and so on. The Sandy role was not one to turn over to a new guy. So PACAF—with good justification, I believe—pressed hard for an A-7D unit of its own. So the 3rd TFS under the 388th TFW was born in February 1973. The 3rd TFS became the sole A-7D unit when the 354th TFW departed in 1974. The A-7Ds of the 3rd TFS participated in the evacuation of Phnom Penh and Saigon and in the rescue of the SS *Mayaguez* [in 1975]'.

The war in Vietnam might have been over but men flying combat into Cambodia didn't know it. Typical incident: on 4 May 1973, an A-7D (71-305) of the 3rd TFS, callsign PHILO 2, was on a close air support mission in Cambodia and was pulling off its target (boat traffic) when it was hit by small-arms fire. The engine seized. The pilot, 1st Lt Thomas Dickens, ejected and was rescued by Jolly Green helicopter. By coincidence, Arnie Clarke and Tom Dickens were to

A-7D (72-193) of the 23rd TFW, England AFB, La., wearing the wraparound camouflage and black tailcodes which came into use in the late 1970s (Don Spering)

fly together with the Air National Guard in the late 1970s.

The final combat mission for Americans in Southeast Asia came on 15 August 1973 when people with ordinary radios in Phnom Penh heard a US command aircraft chattering with FACs and A-7D pilots. 'I guess this is just about it,' one pilot radioed. 'That's affirmative,' said another. 'See you in the next war, buddy.'

Maj John H Hoskins and Capt Lonnie O Ratley, both flying MB-coded A-7Ds of the 354th TFW dropped the last US bomb and fired the last US shots of the war around noon on 15 August 1973, 40 miles northeast of Phnom Penh. The two A-7Ds, callsigns SLAM 1 and 2, returned to Korat with all but 20 of their 2,000 rounds of 20 mm ammunition expended. For Hoskins, it was the 240th combat mission in the theatre. Technically, theirs was not the very last mission of the war—an EC-121 Warning Star surveillance aircraft earned that niche—but they were the last to use ordnance.

The A-7D remained in Southeast Asia until the bitter end. On 30 April 1975, it seemed to be over as 3rd TFS aircraft covered the sad, chaotic evacuation of Saigon. But on 12 May 1975, the American-registered cargo ship *Mayaguez* was seized by Cambodian naval forces and President Ford ordered military operations to rescue Capt Charles T Miller and his 39-man crew. As a helicopter-borne rescue force moved in, A-7Ds strafed and sank a Cambodian

Carrying Snakeye bombs, FLIRed A-7D (70-955) of the 23rd TFW heads for the range (USAF)

vessel. The same flight of A-7Ds spotted a vessel carrying the *Mayaguez* crew and covered a pick-up, while other A-7Ds covered the supporting helicopter assault on nearby Koh Tang Island.

Records show one A-7D lost in combat in North Vietnam (71-310, on 2 December 1972), two in Laos (71-312, on 24 December 1972; 70-949 on 17 February 1973) and two in Cambodia (Dickens' 71-305 on 4 May 1973; 70-945 on 25 May 1973). Given their combat career of about four months in the Vietnam war itself with holdover actions elsewhere, this was testimony to the ruggedness and survivability of the A-7D in a high threat environment. Only one A-7D (71-316, on 11 January 1973) is listed as a non-combat operational loss in the Vietnam conflict.

Once the smoke had settled, the A-7D served the US Air Force well in worldwide operations and racked up an impressive roster of achievements. One milestone was reached in October 1977 when A-7Ds of the 23rd TFW from England AFB, Louisiana travelled overseas to win all the awards available to them in the Royal Air Force Tactical Bombing Competition (TACOMP) held at Lossiemouth, Scotland, beating the RAF's new SEPECAT Jaguar aircraft. Also in 1977, the Air Force began a programme to improve A-7D capabilities by fitting the last two production airplanes with Automatic Manoeuvring Flaps (AMF), later retrofitted to all machines.

When it became clear that the Air Force wanted an attack aircraft especially intended to cope with the armoured threat in Europe and Korea, tests were carried out in 1979 with two 'strap on' gun pods, each containing a lightweight version of the GAU-8/A 30 mm Gatling-type cannon. The aircraft and the weapon proved effective against tanks but no more so than a newer design which was already well along by that time. The anti-tank SLUF was simply a late attempt to keep the A-7D in production and to stave off its replacement by a new airplane coming from Fairchild.

This didn't happen. By the early 1980s, the A-7D had been replaced in front line Air Force squadrons by the Fairchild A-10A Thunderbolt II, carrying that same GAU-8/A cannon. The A-7D, never officially named Corsair, departed active duty but continued to provide yeoman service with the Air National Guard.

Chapter 6
Walk-Around Check
A Technical Description of the Airplane

It starts up front, of course.

Like the gaping jaw of a predatory animal, the open mouth of the A-7—its unusually large, low air intake—threatens to devour everything in front of it. And it does. More than other aircraft, the A-7 is literally wide-open to trouble, unwillingly taking-in more than it can digest. Foreign object damage (FOD) is an alimentary affliction to which most modern aircraft are susceptible, but most engine intakes consume only ballpoint pens, screwdrivers, wrenches. The very large, very low intake for the A-7 eats *people.*

What's worse, the aircraft was designed without any imbedded grill or screen between the intake and the turbofan stator blades. A man who gets sucked into an A-7 also gets chewed up. No other combat aircraft in the American inventory has made so much minced meat of ground and deck crews.

It really happens. Despite the noblest efforts of safety people, it happens regularly. On the September 1971–March 1972 Mediterranean cruise of USS *Independence* (CVA-62), with Carrier Air Wing Seven embarked, including A-7E squadrons VA-12 and VA-66, it happened. Just after the carrier had secured from nightime flight recoveries at 0145 hours on 2 November 1971, Aviation Structural Mechanic Third Class Arthur Q Wigglesworth was working on an A-7E and was sent to Flight Deck Control to get permission to turn up its engine. Apparently, it was almost black on deck as *Indy* ploughed through calm waters near Greece. As Wigglesworth walked in front of another A-7E (157580), coded AG-313 of the 'Waldomen' of VA-66, already being turned at low power, he was caught in the intake suction and drawn into the engine duct. Another member of VA-66, Airman Terry Tennis, saw Wigglesworth in trouble and ran to help him, but was unable to keep him from being pulled into the intake duct. Wigglesworth was killed instantly.

Lt Cdr R D Musfeldt of the 'War Hawks' of VA-97 on USS *Coral Sea* (CV-43) pointed out to squadron mates the folly of disregarding FOD. Musfeldt cited an absurd example of poor deck practice—holding a mop in front of an A-7 intake to determine if the engine was running. On *Coral Sea*, safety officers emphasized to deck crews that A-7 intakes can ingest people by creating an initial suction on their headgear, jackets, hoods, etc . . . pulling them off balance. Deck crew personnel were taken to an A-7 where an experienced plane captain jointly crawled inside the intake with each crewman for an edifying close-up look at the razor-sharp blades of the engine. These training sessions were, in Musfeldt's pun, an '*object* lesson' in how easily the A-7 can eat not only foreign objects but the men themselves. Musfeldt's warning about the jet intake—the first and most obvious feature of the A-7—was disseminated throughout the US Navy.

The problem of catapult steam ingestion by early A-7 aircraft is addressed elsewhere in this text. Considerable effort has been expended to demonstrate that the TF41-powered A-7E does not suffer from the engine stalls attributed to sucking up steam on the carrier deck. The problem has always received more bad publicity than it warrants and, today, is merely an item of past history.

Airframe

Doing a 'walk-around,' staring in bright sunlight at an Air National Guard A-7D or US Navy A-7E Corsair II, the observer is struck with how unremarkable, how very conventional, the airplane actually is. Its resemblance to the F-8 Crusader is apparent, yet the A-7 lacks the variable-incidence wing of the Crusader, able to pivot on the fuselage to change angle of attack while the attitude of the fuselage remains constant. The SLUF has the open-mouthed, high-wing appearance of the Crusuder but is shorter and sturdier. You have to sit in the cockpit to appreciate that it is not *really* a small aircraft. Sitting in the cockpit and looking back over your shoulder, you can just see the leading edge of the wing which seems very far back indeed.

The A-7's dual-wheeled nose gear is an air-oil energy-absorbing strut which retracts aft and upward into the fuselage front section. The two main landing gears consist of single-wheel tripod struts with associated tyres and brakes. They retract forward, upward and inward into the lower fuselage section below the wing. To prevent accidental landing with the speed brake extended (that is, below the surface level of the undercarriage), extension of the landing gear automatically retracts and locks the speed brake. The A-7E structure and gear are designed for field landing at 32,251 lb (14,628 kg) gross weight at sink rates of up to 10 ft (3.04 m) per second, and carrier landing at 25,300 lb (11,475 kg) gross weight at sink rates up to 26 ft (7.92 m) per second. Maximum take-off gross weight on a typical mission with full fuel and ordnance is 42,000 lb (19,050 kg).

The A-7 fixed wing, considerably less complex than the variable-incidence wing of the F-8, is swept back at 35 degrees and has a wing area of 375 sq ft (34.83 m^2). It consists of a fixed centre wing section. Lateral control is provided by an arrangement of inboard spoiler-slot-deflectors and conventional outer panel ailerons. For optimum cruise, manoeuvre and air combat performance the wing has a built-in

On the deck of USS Eisenhower *(CVN-69) in the Indian Ocean in July 1980, alert catapult deck crewmen prepare an A-7E for launch while remaining wary of its gaping nose jet intake. Nose details of this A-7E of the 'Waldos' of attack squadron VA-66 include refuelling probe and launch bridle affixed to nosewheel*
(USN)

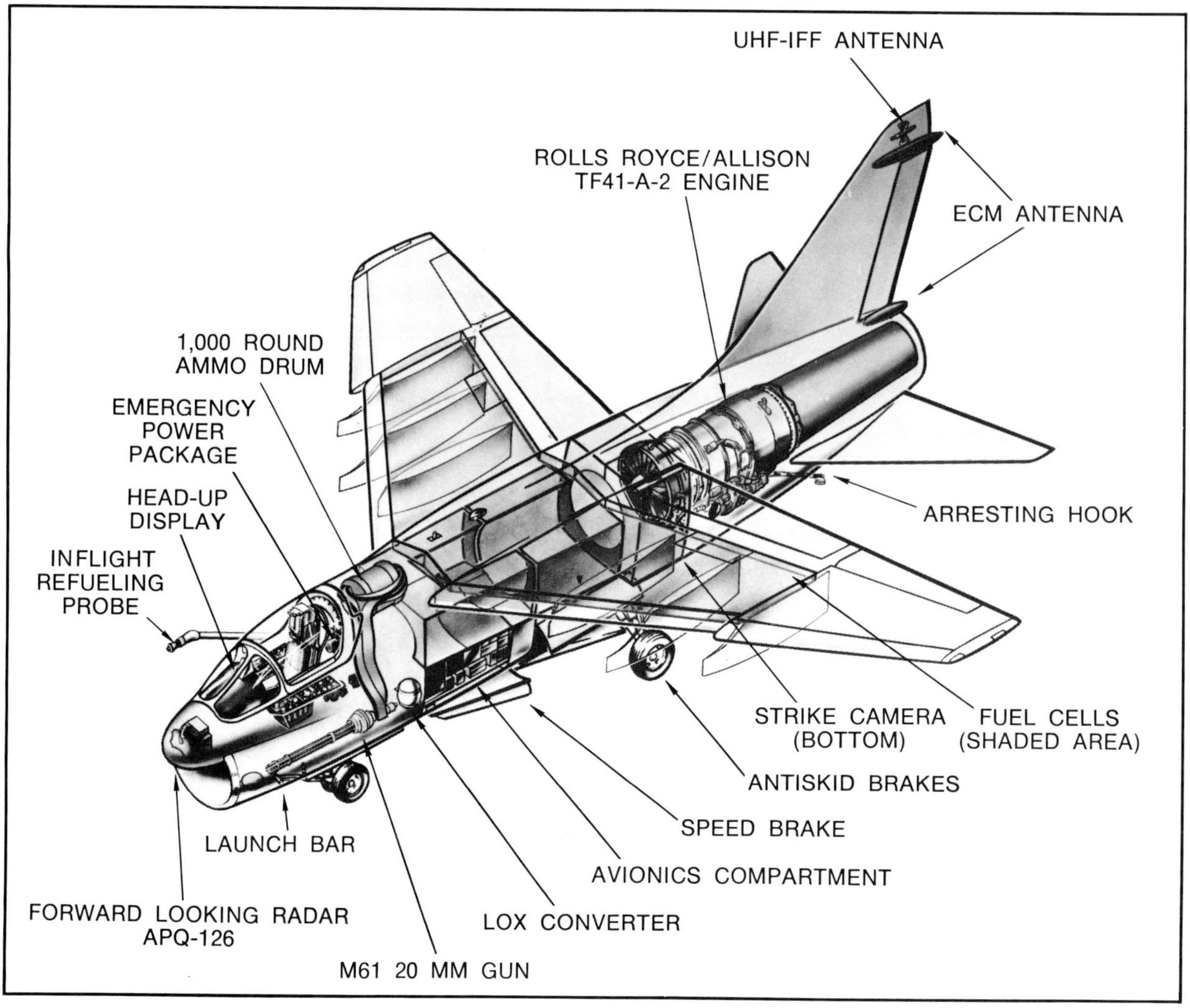

UHF-IFF ANTENNA
ROLLS ROYCE/ALLISON
TF41-A-2 ENGINE
ECM ANTENNA
1,000 ROUND
AMMO DRUM
EMERGENCY
POWER
PACKAGE
HEAD-UP
DISPLAY
INFLIGHT
REFUELING
PROBE
ARRESTING HOOK
STRIKE CAMERA
(BOTTOM)
FUEL CELLS
(SHADED AREA)
ANTISKID BRAKES
SPEED BRAKE
LAUNCH BAR
AVIONICS COMPARTMENT
FORWARD LOOKING RADAR
APQ-126
LOX CONVERTER
M61 20 MM GUN

fixed leading edge camber. There are six wing and two fuselage station pylons.

The fuselage is of conventional design, comprising redistribution bulkheads, continuous longerons and shear-carrying skins stiffened by frames. The single T-shaped speed brake is centrally located on the bottom of the fuselage. The arresting gear hook for cable engagement retracts into the fuselage aft section.

Tail section components are two separate but synchronized unit horizontal tails, vertical stabilizer, and a conventional rudder at the trailing edge of the vertical stabilizer.

According to Vought, the A-7E is designed for a service life of 4,000 flight hours and a load factor of 7G at a combat weight of 29,575 lb (13,414 kg).

The cockpit is intended to be 'ergonometric,' or man-efficient, with good visibility (though perhaps less than 'excellent,' the manufacturer's term, particularly to the rear), roominess, and ease of occupancy. Radar scope, projected Map Display and ECM Threat-Analyzer are located on the right-hand side of the main instrument panel, preserving proper pilot instrument scan of basic instruments. The Head-Up Display (HUD) permits the pilot to keep his principal readings in front of him and is also used to aim ordnance. The exceptional accuracy of aim is one of the A-7's strongest assets.

Ejection System

In his far-forward cockpit, the A-7 pilot inhabits a survival system intended to get him down safely if the caprice of circumstance forces him to leave his airplane. The A-7E employs the McDonnell Douglas

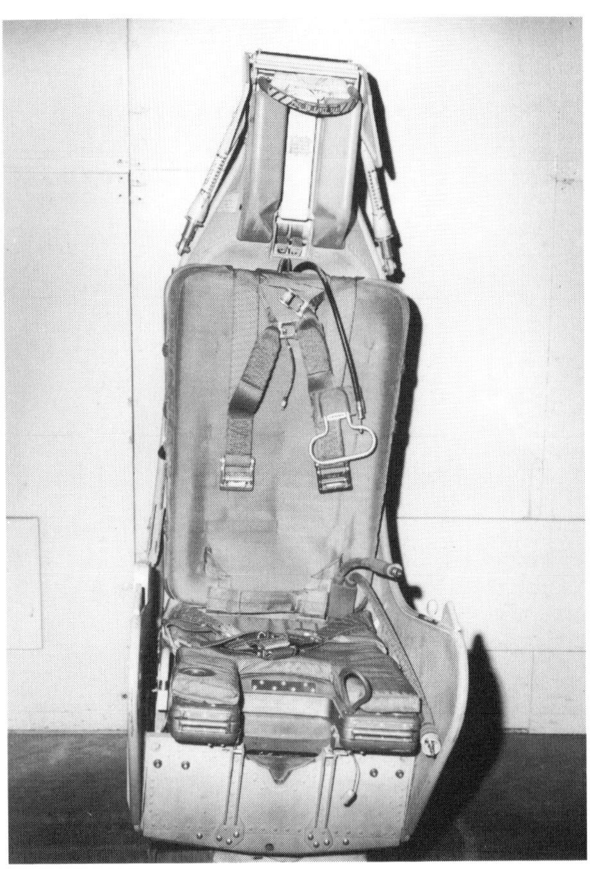

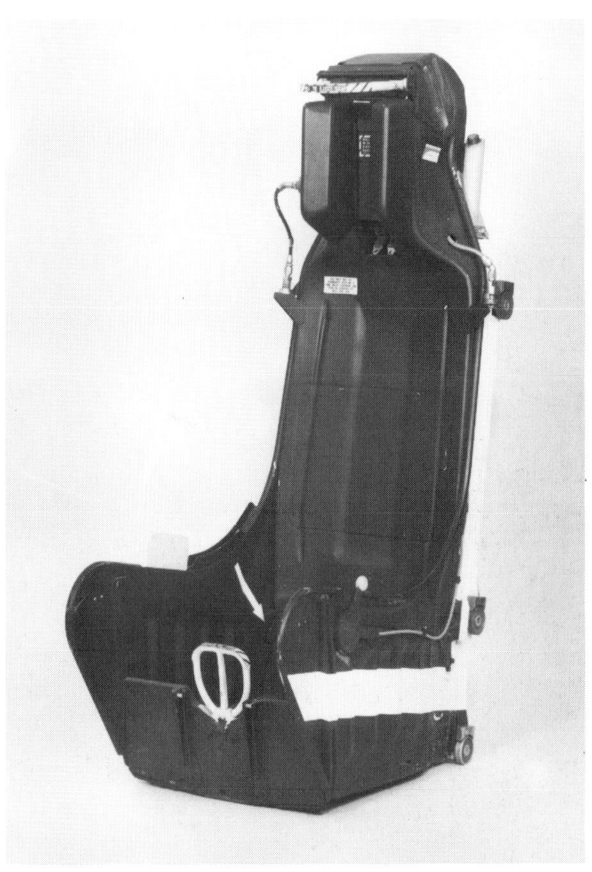

TOP LEFT
Internal arrangement drawing of A-7E
(LTV)

BOTTOM LEFT
Corsair is designed to make no-flare carrier landings with hook engaging carrier's arresting gear. A few weeks after the unsuccessful attempt to rescue American hostages in Iran, an A-7E with full flaps down engages the wire during 30 July 1980 landing aboard USS Eisenhower *(CVN-69)*
(USN)

TOP RIGHT
McDonnell Douglas Escapac 1C2 rocket-propelled zero-zero ejection seat used on A-7D aircraft
(MDC)

BOTTOM RIGHT
McDonnell Douglas 1G3 Escapac rocket-propelled zero-zero ejection seat used on Navy A-7E aircraft
(MDC)

OVERLEAF
Sequence shows TF41-powered A-7E being launched through a large volume of steam on a ground-installed catapult at NATC Patuxent River, Maryland. According to Allison, the TF41-powered Corsair has none of the problems with steam ingestion attributed to earlier, TF30-powered machines
(Allison)

TF41 TURBOFAN AIRCRAFT ENGINE
14,250 LBS. THRUST AND 15,000 LBS. THRUST
FOR US AIR FORCE AND US NAVY
PRODUCED BY
Allison
GM

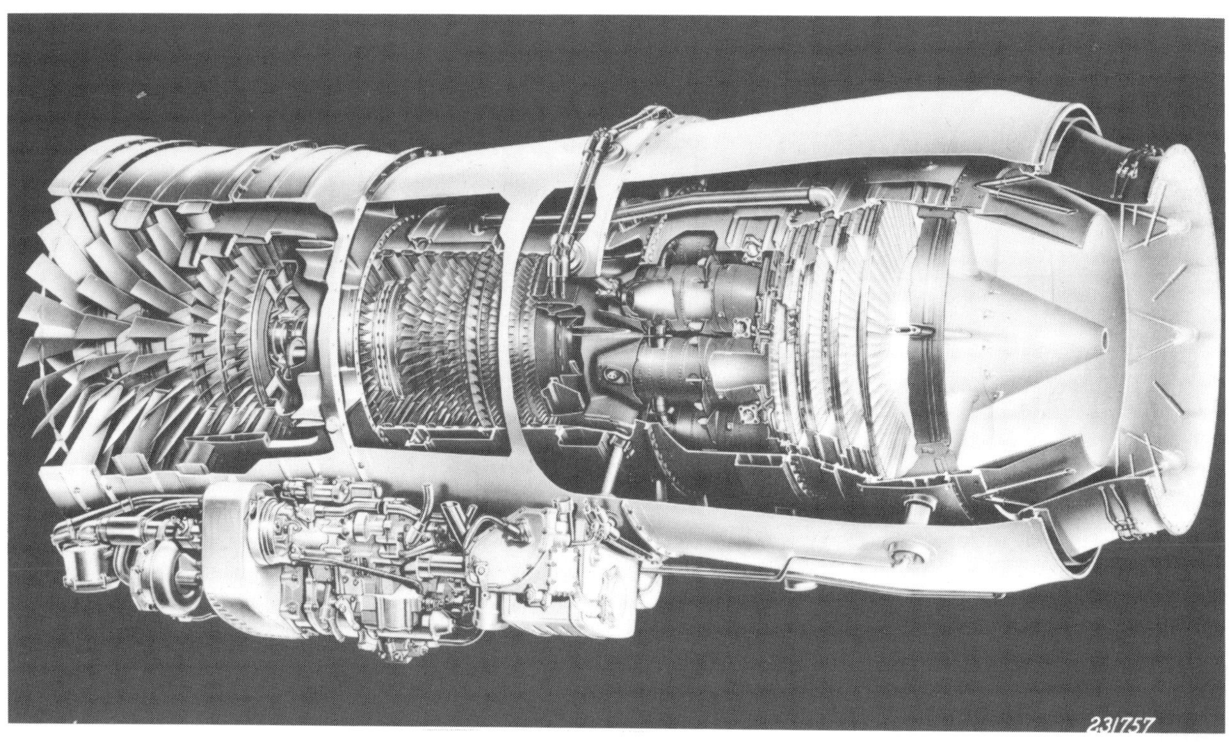
231757

ESCAPAC Model 1G2 rocket-propelled ejection seat (Model 1C2 on the A-7D), an NES-12M parachute with a 28 ft (8.53 m) flat circular canopy (A/P28S-20 parachute on the A-7D), an automatically deployable survival kit and a ballistically initiated canopy ejection system. The escape sequence is initiated by either a face curtain or a lower ejection handle situated on the forward edge of the seat bucket. Once the pilot has initiated the sequence, all functions which follow are fully automatic.

The system is intended to provide safe egress from 0 to 660 mph (1062 km/h) indicated airspeed (IAS) at altitudes from sea level through 50,000 ft (15,240 m). Although some aircraft types such as the F-4 Phantom do not permit crewmen to eject through the canopy, the A-7 is more forgiving: automatic flip-up canopy breakers are installed to allow safe ejection through the canopy. Eliminating the time lag between canopy ejection and seat ejection allows the system to accommodate high sink rates.

The system is generally considered effective and pilots have swum out of Haiphong harbour, and in one case landed safely in down-town Beirut, because it works. Ejecting is never fun, of course. In a two-seat TA-7C (buno 154410), coded NJ-203 of the 'Flying Eagles' of VA-122, the replacement air group (RAG) at NAS Lemoore California on 17 January 1984, Lt K C Hutchinson realized that engine trouble caused by foreign object damage (FOD) was going to provide him with an unexpected chance to try something he'd once done for sport—using his parachute. Hutchinson recalled that the moments immediately preceding his ejection were far from comfortable. He started to prepare to eject: knee-board off, lap belts tight, harness locked. He struggled to arrange the harness straps going between his knees so that he wouldn't receive an unwanted jolt during the opening shock.

As Hutchinson's TA-7C bored inexorably toward the desert near China Lake, ejection was initiated from the rear seat while he, up front, held his hands on the lower ejection handle, ready to pull if the sequence didn't start immediately. The canopy fracturing system (explosive cord) on the canopy went off, splattering the hood and striking him with windblast. Hutchinson was hurled out of the aircraft. Almost immediately, he had the good sense to rip off his mask and look up at his canopy. Both Hutchinson and his instructor landed safely and were rescued.

In the single-seat A-7E Corsair II which is in most respects identical to Hutchinson's TA-7C, manual ejection can be accomplished in either of two modes: (1) with parachute and survival kit, or (2) with parachute only. The second mode is attained by

LEFT
Allison TF41 turbofan (Rolls-Royce RB. 168-62 Spey) used on A-7D and A-7E aircraft. Maximum thrust is 15,000 lb (6804 kg)

Forward-Looking Infrared Receiver (FLIR). The 'Sunliners' of attack squadron VA-81 were the first Atlantic Fleet squadron to be equipped with the FLIR installation. Here, a FLIR-equipped A-7E (underwing pod) prepares to launch from USS Forrestal *(CV-59) (LTV)*

The 'Golden Dragons' of VA-192 converted to FLIR-equipped A-7E aircraft just before a 1982 Indian Ocean cruise aboard USS Ranger *(CV-61). These two 'Golden Dragon' Corsairs with FLIR pods are seen over the western desert in the United States (USN)*

pulling the survival kit deployment handle and the seat-mounted harness release handle; the first mode is accomplished by pulling only the seat-mounted harness release handle.

Company literature on the cockpit provisions of the A-7E makes it clear that the aircraft has another, little-publicized feature: the pilot is protected from the heat and light effects of a nuclear explosion by a fibreglass cockpit closure.

Propulsion

Early A-7A and A-7B Corsairs with the Pratt & Whitney TF30 engine were unquestionably underpowered. In fact, remarks made about the TF30-powered Corsair by seasoned veterans are far from charitable. But it must be remembered that the TF30 was the first practical military turbofan engine, the creation of the 1960s which was the first real innovation since the turbojet of the 1940s. For the first time a straight-through engine could use extra energy from larger turbines operating at higher temperatures, with much of the engine mass flow bypassing the main part of the engine, to produce exhaust thrust at much greater fuel-efficiency. The TF30, originally for the F-111 and later for the F-14, set the standard for high specific thrust and low specific fuel consumption, this as much as fuel capacity contributing to the A-7's marathon endurance. Rated upwards from 12,350 lb (550 kN) static thrust, the TF30 was rugged and durable in operational service and in combat.

The A-7D is powered by the Allison TF41-A-1 rated at 14,250 lb (6463 kg) thrust and all A-7E aircraft from number 68 (buno 158601) are powered by the Allison TF41-A-2 with a static thrust rating of 15,000 lb (6803 kg), both being license-built Rolls-Royce RB.168-62 Spey 25 turbofan engines. Again, the high fuel efficiency of the turbofan engine is exploited. Vought says that this engine was selected for optimum low-altitude performance, shorter take-off distances, increased pop-up capability, higher cruise ceilings and speeds, and increased manoeuvrability. Pilots consider TF41-powered A-7s a vast improvement over earlier A-7A and A-7B machines with TF30 powerplant, but even the more advanced airplanes are regarded by some as underpowered.

The engine design comprises a two-spool axial-flow compressor driven by a low-pressure and a high-pressure turbine. A bypass duct directs a portion of the air from the three fan stages around the combustion section and back into the exhaust. An annular mixer blends bypass air with turbine exhaust gas for more efficiency and a cooler exit nozzle, which provides major advantages in terms of increased survivability against heat-seeking missiles.

The TF41 can be restarted in flight by either an automatic relight system or a manually controlled ignition air start. In the automatic relight system, a flameout sensor (simply a differential pressure diaphragm with one chamber restricted) rapidly senses any change in pressure caused by a flameout. The diaphragm then moves to operate a switch which turns on the ignition.

Navigation/Weapon Delivery System

The A-7 navigation/weapon delivery system frees the pilot of most of the constraints previously imposed by manual bombing, augments his ability to find targets, and permits attack from arbitrary manoeuvres. The system can generate guidance to other targets or back home by the safest route. Before the A-7, no other aircraft, none, was designed with so sophisticated a computerized system to enable its pilot to navigate to the target and deliver his ordnance. In fact, Sweden's SAAB 37 Viggen, which first flew on 8 February 1967, is the only Western aircraft equipped with anything like the Navigation/Weapon Delivery System (NWDS) which forms the heart of the A-7 Corsair II. The system, as currently employed with A-7D and A-7E aircraft, includes:

AN/ASN-91(V) tactical computer, which functions as the primary element of the system, programmed to compute navigation solutions at a rate of 5 times per second and weapon delivery solutions at 30 times per second;

AN/ASN-90(V) Inertial Measurement Set which senses rotations in the aircraft's roll, pitch and heading axes as well as velocity changes and which functions as a three-axis reference system for navigation and weapons delivery;

AN/APN-190(V) Doppler Radar System, which uses the Doppler effect to continuously measure ground speed and drift angle;

AN/APQ-126(V) Forward Looking Radar (FLR) which provides the pilot with air-to-ground ranging, terrain-following, terrain-avoidance and other display data;

The Air Data Computer (ADC) CP-953A/AJQ, a solid-state, servo-mechanical analogue computer which continuously measures and computes altitude and airspeed information:

AN/AVQ-7(V) Head-Up Display (HUD), the

The Head-Up Display (HUD). USS Tarawa *(LPH-1) was flagship for the 'enemy' force in a war-gaming exercise in the Indian Ocean when A-7Es of the 'Royal Maces' of squadron VA-27 closed in for the kill. Photo shows pilot's-eye view, through the HUD, as A-7E's ordnance is aimed at* Tarawa's *bridge, 'killing' the commander of the simulated enemy force*
(USN)

first HUD in any American combat aircraft which displays symbols in front of the pilot's gaze giving him attack, navigation and landing data.

The Armament Station Control Unit (ASCU) which (1) supplies electrical signals to arm and release or jettison external stores; (2) controls and fires the fuselage M61A1 internal 20 mm rotary cannon; (3) furnishes store type information to the tactical computer; (4) supplies weapon status information to the pilot; (5) determines release according to the priority of stations; (6) determines the compatibility of the selected release mode with the stores on selected stations;

The Projected Map Display Set (PMDS) which reproduces an actual map, in motion coinciding with that of the aircraft, to guide the pilot.

The PMDS seemed especially impressive to the author on 10 July 1984 when he sat in an A-7E Corsair II (buno 160565) at NATC Patuxent River, Maryland being briefed on the Corsair II's remarkable systems by Strike Test chief test pilot Cdr Dennis V McGinn. It seemed so odd, this masterpiece of aerial wizardry, using an ordinary road map! The PMDS provided full-colour projection of a standard aeronautical chart reproduced on 35 mm film (well, *almost* a road map) of the region around the picturesque Chesapeake Bay in southern Maryland where naval officers have tested the newest of carrier-based warplanes for 42 years. McGinn showed how, in response to computer signals, the PMDS moves the film to keep the aircraft's present position on the map. This kind of 'moving road map' is available in much more recent strike aircraft, the Panavia Tornado for example, but as McGinn says, 'When the A-7 got it, nobody else had it.'

In the 1980s, terrain-hugging, computerized navigation and pinpoint, low-level ordnance delivery are routine. In the 1960s, the A-7 Corsair II pioneered these capabilities and pilots were impressed. Men who had *thought* they wanted to be fighter jocks suddenly discovered that the 'mud-

Cannon armament. The A-7D and A-7E are armed with the 20 mm M61A1 rotary-type 'Gatling' cannon using linkless cartridges. In the Gulf of Tonkin, deck crewmen feed ammunition into the magazine of a Corsair which has already been bombed up for strikes against North Vietnam (LTV)

moving' air-to-ground strike job could be as exciting as flying a Phantom. 'It's the mission that makes you want to fly the A-7,' says Cdr Michael A Ruth.

Col Erv Ethell, who played a key role in 'working up' the 354th TFW, became an LTV consultant and later the firm's east coast manager after retiring from the Air Force. 'I still firmly believe that the A-7 is the best close-support aircraft flying today,' says Ethell, who is not enthusiastic about the Air Force replacing the A-7D with the A-10A. 'The A-7D was manufactured with a 10-mil error or less. That was part of the specs. LTV met those specs and more. The pilot average was better than that, including flying combat in Southeast Asia. The accuracy was closer to 7 mils.'

To its Navy users, the Navigation/Weapon Delivery System is considered one of the most reliable and useful in the Fleet. But it can always be improved. Says Paul C Clements of the Naval Research Laboratory (NRL) in Washington, 'Like most software products of its vintage, (the computer) suffers from not having enough memory and being too difficult to understand and far too expensive and complex to modify.' In 1979, the NRL undertook to develop and demonstrate advanced software engineering techniques that promise to solve these problems for the A-7 and later aircraft with embedded tactical computers. Says Clements, 'We chose the A-7E program as the application model on which we would demonstrate our methods. We're producing a new program for the A-7 computer, developed in accordance with strict state-of-the-art engineering techniques, that will demonstrate the benefits of new software technologies.' Clements' project, called Software Cost Reduction (SCR) will improve the A-7 system and will also, in his words, 'serve as a model of software development for others to follow.'

Vought test pilot Nelson Gillette (left) and Col Wess Chambers of the Arizona Air National Guard hunker beneath the General Electric gun pod used to carry the 30 mm GAU-8/A cannon in April 1979 tests with the two-seat YA-7E (156801). Gillette evaluated this aircraft with one gun pod under each wing in an apparent bid to compete with the Fairchild A-10A's anti-tank capability. In separate tests, the A-7 was also evaluated with a gun pod carrying 30 mm Oerlikon KCA cannon (LTV)

65

The Goodyear AN/ALE-39 Countermeasures Dispensing System (CDS), mounted on the wing pylon above an MER of the eighth A-7A built (152651) at the Naval Weapons Center, China Lake, California may have been used in Corsair actions in Lebanon. The system accommodates RR-129 chaff packs, Mk 46 flares, and the AM/6988/A active jamming device. The system does not interfere with the placing of ordnance on the underwing pylon (Goodyear)

REMOVE BEFORE FLIGHT

Deck crewmen aboard USS Kitty Hawk *(CVA-63) in the Gulf of Tonkin in 1972 load an A-7E Corsair of the 'Golden Dragons' of attack squadron VA-192 with ordnance for a mission against North Vietnam (LTV)*

Armament

The Air Force A-7D and Navy A-7E incorporate the definitive gun armament for the Corsair series. Whereas the A-7A and A-7B mounted two 20 mm Mk 12 cannon with 680 rounds, the A-7D and A-7E have the 20 mm M61A1 six-barrel rotary cannon with a 1,000 round-capacity drum mounted behind the pilot's head, this drum employing a linkless feed, spent cartridges being returned to the drum instead of being jettisoned with possible damage to the aircraft's external surfaces.

The Corsair routinely carries two AIM-9 Sidewinder IR missiles on LAU-7/A fuselage launch rails. Though no A-7 has ever shot down an enemy aircraft, pilots regard its air combat capability as outstanding; A-7s are used for carrier combat air patrols when wind conditions are not favourable for launching F-14As, or when a ship's catapults are down, since the A-7 can be launched without catapult assistance but the F-14A cannot.

The active defence capability of the A-7D/A-7E is augmented by the high standard of manoeuvrability permitted by its 7G flight envelope, a roll rate of 140 deg/sec and, as has been said, sufficient fuel to enable it to outstay an enemy interceptor in low-altitude, fast-manoeuvring combat. As a passive defence measure, 430 lb (195 kg) of armour is provided for the pilot, engine and fuel lines, and a special pilot-operated valve can isolate non-essential hydraulic systems from the flight-control system, minimizing

Confederate flag identifies this A-7D as belonging to the Virginia Air National Guard's 192nd TFG. Pave Penny is fitted under the intake. In 1985, Virginia was the only A-7D user not to be assigned a two-letter tailcode, although it was reported that a VA code would eventually be adopted
(Va. ANG)

hydraulic fluid loss in the event of battle damage. The A-7D/A-7E can also carry a variety of electronic countermeasures (ECM) equipment to sense enemy ground and aircraft radar scanning and lock-on, and enemy missile radar pulsing and lock-on, and provide the right signals to enable the lock to be broken.

For the passive electronic warfare task, the A-7E carries the Goodyear ALE-39 chaff/flare dispenser. A recent addition to this system is Sanders Associates' POET (Primed Oscillator Expendable Transponder) which is physically interchangeable with chaff/IR rounds and is a self-contained, expendable miniature jammer which can modify and repeat an incoming radar signal. The ALE-39 is carried on a parent rack on station six under the A-7E wing and its chaff, flares and expendable jammers, packed in identical cartridges, are interchangeable with each other. In addition to parent racks (ie, ordnance station pylons), the aircraft carries triple ejector racks (TER) and multiple ejector racks (MER) which fit beneath the basic pylon to increase the variety of ordnance stores.

An encyclopedia could be written solely about the various kinds of ordnance with can be fitted beneath those parent racks, TERs and MERs. A typical sampling of A-7 ordnance loads would include the following (all without external fuel and with two fuselage-mounted Sidewinders):

Six each Mk 81 250 lb (114 kg), Mk 82 500 lb (227 kg), or Mk 83 1,000 lb (454 kg) laser-guided general-purpose bombs.
Six each Mk 81 or Mk 82 with Snakeye drag-retardation fins.
Six each Mk 20 Rockeye II cluster bomb units;
Four each AGM-45 Shrike anti-radiation missiles;
Two additional AIM-9 Sidewinders plus two GPU-5/A pods carrying one each 30 mm General Electric GAU-8/A cannon.

The A-7 Corsair also routinely carries the KB-18A panoramic 70 mm strike camera provided for strike assessment and documentation. The KB-18A is intended for daylight, low-level photography. Standard 70 mm film provides a forward-to-rear photographic coverage of 180 degrees along the line-of-flight and 20 degrees to either side. The camera is installed in an environmentally controlled compartment in the lower, forward right-hand engine compartment. Camera operation is essentially automatic and it begins running when the pilot hits RELEASE ENABLE prior to releasing stores or firing the gun. Pilots have noted that even minor hydraulics leaks can slosh hydraulic fluid into the camera and render it useless.

Guardsmen

Air National Guard A-7Ds have been retrofitted with the Pave Penny laser target locating device, housed in a distinct chin fairing beneath the nose intake inlet. A-7D aircraft Nos 458 and 459 (75-408/409) which went from the production line to the 162nd Tactical Fighter Training Group, Arizona ANG, introduced the Advanced Manoeuvring Flap (AMF), aimed at improving performance at critical attitudes and airspeeds. AMF-equipped aircraft cannot be made to depart. AMF has been retrofitted to ANG A-7Ds.

In the mid-1980s, A-7D aircraft of the Air National Guard and A-7Es of the US Navy were being retrofitted with an LTV forward-looking infrared receiver (FLIR), recognized by its slant-nosed underwing pod but, in fact, integral with the airplane's systems. The FLIR system includes wing-mounted pod, expanded NWDS computer with software, and airframe changes to incorporate associated FLIR switches and controls.

Mounted on wing station six, the FLIR pod houses the IR sensors, scanner array, pointing servos, an on-board air refrigeration unit and provision for a video tape recorder. The pilot controls FLIR through the NWDS computer. The FLIR scene can be viewed in either a narrow or a wide field of view on the pilot display unit. It is so well integrated with the existing weapons system that there are few FLIR-only associated controls, easing the pilot's transition to the FLIR system. The pilot soon becomes comfortable with it, relying primarily on the head-up display for altitude, airspeed, heading and range-to-target information.

FLIR navigation relies mainly on the A-7's inertial navigation system, using the FLIR scene to positively identify checkpoints. It also gives the A-7 a low altitude capability at night, allowing the pilot to navigate as he would during the day.

Weapons delivery with FLIR uses all current attack modes. The pilot can make a FLIR or non-FLIR delivery by selecting one switch. Using FLIR, night deliveries have proven to be as accurate as day deliveries.

FLIR was introduced to the Navy by the 'Sunliners' of VA-81 in the Mediterranean and the 'Blue Diamonds' of VA-146 in the Western Pacific. It appears that the Navy plans to have one A-7E squadron on each carrier (out of two) equipped with FLIR. In 1985, LTV was awarded an $86.6 million (£80 million) contract to equip two Air National Guard squadrons with night-attack capability by installing FLIR and related equipment in 48 A-7Ds and four two-seat A-7Ks, with the capability eventually to be acquired by nearly all of the ANG fleet.

The diverse ordnance loads carried by the A-7 are remarked upon throughout the text; they range from the anti-shipping mines used in Haiphong harbour to the TV-guided AGM-62 Walleye glide bomb.

In walking around an A-7 parked on the ground or on a carrier deck, one is impressed that the SLUF isn't as little as it was supposed to be. And while far from graceful, the A-7 isn't as ugly as it's supposed to be, either. Viewed from behind, rear fuselage and engine exhaust low to the ground, the Corsair II looks ready to leap into the sky. The rear tail shape on the A-7D and A-7E has been altered somewhat by the addition of radar warning receivers (RWR) but the airplane remains an impressive sight from this angle. And having begun at the nose, it is fitting to conclude this walk-around check at the tail, one of the angles from which the A-7 Corsair is far from unattractive.

Chapter 7
Corsairs and Carriers
A-7E in the Fleet and the Fight

'16 September 1971. Thursday. The USS *Independence* departed Pier 12, NS Norfolk at 1630. It was a rather anti-climactic moment for the Jacksonville people since we'd said our goodbyes three days ago. Most of the fellows went up to the flight deck anyway to see the last-minute kisses and goodbyes. As the skipper remarked, 'Let's get this thing underway. The quicker we get going, the quicker we will be back. . .'

With these jottings in a personal diary, an American naval aviator sets forth on a carrier cruise with an A-7E Corsair squadron. The 'Jacksonville people' are the members of the A-7E community aboard ship who left home at Cecil Field to join *Independence* (CVA-62) at Norfolk. As happens again and again, year after year, sailors head forth to sea and sky hoping for safe haven from the dangers of both. The diary-keeper has done it before, setting forth not merely to sea but to war, in A-4C Skyhawks. This time, nobody will be shooting at him but departure is still a somber occasion. 'It is always a sad and silent time when a ship pulls away from the pier for a long deployment. In 1965, I departed for a combat cruise aboard this same ship, leaving a wife and little boy waving from this same pier. We'll be back in six months. . .'

This time the 'Flying Ubangis' of attack squadron VA-12, soon to be renamed 'Clinchers' and led by Lt

TOP RIGHT
A-7E Corsair touching down on USS Eisenhower *(CVN-69) in the Indian Ocean, 12 September 1980. With the A-7E model, the Navy acquired new navigation/bombing system, engine, and cannon. Current plans are for A-7Es to remain operational at least through 1992*
(USN)

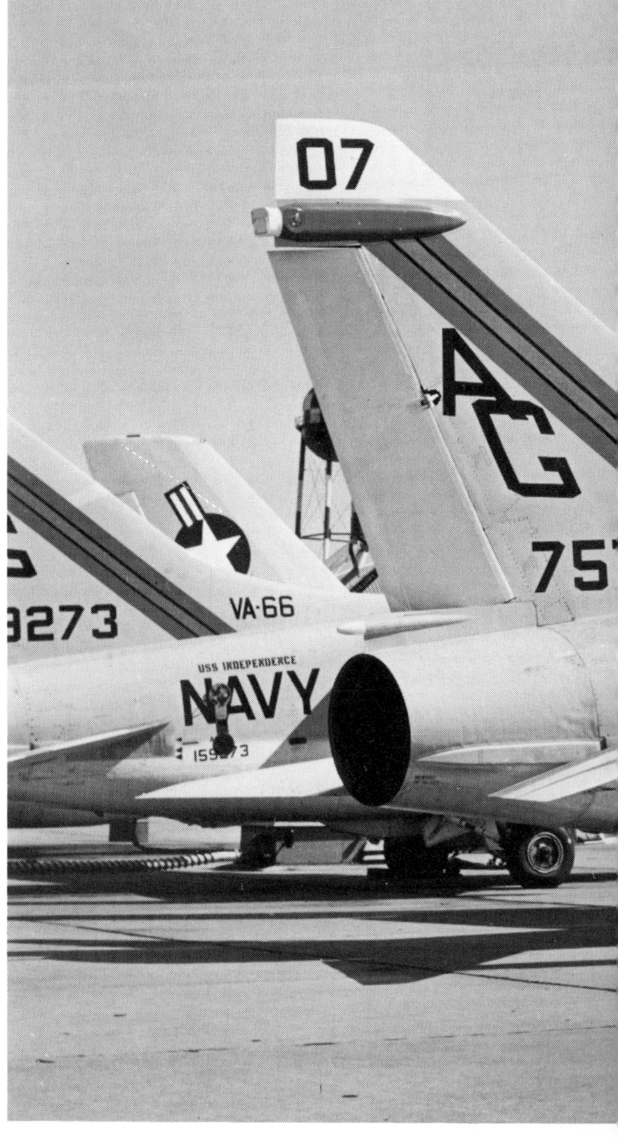

A-7E (157570), side number AG-307, of the 'Waldomen' of attack squadron VA-66 at NAS Oceana, Virginia on 25 April 1974. Squadron has since shifted to low visibility paint scheme
(Jim Sullivan)

311

VA-66
USS INDEPENDENCE
NAVY
307

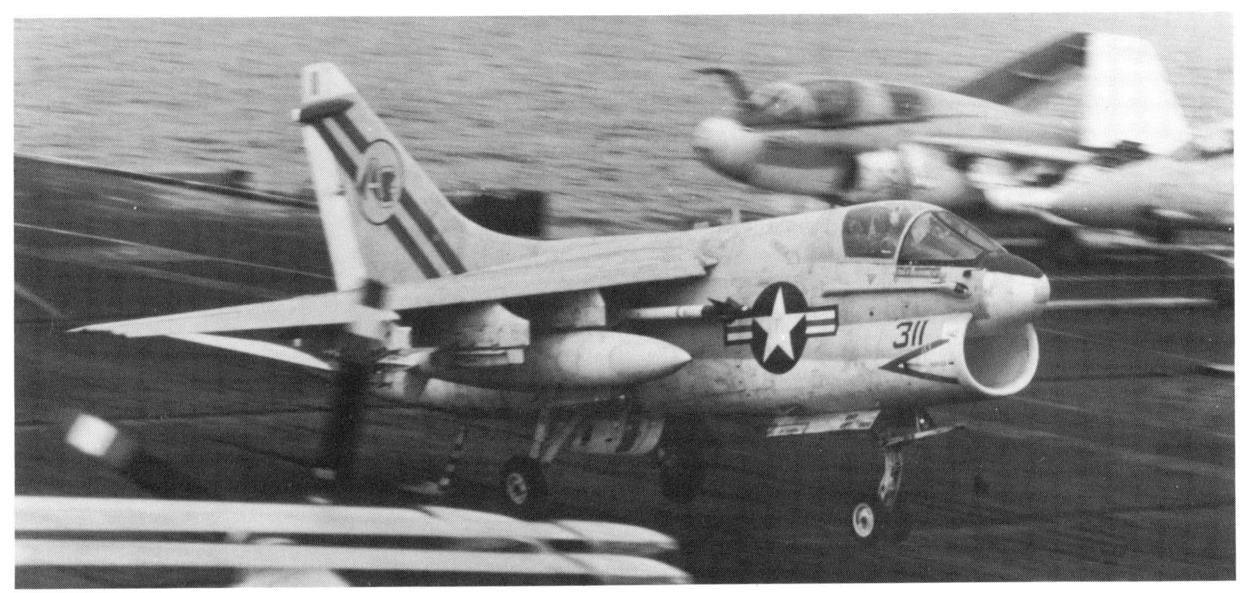

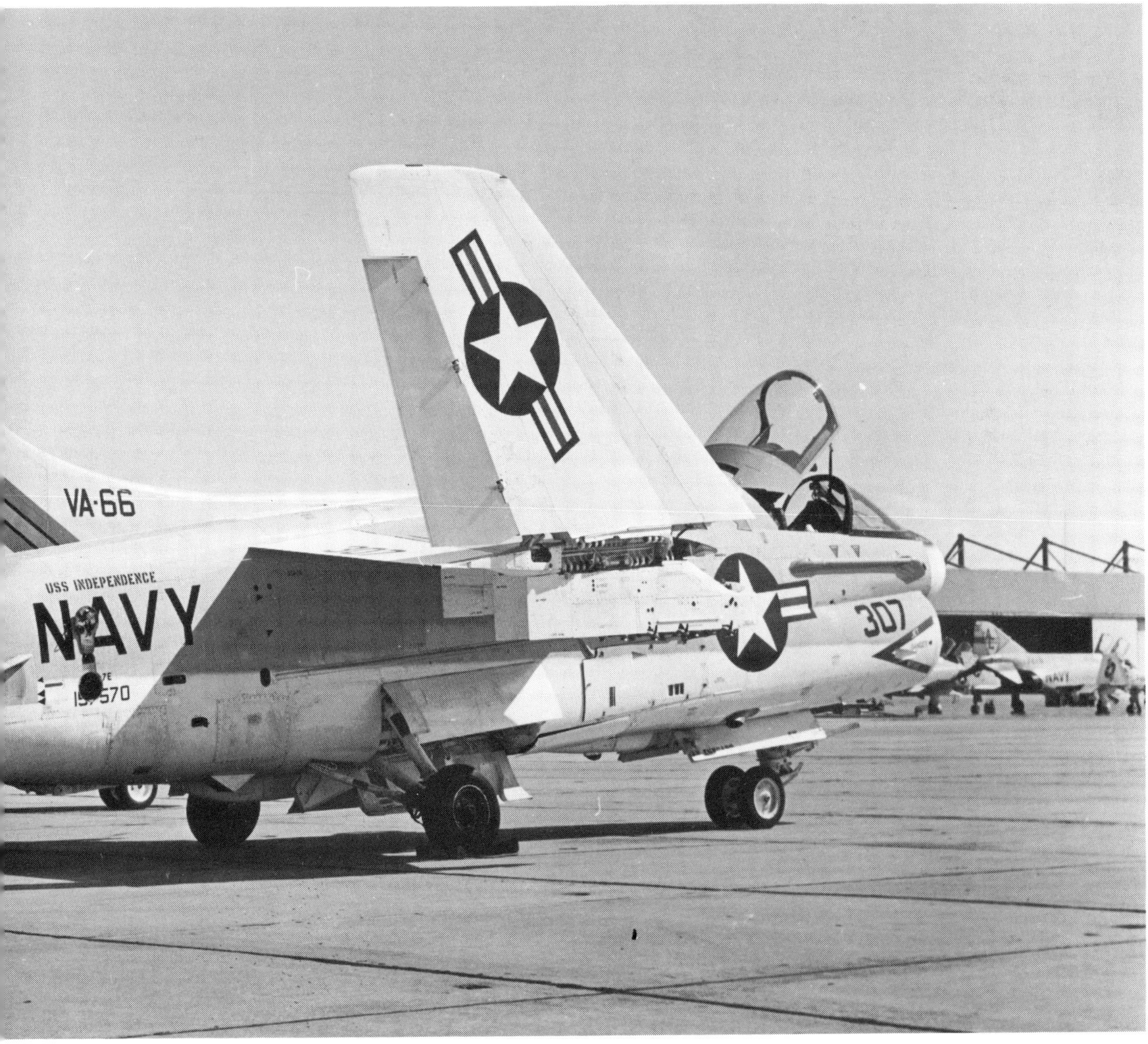

Cdr H E Nelson (the first time a Corsair squadron has been skippered by a lieutenant commander) are putting forth on *Indy* for a Mediterranean cruise which will test their A-7Es and their own mettle to the limit. During workups aboard *Independence*, the squadron has already lost a man. On 24 June 1971, Lt (jg) J M Gibson was catapulted on a night launch in an A-7E (157588), side number AG-513, callsign CLINCHER 513. A night launch requires intense concentration. In a marginal sea state, an airplane can fly right into the waves. Gibson's A-7E is on radar until a mile ahead of the carrier's bow. Then, abruptly, it disappears. Nothing is ever found.

A hundred other diaries, a hundred other cruises. . .

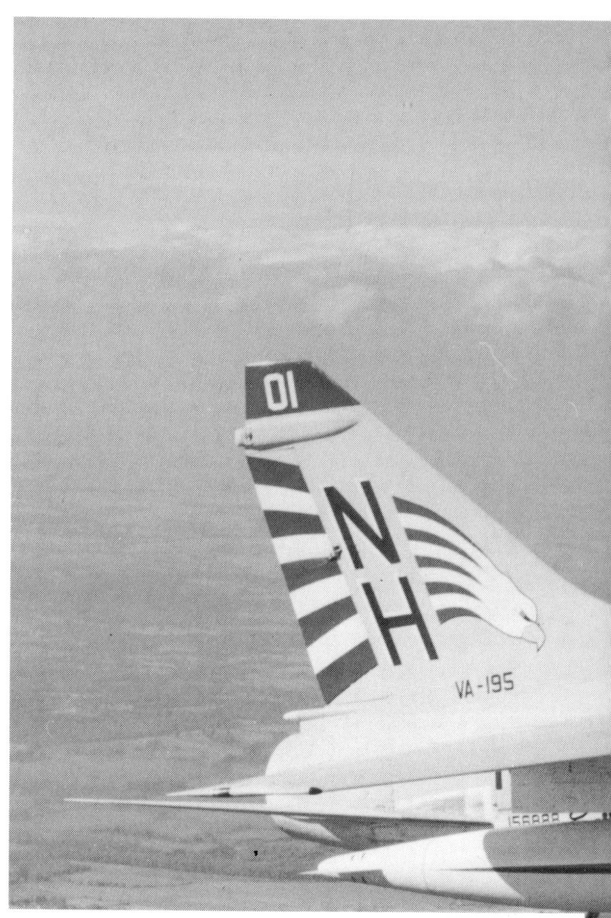

Cdr D D Hicks of the 'Dam Busters' of VA-195 in the vicinity of Farnborough during the 1970 air show in A-7E (156888), side number NH-401. VA-195 made a Westpac cruise in 1972 and spent five months on the line attacking targets in North Vietnam from USS Kittyhawk *(CVA-63). Features visible in this clean flying view of the A-7E include ECM antenna mounted at rear base of tail and upper vertical tailplane, and inflight refuelling probe (Tom Hamill,* Flight International*)*

BELOW
Busy flight deck of USS Kitty Hawk *(CVA-63) during Linebacker combat operations against North Vietnam in 1972. Four A-7Es of the 'Dam Busters' of VA-195 are lined up at upper left while A-7Es of the 'Golden Dragons' of VA-192 occupy centre of picture. Also visible are F-4J Phantoms and A-6E Intruders from Cdr Huntington Hardisty's carrier air wing (LTV)*

RESCUE
401

A-7E Corsair (157545), side number NH-400, of the 'Dam Busters' of attack squadron VA-195, after the squadron's first deployment to Vietnam but before the events in this narrative, seen at NAS Lemoore, California on 9 October 1971
(Peter Mancus via Jim Sullivan)

Life with an A-7E squadron on a cruise aboard a US Navy carrier means separation and sacrifice. It entails hard work under pressure in close quarters, danger on a crowded and unforgiving flight deck, and constant flying, including night flying. The men with billets beneath the steam catapult will be kept awake by the slamming noise or forced away by the heat. Life on the carrier can include coping with incursions by Soviet naval and air units, the A-7E being often used for barrier combat air patrol (BARCAP), especially when the catapults are down or when wind conditions do not favour F-14A launch, and thus being called upon to intercept Russian *Badger*, *Bear*, *Moss* and *May* reconnaissance aircraft.

A typical cruise lasts five to seven months, the longest-ever surpassing the latter figure when USS *Nimitz* (CVN-68), with two A-7E squadrons aboard, prowled the Persian Gulf in 1980 and launched the unsuccessful attempt to rescue American hostages in Tehran. The rigours of shipboard life and the demands of 'round-the-clock' flying are broken during an extended cruise by a half-dozen or more port calls, but even pulling into port can mean added chores, 'manning the rail' in dress whites or arranging protocol formalities. Shore liberty can be lonely and unfulfilling, yielding a sterile guided tour to some tourist site or a night out in a flashy, noisy bar district when a man would rather be with his family.

At any time, half the US Navy's fleet of 13 carriers (CVs), each at the helm of a carrier battle group, is

embarked on Med, Westpac or IO cruises, the Mediterranean, Western Pacific and Indian Oceans being the key regions for projection of American naval power. A cruise reaches its critical period when the ship arrives 'on the line' at Gonzo Station (the Persian Gulf), Bagel Station (off Beirut) or one of the other zones designated for sustained operations.

Some ports of call become all to familiar to the A-7E sailor: the drab bars and pasta shops of Catania, Sicily, with its side trips to Palermo and Mount Etna; the noisier, naughtier red light district in Hong Kong's Wanchai with floating sea food at Aberdeen; the raunchiest, rowdiest 'sin town' at Subic Bay, Philippines. Such are the travels of an A-7E aviator who can put in a 20-year career without ever seeing Paris, Berlin or Delhi.

In the late 1980s, eleven of the thirteen carriers had two each A-7E squadrons assigned. USS *Coral Sea* (CV-43) was scheduled to become the first fleet carrier with F/A-18A Hornets embarked in the light attack role while *Kennedy* (CV-67), under a mixed-force evaluation begun by Secretary of the Navy John Lehman, carried only medium-attack A-6E Intruders. The A-7E remained very much the Navy's principal carrier-based light attack aircraft and, while scheduled for gradual replacement by the F/A-18A, will remain so well into the 1990s.

On any carrier, the men of the paired A-7E squadrons enjoy close camaraderie and shared

BELOW
A-7E Corsair (157523), side number NH-407, of the 'Dam Busters' of VA-195, flying from USS Kitty Hawk *(CVA-63)*
(USN, via M J Kasiuba)

OVERLEAF
'Dam Busters' Corsair is set up on Kitty Hawk*'s catapult for combat launch*
(LTV)

INSET OVERLEAF
'Dam Busters' pilot of VA-195 climbs aboard A-7E for combat mission against North Vietnam
(LTV)

605

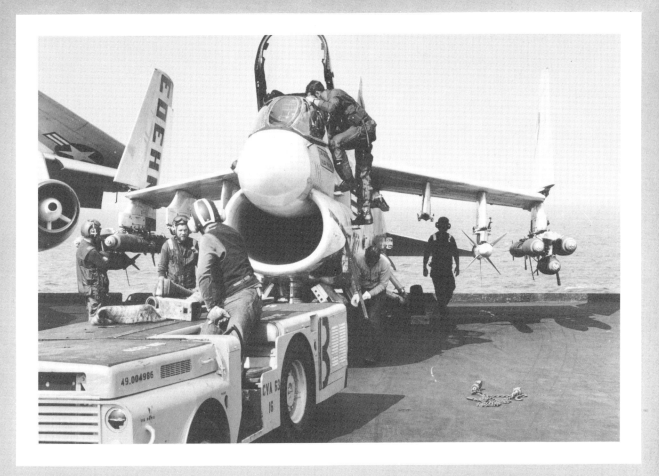

Classic pose for a Corsair at war. A-7E (157530), side number NH-300, a CAG airplane of the 'Golden Dragons' of attack squadron VA-192, en route to the target (LTV)

purpose but also a keen sense of competition for best maintenance record, best flying performance, and fewest bolters (unplanned go-arounds on landing approach). A heavy dosage of administrative detail, paperwork and 'people problems' comes with the flying job and the A-7E squadron commander must meet the watchful demands of the carrier air wing commander (CAG) who may, by chance, be an old hand in the A-7E community himself but, even if not, will have made familiarization flights in the aircraft.

During the long period of US combat operations in Vietnam from 1964 to 1973, a Westpac cruise meant weeks or months at Dixie Station in the South China Sea facing embattled South Vietnam or Yankee Station in the Gulf of Tonkin flying against North Vietnam. A naval aviator might spend months flying over the country, but might see Vietnam from the ground only if forced to divert to Da Nang with battle damage. The jargon of the period includes the Rolling Thunder campaign against North Vietnam (1965–68), close support and other combat missions in the south (through January 1973), Steel Tiger missions into Laos, Barrel Roll operations in Cambodia (through August 1973) and the final Linebacker campaign against North Vietnam fought from May 1972 through war's end in January 1973. A-7E aviators returned to the fray for Operation Eagle Pull, the evacuation of Phnom Penh in March 1975; Operation Frequent Wind, the pullout from Saigon in April 1975, and combat operations to recover the crew of the merchant vessel *Mayaguez*, seized by Cambodian communist forces in May 1975.

Until now, the A-7 story, including the US Navy's part of the Corsair story, has been presented more or less in chronological order. At this point, however, it is time to revert to parts of the seagoing Corsair saga which begin before the major events in the Air Force's A-7D experience (chapter five) and which will continue to unfold long after the conclusion of that experience. Thus, it is necessary now to back up in time to the 1972 Linebacker operations against North Vietnam.

Baptism of Fire: A-7E

Eight months after the first flight of the TF41-powered A-7E for the US Navy (page 96), Cdr Marvin Quaid, skipper of VA-122, came to Dallas to accept the first operational A-7E for the west coast RAG. Now, Navy Corsair squadrons were proliferating. The A-7E, very simply, would be the standard carrier-borne light attack aircraft for a generation. When Quaid taxied out from the LTV flight line on 14 July 1969, he knew something no attack pilot had ever known before—his exact latitude and longitude on Earth, precisely to the foot. So finely tuned is the navigation and weapons delivery system (NWDS) on the A-7E that each aircraft parking spot on the ramp has a different latitude and longitude designation in degrees, minutes and seconds. Since a second of longitude is about 100 ft (30.5 m), each spot differs in one second from the next.

The definitive Navy variant, the A-7E, was

heading to war, following in the path of the A-7A and A-7B. The paired 'Blue Diamonds' of VA-146 and 'Argonauts' of VA-147, under Cdr Wayne L Stephens and Cdr Robert N Livingston, were to take the E model into the fray from an Atlantic Fleet carrier, USS *America* (CVA-66)

Following a shakedown cruise in March 1970, *America* transited the Panama Canal and made the long crossing to Dixie Station. At 1201 hours on 26 May 1970, Lt (jg) Dave Lichetermann of VA-146 was catapulted from *America*'s deck in the first A-7E ever to be launched in combat. Stephens followed and led a strafing attack against a Viet Cong emplacement. An hour later, Livingston and Lt Cdr Tom Gravely of VA-147 rolled in on an enemy supply route to deliver the first bombs in combat in an A-7E. Theirs, of course, was the squadron which had introduced the A-7A to combat three years earlier.

The Dam Busters (I)

Each of the US Navy's three dozen A-7E squadrons considers itself first and best, but few are better known in Corsair lore than the 'Dam Busters' of VA-195. The squadron's nickname comes from its assault in prop-driven Skyraiders on the Hwachon Dam in the 1950–53 Korean conflict.

In March 1972, equipped with A-7E Corsairs, the squadron was at sea just off the Philippines aboard USS *Kitty Hawk* (CVA-63) just as North Vietnam invaded the south and US warplanes returned to the North. As usual paired with sister squadron the 'Golden Dragons' of VA-192, the men and machines of VA-195 headed for the fight. It often happens that tragedy occurs at the front end of a cruise but while heading for Vietnam the 'Dam Busters' suffered an especially saddening loss. On 6 March 1972, VA-195's skipper, Cdr Donald L Hall, was on a routine night flight in an A-7E (158655), side number NH-404, callsign CHIPPIE 404. In an incident described by a shipmate as 'spooky,' Don Hall was on approach when the night and the sea swallowed up his aircraft. Before the first shots were ever fired at them, VA-195

Michael A Ruth flew 151 combat missions in the Vietnam war zone with the 'Dam Busters' of VA-195 and one of his scariest experiences occurred when he accidentally fired his own Sidewinder. Commander Ruth returned for a second tour with VA-195 in 1982, when this photo was taken
(USN)

66
12
NG
VA-146
USS AMERICA

had lost a squadron commander. Cdr Mason L 'Mace' Gilfry took the helm.

Soon it was Gilfry's turn. On 6 April 1972, leading an air strike against the heavily defended Dong Hoi area 45 miles (60 km) north of the DMZ in North Vietnam, Gilfry's A-7E (158006) was hit and crippled by a SAM. It was Gilfry's third combat cruise. 'I successfully dodged the first two SAMs and had put my aircraft into full power when I heard the CAG [Cdr Huntington Hardisty] in the number three slot alert me with, 'Here comes another one, Mace!' So I rolled into a hard turn, saw it, and it was too late.' The receptiveness of the A-7E to a pilot's touch was often a valuable defence against a SAM, but not this time. 'My engine and tail were on fire and I began to lose power.

'As I was coasting out, heading for the water, I pickled off my bombs and hit a storage area which was known to have about 65 guns, and continued coasting my aircraft to an area about two miles out to sea before the airplane became uncontrollable.'

Gilfry ejected. 'Three or four SAMs passed me as I was floating down. I could hear big coastal guns clacking away at their target which I assumed was me since the shells, at least thirty of them, splashed into the sea below me.'

Gilfry was scooped out of the water by an HH-3A helicopter flown by Lt Frank Lockett of Helicopter Squadron 7. Described by a shipmate as 'utterly fearless,' Gilfry arrived back on *Kitty Hawk* soaking wet to be greeted by CAG Hardisty and went on to command VA-195 throughout the carrier's 1972 cruise.

Perhaps the best-known A-7E mission of the war, though described by participants merely as 'typical,' happened on 10 May 1972, the first day of the enlarged Linebacker campaign against North Vietnam. As part of a larger A-6 and A-7 operation around Hanoi, Lts Charles W Brewer and Michael A Ruth attacked the Hai Duong bridge outside Hanoi and broke its spans with Mk 83 1,000 lb (454 kg) bombs.

Mike Ruth is soft-spoken and relaxed but is, like Gilfry, totally without fear in the driver's seat of an A-7E. In the dark, up high, Mike had one memorable experience which would have shaken most people.

Every night, VA-195 routinely sent up two A-7Es to orbit at anchor points looking for evidence of North Vietnamese surface vessels offloading supplies. It all went back to the original justification for the US role in Vietnam, the notion that the North was using sea lanes to ship supplies, arms and encouragement to the indigenous Viet Cong uprising in the

A familiar sight aboard USS America *(CVA-66) during its combat cruise with Corsair squadrons VA-146 and VA-147 in Vietnamese waters. On 13 July 1970, A-7E of VA-146 misses the second wire after a combat mission. RA-3B Skywarrior and F-4B Phantoms in background (LTV)*

A carrier landing is abrupt. On 1 May 1975, an A-7E (159284), side number NE-416, of the 'Fist of the Fleet', squadron VA-25, is recovered aboard USS Ranger *(CV-61). Squadron has more recently become VFA-25 and now operates the F/A-18A Hornet*
(USN)

South. Catch the ships offloading supplies and you'll break that supply line, everybody had been told. Up there at night, Mike thought he'd found an NVA supply vessel. Mike set his master arm selector. Then, intending to illuminate his nautical target, Mike pushed the switch to fire SUU-44 flares dangling from a pod on ordnance station one.

Abruptly, a brilliant flash exploded around him. Not the expected flash from a flare but a stunning, blinding blast of light. Before regaining his night vision, Mike was certain that a flare had exploded in the station one pod and that his A-7E was on fire.

He smelled smoke. Convinced that he was burning, he looked back. Although the pilot sits far forward in the A-7E, all underwing ordnance stations are visible. Mike could see no fire, at station one or anywhere else. More confused than afraid, Mike made a prompt and businesslike return to *Kitty Hawk*'s deck and was greeted by a deck crewman.

'What did you do with your missing Sidewinder, sir?'

'Oh, I don't *believe* this!'

'I guess you pushed the wrong switch, lieutenant, right?'

'Sidewinder,' Mike uttered the noun slowly the first time. '*Sidewinder*?' Even in the darkness on deck, it was plainly visible that one missing AIM-9 IR missile was no longer hanging on the A-7E's fuselage LAU-7 launch rail where it was supposed to be.

'I pushed the switch for a *flare*!' Mike insisted.

A quick check revealed a cross-circuited wire and confirmed that Mike had made no mistake. In 151

combat missions, in over a decade in Corsairs, it was the only time Mike ever fired a Sidewinder—because of a wiring problem not characteristic of the usually trouble-free A-7E.

Many years later, almost no emotion is visible when Mike Ruth collects some businesslike thoughts and recalls an Alpha Strike on 14 June 1972. 26 aircraft from *Kitty Hawk* are attacking targets 12 miles (19.4 km) inland in the ever-familiar Thanh Hoa region. Cdr Norman D Campbell is division leader for VA-195's four-ship contribution to the strike. Ruth is number two in his A-7E (157539). Lt Cdr Rex R Arnett is section lead in number three and the fourth pilot is Lt Michael E Leppert.

Pilots assemble in their ready room 2½ hours before launch. Campbell, the division lead, attends a briefing held by the overall strike leader, while the others remain in the ready room and get the brief over closed-circuit TV. It takes about 1 hour 45 minutes to go through the intelligence brief, weather brief, and discussion of targets. Then Ruth and the other pilots check out their gear—torso harnesses, G-suits, survival radios and equipment—and head up to the flight deck 45 minutes before launch. Each pilot will check his yellow sheet, a log of maintenance problems on his particular aircraft in the past 10 days. The pilot then performs a thorough preflight of his aircraft. Today, Mike Ruth is carrying twelve Mk 82 500 lb (227 kg) bombs.

BELOW
Still catching sunlight after dusk has fallen on the fleet below, an A-7E of the 'Royal Maces' of attack squadron VA-27 prepares to land during 1980 Indian Ocean cruise (USN)

OVERLEAF
In 1974, with colourful markings still in vogue, A-7E Corsairs of the 'Royal Maces' of VA-27 stack up over Utah's Great Salt Lake. Inset: Lt Cdr Rosemary Conatser Mariner is the only woman to have flown an A-7 (LTV)

00
NK
400
E
NAVY
402

NK
NAVY
NK
NAVY
NK
404
NK
405
NK
NK

Today, something unusual happens.

At the last possible instant, VA-195's target is changed. Just before manning the aircraft on deck, Cdr Campbell hands around photos of the thermal power plant at Thanh Hoa which came from post-strike recce of an attack earlier in the morning. It is a bright, cold, sunny day, a wind rustling the photos which are handled with extreme care by the VA-195 pilots, and Mike Ruth will always remember the unusual situation of being briefed on the target in open air just before climbing into his A-7E.

With a nod to his plane captain, Ruth climbs into his aircraft. He goes through start procedures, gets the TF41 engine turning over, and does a post-start plane captain check. Flight controls. Engine instruments. He gives a thumbs-up to the plane captain, who turns him over to a yellow-shirted flight deck director. He taxies to *Kitty Hawk*'s steam catapult. The weight-board man holds up a slate telling him what the weight of his aircraft should be for the catapult setting and Mike negotiates with hand signals until it's right. Mike unfolds his wings and checks the wing spread and lock. He taxies the last few feet to the catapult and hooks up. At 100% power, his A-7E is taken under tension on the catapult. Ruth salutes the catapult officer, who returns the salute and authorizes the launch.

For split-seconds, the sheer force of the catapult launch puts Mike into a kind of suspended animation. His aircraft goes from zero to 160 mph (256 km/h) in two seconds. Mike collects airspeed, heads out at an altitude of 500 ft (152.4 m) to a distance of 10 miles (16.1 km), then picks up altitude and returns over the ship for rendezvous. All four of VA-195's Corsairs (callsign CHIPPIE) are into the mission as the 26-plane Alpha Strike assemblies at 5,000 ft (1524 m) above the marshalling point, which is directly over *Kitty Hawk*. Ruth tucks in on Campbell's wing as the overall flight leader checks his force. Campbell reports that, 'CHIPPIES are aboard with four.'

En route to the target, there is minimal radio chatter. Campbell is setting up his VA-195 four-ship to separate from the rest of the strike and ingress to its

Walleye television-guided air-to-surface missile arms A-7E Corsair of VA-27 over the Indian Ocean (Cdr Dennis McGinn)

own target. Close to the coast, radio calls report lock-on by the *Fan Song* radar associated with North Vietnamese SA-2 missile sites. In A-7 number two, Ruth is attentive to tight formation on his division lead, Campbell. Campbell ingresses, crossing the beach due east from Thanh Hoa, and there are more SAM warning calls but apparently no SAMs are fired. Ruth and his wingmen are aware of an inordinate amount of flak coming up at them. 23 mm and 37 mm shells are small, fast beads of fire whipping around them. The larger rounds from 57 mm and 85 mm guns leave cloudbursts and entrails of shrapnel arching through the air.

Campbell rolls in on the target. Ruth follows almost simultaneously. Ruth acquires the target visually, makes a mental note of the thermal power plant complex as compared with the photos he'd examined back on the flight deck. He hits his master arm selector. He places his aiming diamond on the target. Designates it. Hits his RELEASE ENABLE.

Surrounded by swirling triple-A fire, he releases ordnance and pulls off the target, maintaining section integrity on Campbell's wing. When their bombs come off, Campbell and Ruth begin jinking to avoid AAA. They continue a turn to the left, jinking from left to right, moving to an easterly heading and heading back for the beach. Today, the 'Dam Busters' of VA-195 suffer no casualties and the four A-7Es are soon 'feet wet,' ie back over the Gulf of Tonkin.

Once over the Gulf and out of the SAM envelope, Ruth is able to relax somewhat. Campbell is in radio contact with the PIRAZ ship (Pilot Information Radar Advisory Zone), callsign RED CROWN, mindful that MiGs could appear and tuck into their formation heading back to *Kitty Hawk*. The return to the carrier is coordinated with a Grumman E-2 Hawkeye early-warning aircraft circling over the Gulf, also watching for MiGs. PIRAZ identifies CHIPPIE flight from its IFF squawks (identifi-

Captain Lew Dunton's squadron, the 'Bulls' of VA-37, was one of the east coast units which flew the A-7A model in combat in Vietnam. Later, the squadron converted to the A-7E model, illustrated by the CAG's aircraft (158826), side number AC-300, at NAS Cecil Field, Florida in October 1973
(Duane E Kasulka)

cation, friend or foe). Today, no MiGs are sneaking back with the A-7Es.

CHIPPIE Flight marshals over the carrier, waiting for the ship's next launch to be completed before stacking up to land. The aircraft formate for approach. CHIPPIE Flight works into the break, Campbell breaking first, the others following at ten-second intervals for ideal spacing downwind from *Kitty Hawk*'s deck. This will bring the Corsairs 'on the boat'—their tail-hooks trapping on the carrier—at 45-second spreads. Research has shown that A-7 pilots feel more apprehensive on approach to the flat-top than when being shot at over North Vietnam, but the Air Wing has gotten very efficient at hitting those 42- to 45-second intervals.

Mike Ruth makes a routine arrested landing. He taxies, parks, ties down, walks around looking for damage, then clears the flight deck expeditiously. Below decks, Mike will write up any maintenance gripes in the aircraft maintenance log for the next pilot to check.

The men are debriefed. In the ready room, they report on hostile fire for the benefit of others who will follow. Post-strike photography from the KB-18A cameras carried by their A-7Es show that bombs from all four aircraft struck in the powerplant complex. In the ready room, Campbell leads a candid, honest bull session to encourage each pilot to bring up anything done wrong by anybody during the

A-7E Corsair (157446), side number AG-400, of the 'Sunliners' of VA-81 in flight near Jacksonville, Florida, 19 August 1970
(USN, via M J Kasiuba)

flight. Campbell then writes up the mission and prepares the recommendations for awards (air medals) which are a routine part of the paperwork. After debriefing, these 'Dam Busters' pilots may have another mission coming up, or other squadron duties, or (rare during a combat cruise) a few hours of leisure time. Today's mission has been relatively uneventful, yet typical of hundreds flown again and again by relentless and dauntless Corsair pilots. Back at Thanh Hoa, the North Vietnamese will begin repairing their thermal power plant in the knowledge that another strike may come in an hour or a day.

The High-Hour Flier

Capt Lewis W Dunton III has done more flying in the Vought A-7 than anybody. Dunton, head of Strike Test at NATC Patuxent River, Maryland has accumulated over 4,000 Corsair flight hours in his logbook making him the current high-hour A-7 flier, although he is quick to suggest that today's skipper of *America*, Capt Leighton W 'Snuffy' Smith will probably catch up and pass him. Lew Dunton, dark-haired and deliberate, an intent man visibily happy

Flying from the deck of USS Nimitz *(CVN-68), the carrier which mounted the abortive April 1980 mission to rescue hostages in Tehran, A-7E (159289), side number AJ-300, assigned to the air wing commander (CAG) banks in bright sunlight*
(USN)

with what he does for a living, has just about done it all. He remembers a day when he crossed the beach into North Vietnam without Sidewinders, got chased 'through the weeds' (at near-zero altitude) by a gaggle of MiG-17s, and simply outlasted the limited endurance of the MiGs without even getting down to bingo fuel.

Dunton earned his wings in 1965, did two cruises in the A-4C Skyhawk in 1966–67, and afterward joined the 'Bulls' of VA-37, the first A-7 squadron to be formed from the beginning without a history of operating earlier types. Dunton did a Southeast Asia cruise on USS *Kitty Hawk* (CVA-63) in 1968–69, spent the next two years instructing in the A-7A at Cecil Field, and returned to VA-37 in January 1971. After a Mediterranean cruise in A-7As on *Saratoga* (CVA-60), Dunton went forth with ship and squadron again. Still part of east coast/Atlantic Fleet aviation, as he has been throughout his career, Lew was going into combat once more. *Saratoga* departed her usual venue, transited the Indian Ocean, and relieved *Midway* (CVA-41) at Dixie Station in April 1972.

After flying close support at beseiged An Loc, site of one of the major infantry battles following the spring invasion, *Sara* moved north to Yankee Station. 'We went up there to clean out SAMs in RP 3 and RP 6'—Route Packages Three and Six in North Vietnam—'and we flew armed recce against roads, railroads and targets of opportunity.' The last-named are known in the jargon as LUCTARs, or lucrative targets. While other squadrons were operating the A-7E, Dunton's was one of the last with the A-7A model.

Dunton's assessment of the Vought product reiterates familiar praise for a cockpit roomier than the A-4C's, increased fuel, ammo and ordnance, and low 'down' time for maintenance. He found the Mk 12 cannon on the A-7A model at times unreliable and prone to jamming, while the M61A1 rotary gun on the A-7E was both dependable and deadly accurate. The A-7A and A-7B used a roller map with an 8 ft (2.43 m) cartridge, not bad but not as good as the repeatedly-praised NWDS system of the A-7E. Dunton's squadron encountered deficiencies with the unit horizontal tail (UHT) hydraulics, where cylinders were splitting on top causing hydraulic loss, a problem eventually solved by adding a redundant system. Dunton notes that on the TF30-powered A-7A and A-7B, Zuni rocket pods could not be carried on the fuselage Sidewinder stations because of engine compression stall caused by the rocket gases—a problem closely related to the Corsair's teething trouble with catapult steam ingestion.

A typical mission during Dunton's VA-37 cruise amid the Linebacker campaign of 1972: Late June 1972. The squadron XO (executive officer) leads a strike from *Sara*'s deck against SAM storage areas behind Haiphong. They coast in, eight A-7As against one target, six Grumman A-6 Intruders against another. The Corsair bombload is four Mk 82 500 lb (227 kg) and two Mk 83 1,000 lb (454 kg) iron bombs. Coming off the target, radar warning receivers (RWR) tell of SAM sites locking-on with the ubiquitous *Fan Song* guidance radar for their deadly SA-2 *Guideline* missiles. Flight discipline is momentarily lost. There is some confusion as Corsairs and Intruders pull away and suddenly SAMs are flying around them everywhere. At one point, the XO is watching the bright-red burn of a SAM sustainer engine against the green-brown landscape when his wingman calls out another SAM and he jinks to avoid it at the last moment. The strike returns to *Saratoga* with no losses and recce photos confirm solid hits on target.

The Linebacker campaign from May 1972 to January 1973, the all-out effort which ultimately ended the war, was an intense period for carrier aviators. Though the A-7E was now *the* Corsair, three squadrons in the combat zone still operated the TF30-powered A-7A—Dunton's VA-37 and VA-105 on *Saratoga* and VA-153 on USS *Oriskany* (CVA-34). The three squadrons were 'moving mud' in North Vietnam when the US Navy, incredibly, ran out of TF30-P-6 engines. As often happens in government, the problem was solved by writing a memorandum. The Navy administratively allowed 100 more hours on the TF30-P-6 than had previously been authorized. Still, when Dunton returned from that cruise, because of engine hours, he landed at Cecil Field in a 'downed' airplane.

But first, Linebacker II. The Christmas bombing campaign. 18 December 1972. At night under a bone-white full moon, Lew Dunton and Whitey Drossel take two A-7As north of Thanh Hoa up behind Nam Dinh, southwest of Hanoi. They are flying an 'Iron Hand' SAM suppression mission, each with four AGM-65 Shrike anti-radiation missiles. As they coast in, criss-crossing tracers flitter through the darkness around them. Dunton and Drossel pop their targets, climb away, and recover on *Saratoga* in the dark. Scratch several SAM sites. Many years later, on a peacetime daylight strike against unresisting rocks in the Aegean in October 1979, finally at the controls

of an A-7E, Lew Dunton makes a far easier arrested landing aboard USS *Independence* (CV-62) in the Ionian Sea, becoming one of only about three dozen men in all naval aviation to achieve 1,000 carrier landings.

The Dam Busters (II)

The day after Halloween, 1 November 1982, USS *Ranger* (CV-61) was steaming in the Indian Ocean. Morale was at an ebb, a planned crossing of the equator and resulting 'shellback' party cancelled when the crew learned that a replacement carrier was late and their time on the line would be extended. At 0800 hours, *Ranger* recovered A-7E Corsairs of Cdr David Pierce's 'Dam Busters' of VA-195 which had made an 0430 launch to escort Soviet *Bears* prowling the region. A few minutes later, all hell broke loose when a fuel oil leak was followed by an explosion, fire, and thick black smoke spewing through the ship's air-conditioning system. Medical corpsman HM2 Martye Dixon found himself with two patients in the below-decks dispensary, thrown into darkness, smoke everywhere, with no way to get out and one oxygen respirator for the three men to share. The metal bulkheads of the ship were becoming too hot to touch. Six *Ranger* sailors had already died. The whole ship seemed to be going up.

A-7E (157496), side number NE-310, of the 'Stingers' of VA-113, operating from USS Ranger *(CV-61), at NAS Miramar, California in 1974. Squadron has since become VFA-113 and converted to the F/A-18A Hornet (Duane A Kasulka)*

For every officer piloting an A-7 Corsair, hundreds of men labour with pride and dedication to keep man and machine in the air—armourers, catapult crews, electronics mates, mechanics. Few are as important as the single aviation medical technician assigned to each A-7 unit, the only medical man in a 336-man attack squadron. Martye Dixon has never flown in a Corsair except as a back-seat passenger in a TA-7C, but Dixon has done two cruises with VA-195 as the squadron's only expert on cut fingers, altitude chamber tests, anatomy (including an A-7E pilot's ability to pull Gs in air combat manoeuvring) and the whole myriad of medical problems which must be monitored if men are to fly and fight. ('An aircraft accident takes two seconds; the investigation takes two months.') Martye joined VA-195 for its 1981 IO cruise the hard way, by travelling from Lemoore to Diego Garcia and reaching *America* (CV-66) aboard its COD, the carrier on-board delivery Grumman C-1A Trader supplying the vessel. (The CVA designation was changed to CV with the addition of anti-submarine warfare (ASW) capability to all carriers beginning in 1973). One of Martye's first jobs was to ground an A-7E pilot who couldn't hack night landings.

It was not Dixon's introduction to the carrier. He'd been aboard *America* during workups in the Caribbean. Cdr Rose of VA-195's sister squadron, the 'Golden Dragons' of VA-192, came in for a landing, missed *America*'s wire, and hit the 'round-down,' a hump on the ship's fantail. Rose was on a refuelling mission and carrying a buddy store under the left wing. He went careening into a 'six pack' of F-14A Tomcats (the term for a half-dozen airplanes parked stem to stern) and a furious fire erupted. Rose scrambled out of his A-7E surrounded by smoke as firemen closed in to extinguish the blaze which destroyed the Corsair and damaged one F-14A. Dixon administered first aid but Rose was all right. The incident was left behind as *America* made her IO cruise and HM2 Dixon attended to his own A-7E squadron, the 'Dam Busters' of VA-195.

Dixon is proud that the squadron came back from that cruise with all its men, all its aircraft. This was partly due to his own efforts—monitoring ejection seat training, checking the flight status of pilots, giving lectures at briefings.

In the summer of 1982, the 'Dam Busters' A-7Es went to NAS Fallon, Nevada for rigorous exercises on the bombing range, 'a 24-hour job,' and then participated in workups for the USS *Carl Vinson* (CVN-70). The squadron never deployed on *Vinson* but during the Nevada phase Dixon became one of the privileged few to go out on the bomb range when ordnance was actually being dropped. 'Low visibility' paint schemes were coming into use then, and Dixon watched as a sky-blue 'low viz' A-7E piloted by VA-195's administrative officer, Cdr Michael A Ruth (on his second tour in the squadron) smeared the desert with Mk 83 bombs. 'You could feel the earth shake.' It had been ten years since Mike Ruth had attacked targets in North Vietnam.

Dixon, VA-195 and their A-7Es shifted to *Ranger* for its fall 1982 cruise, were briefly diverted to Central America (where A-7Es discovered a Soviet freighter carrying arms to Nicaragua), then steamed for the Indian Ocean. *Ranger* was on the line for 132 days, a hectic period, constantly under surveillance by Soviet ships and aircraft. VA-195's sister squadron, the 'Golden Dragon's of VA-192, were using some of the first FLIR-equipped A-7Es and pilots were enthusiastic about the Corsair's improved night and bad-weather capability. Morale was high throughout most of the line period. There was an annoying moment when a Sidewinder dropped from an A-7E, rolled across the deck, and injured a foot (Dixon to the scene with bandages), but there were no serious accidents. Spirits were high until 1 November 1982 when an extension of the line period led to doldrums and *Ranger* caught fire.

Earlier in this narrative, mention was made of a carrier fire which delayed the A-7B variant getting into action. Nothing at sea can be worse. The first alarm came with the fuel-oil leak, the second with the blaze itself. Suddenly, squadron commanders were leading fire parties, A-7E pilots became fire-fighters, and every man-jack on *Ranger* was struggling in heat, smoke and grime to contain the conflagration. The blaze was in *Ranger*'s own engine area, far from any aircraft, but aviators suffered as many burns, as much smoke exhaustion, as anyone.

Below decks, Martye Dixon and his two patients were joined in the smoke-filled darkness by three other men. With two oxygen respirator bags to be shared, now, by six men, Dixon led the others as they crawled on their stomachs through the labyrinthian interior of the great vessel, choking, gasping, navigating by touch against hot metal. The men reached a hangar bay and safety only after a supreme effort. They joined the firefighting operation until the blaze was extinguished. Casualties: six dead, forty injured. In a miraculous feat of seamanship, while under constant scrutiny from Soviet aircraft lured by the blaze, *Ranger*'s crew kept the carrier operational and remained on station until relieved, despite grave damage. Dixon's 'Dam Busters,' for the second time in his experience, returned from the cruise with all their men, all their aircraft.

There is a grim footnote, a legitimate part of the A-7 story and illustrative of life in a Corsair squadron as in any military service. Shortly after VA-195 returned to Lemoore from that IO cruise with everyone safe and sound, the losses began. Around the west coast home of A-7 aviation, three men were killed in motorcycle or traffic accidents. One man died in a flight line mishap, another in a fall at his home. VA-195's men had ventured forth to sea and sky in one of the riskiest occupations on this planet, had flown eyeball-to-eyeball with the Russians in the Indian Ocean, had survived *Ranger*'s fire, and had returned safe and sound. 'Then we began losing them all,' says Dixon, whose love for the A-7 Corsair is matched only by his respect for health and safety. 'We lost so many in such a short time. And they had all given so much.'

In a different time, on a different cruise, *Independence* returned to Norfolk in March 1972 after six months in the Med, having lost one aircraft in workups (page 154) and one crewman to the A-7E's ravenous air intake (page 134). The cruise described by the diary keeper at the outset of this chapter ended, as a cruise by Corsairs on carriers always does, with men being reunited with their families. The diary writer's final word: 'Good to be home. . .'

Chapter 8
Air National Guardsman
The A-7, the ANG, and the Future

There is another war. Not in Vietnam, not Grenada, not Lebanon. It's the shadowy war of the terrorist. On Monday, 12 January 1981, it came home in what Col Ramon Lavandero of the Puerto Rico Air National Guard (ANG) called 'the most devastating attack ever carried out on a US military installation on US soil.' Lavandero's 198th Tactical Fighter Squadron was 'virtually wiped out,' according the following day's *San Juan Star*.

With San Juan as its capital, Puerto Rico is, of course, the island wedged between the Caribbean and South Atlantic which belongs to the US but has its own separatist movement. Like any chunk of geography, it has military significance, lying as a kind of stepping stone to Cuba and Latin America. It was a clandestine, pro-independence group, the Boricua Popular Army, also known as the *macheteros*, which claimed responsibility for infiltrating Minoz Air Base with sticks of explosives (irignite, wired to timing mechanisms) and blew up eight A-7Ds. The explosions sent 60 ft (18.3 m) columns of smoke into the air and were heard miles away. In all, 20 aircraft (19 A-7Ds) were damaged or destroyed. It was the latest act of senseless violence in an undercover struggle which never seems to produce arrests, prosecution, or retaliation.

The eight A-7Ds destroyed by the terrorists represented a $90 million loss. They were 72-189, 72-219, 72-221, 72-222, 73-994, 73-1005, 74-1748 and 74-1755. All had very low airframe hours. To add insult to injury, the *macheteros* also blew up a Lockheed F-104C Starfighter being saved for eventual outdoor display.

The Puerto Rico Air National Guard, one of 15 ANG users of the A-7D, has long since rebounded from the Minoz bombing. Puerto Rico was the sixth Guard unit to acquire the A-7D, following New Mexico, Colorado, Ohio, South Carolina and Pennsylvania. Today, the squadron exhibits obvious pride in operating the SLUF and morale is high. Eric Cintron, a former F-4D Phantom pilot who made the shift to the A-7D without regarding it as a step down, is one of the Puerto Rico SLUF drivers. 'We have a real enthusiasm for this airplane,' says Cintron. 'We believe in it. We think we can do the mission assigned to us.'

Eric's comments on the A-7D, given here without editing, provide unique insight into an Air Guard pilot's perspective:

'After 500 hours in the aircraft, these are some of my impressions:

'The aircraft is longitudinally unstable unless flown with its AFCS (automatic flight control system) engaged. The AFCS compensates for this instability and shows the airplane which end needs to go first.

'The [Navy-style] refuelling probe was deleted on the Air Force aircraft and instead a refuelling door was added on the upper left fuselage. When latched to the tanker the aircraft becomes thrust limited and the tanker has to toboggan or pull you along in order to stay on board.

'The computer is the brain behind the aircraft. It allows the pilot an unsurpassed flexibility in delivery tactics. The pilot no longer has to fly the aircraft to a point in space at a pre-determined airspeed, dive angle, altitude and range from the target in order to achieve a hit. The computer has the ability to know all of these and continually updates them in order to display to the pilot in his head-up display (HUD) where the ordnance will land at any given moment. This delivery mode is called CCIP (continuously completed impact point). This allows you to better evade defenses in the target area and dedicate more of your time to other tasks (such as evading those defenses) than insuring that you arrive at that precomputed point in space that is required of all manual bombers (ie, mil-cranking iron sight bom-

PR
AF
72
221

The South Carolina Air National Guard operates both the A-7D and the F-16A Fighting Falcon. Maj Ron Ripley in the A-7D (72-258) with 1980s-style wraparound camouflage seems to be pulling away from 2nd Lt Jody Weston in an F-16A (79-304) on 3 October 1983 (Don Spering)

LEFT
This A-7D (72-221), seen here in May 1977, was one of the eight aircraft destroyed by terrorists at Minoz Air Base, San Juan, Puerto Rico on 12 January 1981 (John Vadas)

bers) in order to hit the target. The accuracy of the system (if kept up properly) is devastating. This reduces the amount of ordnance required and the number of sorties to destroy a target.

'When loaded with bombs in a parent-mounted configuration, the aircraft can top 500+ KIAS (810+ km/h) at low altitude. It is slower with MER [multiple ejector racks] and TER [triple ejector racks].

'The aircraft has excellent range. Fuel is normally not a problem during mission planning as in other fighters. This gives the aircrew more options.'

Cintron and other Puerto Rico Guardsmen also praise the previously-mentioned Advanced Manoeuvering Flaps (AMF) which give the A-7D a 25 to 30 per cent increase in turn performance. And finally: 'Overall the aircraft is easy to fly with no bad habits.'

So the saga continues. No longer in regular Air Force service except for specialized duties at Edwards and Nellis AFBs, the A-7D remains a front-line performer with the Guardsmen who can be called to active duty at any time.

Visit to Virginia

'Last of the Gentlemen Day Fighter Pilots,' it says on Lt Col Ed Gorman's calling-card, a harkening-back to the days of the F-105. As if to accentuate the point, the card also says, 'When you're out of Thuds, you're out of fighters.' Gorman and the other pilots of Col Hartwell Coke's 192nd Tactical Fighter Group, the Virginia Air National Guard unit at Byrd Field outside Richmond, *are* out of Thuds. It's one thing to convert to the A-7D from the F-100D, as most Air Guard units have done, or even from the F-104C, as was done in Puerto Rico. But to shift to the unsung SLUF from the gigantic, howling F-105D Thunderchief requires a propensity for dramatic adjustment. Says Gorman, 'It was a let-down initially. But it was a pleasure to see a sharp improvement in bombing accuracy. And I was pleasantly surprised by the A-7D in ACM. It isn't our primary mission, but I think we can go air-to-air with just about anybody.'

The author visited the citizen-soldiers of the Virginia Air National Guard in July 1984 for a first-hand look at a dedicated breed of men typical of those in Guard squadrons operating the A-7D and A-7K. The visit could have as easily been made to Maj Tom Dicken's 166th TFS, Ohio ANG, at Rickenbacker ANGB, Ohio, or to Lt Col Larry Santerini's 112th TFG, Pennsylvania ANG, at Pittsburgh Airport (and, in fact, both *were* visited in the preparation of this work), but in Virginia one has the added zest of being close to a nation's capital. This was the same month when nearby Washington, D.C. buzzed with cocktail-party talk about a startling article in a local magazine which seriously faulted the American officer corps. I had met *Washingtonian* editor Ken De Cell at one of those parties and he'd told me of the year's research that went into the article, concluding that too many officers were sitting at desks and promoting careers while too few stood ready to lead men in battle. Among his magazine's revelations: too many top-notch Air Force officers were leaving active duty in order to fly better planes, more often, in the Air National Guard.

The sun burned down on the Byrd Field flight line. Ground crews scurried about readying the SLUFs belonging to Lt Col John Shurley, Coke's squadron commander, some of them recently repainted in lizard-green 'Europe One' camouflage. The squadron's sole A-7K (80-288) had now been toned-down in 'Europe One' but still had a first-aid kit and an Australian flag painted on the side of the fuselage by the rear seat, a tribute to the Australian-born flight surgeon, Dr Hudson, who is a frequent occupant in the back of the two-seater. I watched a pair of Virginia ANG A-7Ds taxi to runway's end and hurtle into the bright summer sky. There was no hesitation about staying close, almost wingtip-to-wingtip.

Once called 'weekend warriors,' with the implication that they merely played at the profession of aerial arms, Air Guardsmen today are hard-working veterans who give up a segment of their lives to be ready to fly and fight. Most of the A-7D community, like the Virginians, know that they can be hurled into an intense NATO-Warsaw Pact battle environment on hours' notice. Some, like the Ohio and New Mexico Guard units, make up the A-7D commitment to the US Rapid Deployment Joint Task Force (RDJTF) and could find themselves staving off a Soviet invasion in the Persian Gulf. (Desert camouflage paint schemes for the A-7D have been experimented with, but none has been widely adopted).

To be certain, all of these Guardsmen are civilians with full-time jobs—many fly for airlines—but they can be called up on short notice and it *does* happen. The gist of De Cell's story was that regular Air Force officers were fed up with low flying hours, proliferating paperwork and bureaucratic bullshit. The active-duty Air Force had become sclerotic and had developed tunnel vision at the same time. A man could leave active service, join an Air National Guard unit, and fly *more* hours each year in modern combat aircraft. Although they might be fully active only two weeks a year—during 'Coronet Crest' A-7D readiness deployments to England, for example—they could fly every few days while facing fewer inspections, less paperwork. And Guardsmen like Virginia's Basil 'Buddy' Evans who'd just been promoted to lieutenant colonel retained their military ranks.

A-7D 73-1005 of the Puerto Rico Air National Guard was destroyed by terrorists in the bombing at Minoz Air Base
(via Robert F Dorr)

TOP RIGHT
With wraparound camouflage, low-viz national insignia and black tailcode, A-7D (71-338) of the 175th Tactical Fighter Squadron, South Dakota ANG, based at Sioux Falls, basks in sunlight at Davis-Monthan AFB, Arizona on 27 January 1984
(Douglas E Slowiak)

BOTTOM RIGHT
A-7D (78-960) of the 157th Tactical Fighter Squadron, South Carolina ANG, approaches a tanker in August 1981 with dorsal refuelling receptacle open. Full-colour national insignia on the wing is an anachronism in the low visibility 1980s
(Don Spering)

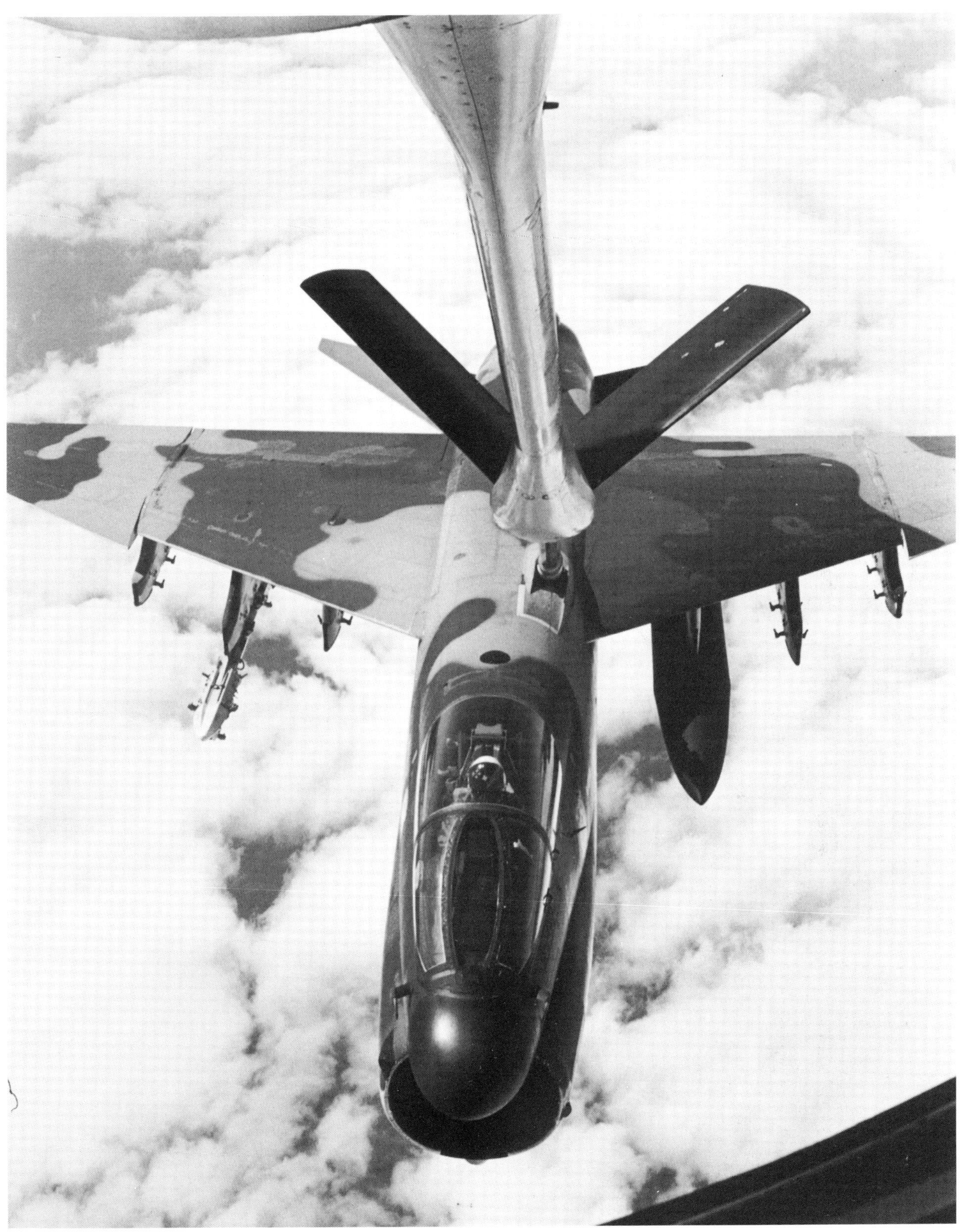

LEFT
A-7D (69-6243) of the 120th Tactical Fighter Squadron, Colorado Air National Guard, leads a formation over the American West on a flight from Buckley Field, Colorado, 24 February 1984
(Don Spering)

Once a familiar sight in Southeast Asian skies, this is now part of Air National Guard routine: an A-7D from Col Lawrence F Santerini's 112th Tactical Fighter Group, Pennsylvania ANG, formates on a KC-135A tanker in April 1983
(Don Linn)

Whatever the other consequences of the critique of American officers, Air Guardsmen came out looking like the cutting edge of an elite force.

Ed Gorman still had a line drawing of the F-105 on his calling cards, but the A-7D was very much his airplane now. After 'Buddy' Evans walked me along the flight line, Gorman and I sat down in the coffee mess and Ed described flying the SLUF.

On range: 'We have a combat radius similar to the F-105.'

On that gadget under the chin: 'The TISL or Pave Penny [laser target locator] was actually developed for the A-10. You use it in combination with the HUD, which lays bombing symbology on the target.'

On departure at high angles of attack: 'The F-8 [Crusader] did that. On departure the aircraft tumbles. Your left butt passes over your right shoulder. The aircraft resists the tendency to do this but if you unwittingly overcome the resistance it will depart on you. You get a nose slice, it's not a stall . . . you whip over. Now we have advanced manoeuvring flaps [AMF] which deploy leading edge devices on the wing and extends 15 degrees of trailing edge flap. With AMF deployed, you can fly at high AOA [angle of attack] and not depart.'

On comparison with the Thud: 'Being short, the SLUF is not as stable as the 105. It's not stable enough to allow you to divert your attention from flying it for very long. It tends to roll out in a turn.'

On landing: 'You pick out an impact point and fly to it. You don't flare the A-7D. The tires tend to get worn on the outside when you flare it. It *can* be flared but a blown tyre is a real risk.' This seems to come from the A-7D's genesis as a carrier-based design. 'Landing speed is about 130 knots [200 km/h] with 2,000 lb [907 kg] of fuel. The 105 landed 60 knots [110 km/h] faster. With the slower speed and the HUD, not found in the 105, you can land in much lower weather.'

The SLUFs of Sandston (the Richmond suburb surrounding Byrd Field) have earned awards for flight safety, readiness, and bombing/navigation proficiency. In an interesting sidelight, the Virginia Guard permits cartoons and individual nicknames on each aircraft, some examples being:

Playmate (71-350)
Dollar 99 (69-6199)

Nose art has long been past history in most military units, but the Virginia Air National Guard still permits cartoons and nicknames on the A-7Ds of the 192nd Tactical Fighter Group at Sandston, Va. Playmate *is an A-7D (71-350) frequently flown by squadron commander Lt Col John Shurley*
(Joseph G Handelman)

The Virginia Air National Guard is just a two-hour drive south of the US capital but is still very much a part of the Deep South, hence the Confederate flag on the nose of this A-7D (72-192). Markings on tail have been painted to reflect the coincidence between the aircraft serial and its unit, the 192nd Tactical Fighter Group, commanded by Col Hartwell Coke
(Va. ANG)

Nail It With Finesse (70-942)
Rebel Rider (70-955)
Bad Company (73-376)

The Air National Guard, headed-up by Maj Gen John B Conaway, boasts no fewer than 91 flying units, 4,000 pilots and 1,700 aircraft of all types including 360 A-7s in 14 squadrons (see Appendix). The magnitude of the Air Guard can best be appreciated when, as aviation writer Don Linn points out, it is viewed as the world's fifth largest air force! The Air National Guard has twice as many aircraft and 4,000 more people than Britain's Royal Air Force, even though most of its people are part-timers. Guardsmen can be called to active duty, as noted, and it happened during the Vietnam conflict and during the 1968 *Pueblo* crisis in Korea.

The A-7D was introduced to the Air Guard in October 1975 with initial deliveries to the 188th TFS in New Mexico. At one time, there were 15 A-7 squadrons in the Guard although the 157th TFS in South Carolina subsequently converted to the F-16 Fighting Falcon in 1983. Ed Gorman and his colleagues in Virginia were the last ANG squadron to acquire the A-7D, although one more unit may eventually be created via conversion from the Cessna A-37. As has been noted, Air Guard units received two-seat A-7Ks straight from Vought's factory and none has ever served in the active-duty Air Force.

The Air National Guard A-7D force has been assigned a special mission in defence of the Panama Canal, rotating its aircraft in 'Coronet Cove' deployments to Howard Air Force Base, Panama. As has been noted, A-7Ds also frequently rotate to Europe in support of NATO and are frequent visitors to RAF Wittering in the UK.

A testing of the Rapid Deployment Joint Task Force commitment saw A-7Ds flying in formation over the Pyramids together with troop-carrying US Army UH-60 Blackhawk helicopters in 1981. To reach Egypt, the A-7Ds of Col David L Quinlan's 150th TFG, New Mexico ANG, set a record for mass nonstop flying which makes even Arnie Clarke's legendary Vietnam mission pall—all eight airplanes being airborne for $11\frac{1}{2}$ hours during the final leg of their deployment from New Hampshire to Cairo West, with no fewer than seven aerial refuellings. The A-7Ds participated in Operation Bright Star in Egypt, dropping 500 lb (227 kg) bombs in support of troops of the 101st Airborne Division. Critics asserted that the Bright Star undertaking was too small and too thoroughly rehearsed to constitute a fair test of US contingency plans for rapid reinforcement in the Persian Gulf in the event of a Soviet invasion of Iran. Still, the Air Guard A-7Ds performed their role effectively and the pilots claimed they could handle the 'real thing' if it happened.

A postscript to the Air Guard story, simply to make the point that it is serious business. The following from an official history:

'9 February 1982: An A-7D Corsair aircraft (72-233) crashed at 0930 EST [eastern standard time] off the coast of North Carolina in the vicinity of the Dare County bombing range. The pilot, Maj William J Monahan of the 192nd Tactical Fighter Group, Virginia Air National Guard, was killed in the crash. . .'

Under current force projections, the Air National Guard will have the A-7D and A-7K in its inventory through the year 2004. The US Navy will operate the A-7E from carrier decks through the year 1992, and even longer with land-based Reserve squadrons. Although some attack squadrons (VA) have now converted to strike fighter squadrons (VFA) and have begun re-equipping with the dual-role McDonnell

RIGHT
Demonstrating the easy accessibility of the SLUF design to ground crews, mechanics work on an A-7D (70-1044) of the Iowa Air National Guard on 14 April 1977, before the days of black tailcodes and wraparound camouflage (Clyde Gerdes)

Capt Mark Hettermann of the 149th Tactical Fighter Squadron, Virginia Air National Guard, shuts down at Byrd Field, just outside Richmond, Va. Hettermann's A-7D (69-6199) bears the nickname Dollar 99 *(Va. ANG)*

Douglas F/A-18A Hornet, others are only beginning to receive FLIR-equipped A-7Es. Some Corsairs serve in VFA Hornet squadrons for transitional purposes. A mixed force of Hornets and Corsairs in the attack role will place some burden on operating costs, but will enable Navy planners to effect savings on the more visible (to Congress) cost of obtaining completely new equipment. Navy pilots are understandably enthusiastic about converting to the F/A-18A ('the best tactical airplane flying,' says Cdr Dennis McGinn, skipper of VFA-125) but this does not diminish their fondness for the Corsair which, late in its life, remains a potent and viable weapons system.

Are there other futures for the Corsair? In a world of Fighting Falcons, Hornets, Tigersharks, the 'stretching' potential of the venerable SLUF may depend upon the cost savings that come with refurbishing a proven aircraft, as an alternative to spending more on the newer and less-proven. In

In about 1979, this experimental desert camouflage paint scheme was applied to this A-7D (70-1006), coded AZ, of the 152nd Tactical Fighter Training Squadron, Arizona Air National Guard. Colour details are not known, and the paint scheme was not adopted for widespread service (USAF)

practical terms, the development of additional Corsair variants for further customers may depend on whether the most likely 'start-up' customer, the Air National Guard, can be persuaded to invest in an updated A-7. Vought clearly sees this as a strong possibility and, while no 100 per cent *new* A-7 will ever roll off the Dallas lines again, the manufacturer believes in a bright future for 'rebuilds' of its proven attack aircraft.

The 'Modernized' Corsair

The equipping of Portugal's Air Force with refurbished Corsairs, designated A-7P, has already been noted. These 'rebuilds' retain most of the features of the A-7A and A-7B models, including the TF30 turbofan, twin Mk 12 20 mm cannons and less

A-7D (70-981) of the 125th TFS, Oklahoma Air National Guard, at Tulsa in October 1984 (via Norman Taylor)

BELOW
In the recently-adopted lizard-green 'Europe One' paint scheme, A-7D (70-1028) of the Oklahoma Guard's 125th TFS is depicted at Tulsa in October 1984 (via Norman Taylor)

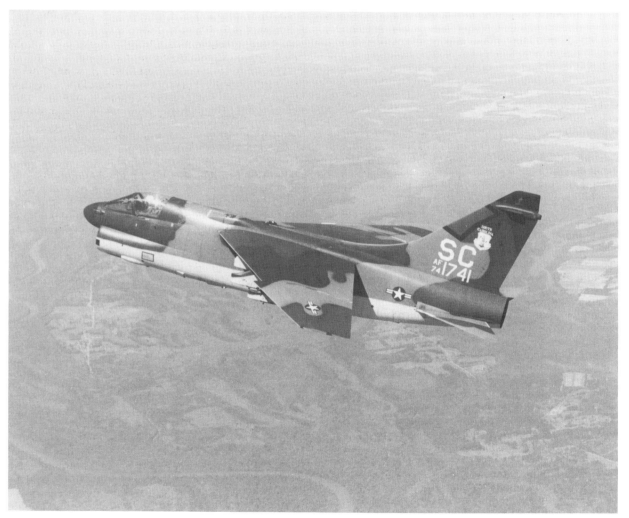

A-7D (74-1747) of the Ohio Air National Guard, in wraparound camouflage and black tailcode, arrives on a deployment to England in 1984
(John Dunnell)

LEFT
A-7D (74-1741), coded SC, of the 157th TFS, South Carolina Air National Guard, which in 1983 converted to the F-16 Fighting Falcon
(via Norman Taylor)

sophisticated navigation and ordnance delivery system. They were attractive to Portugal because of the low cost of updating existing A-7A and A-7B airframes and, very simply, because so many airframes remain in storage ready to be updated. For several years, Vought has been offering the 'modernized' Corsair, essentially identical to the A-7P and powered by the TF30-P-408 turbofan, to those air forces not in need of more advanced machinery. In 1985, Vought had permission to market the 'modernized' Corsair to Thailand, Indonesia, Malaysia, Singapore, New Zealand, Turkey and Venezuela.

The basic making of the 'modernized' Corsair is to be found at the US Military Aircraft Storage and Disposition Center (MASDC) near Tucson, Arizona where unused American warplanes are preserved in a convivial, dry, hot climate. MASDC expert Phil Chinnery estimates that no fewer than 300 airframes are availabe to be taken out of storage and upgraded. Because Vought's planned upgrade is relatively modest—no major changes in configuration or equipment are envisioned—the 'Portuguese formula' could be followed for any additional foreign customer willing to purchase as few as 35 airplanes.

To be feasible, the 'modernized' Corsair would have to compete successfully with other upgrading programmes which offer buyers a state-of-the-art aircraft for no more than the cost of some degree of refurbishment, sometimes modest, sometimes not. Few companies are better at this than Grumman, which has already snatched a portion of the market with rebuilds such as the A-4PTM Skyhawk (peculiar to Malaysia) which has sold successfully to Kuala Lumpur. Also in the running are two separate proposals to upgrade existing F-4 Phantom airframes, one from McDonnell Douglas which envisions modest changes and one from the Boeing Military Airplane Company in Wichita which would include re-engining and installation of completely new avionics and radar. No cost figures have been made public, but it is understood that the 'modernized' Corsair is not significantly less expensive than a rebuilt A-4 or F-4, so the sales job is not likely to be an easy one.

Vought executives candidly acknowledge that their biggest sales hurdle is the obvious one. While men who fly the A-7 Corsair sing its praises to the skies, others have virtually ignored the airplane and its capabilities. 'I mean,' says one, 'how do you compete with a Phantom? The very mention of the name Phantom conjures up an image of might. We know we have a better airplane for the cost-effective, pinpoint ground attack role but outside the Corsair community the airplane's reputation is not something which precedes it.' Some selling points are equally persuasive, including the generally good reputation of the A-7P in Portuguese service. But another drawback is that the rebuild programme for the F-8 Crusader for the Philippines is not universally regarded as a total success. 'In all, it's a mixed bag and while we're confident of our product, it's a competitive marketplace out there.'

Which is why the strongest likelihood for the future is not the 'modernized' Corsair but the more costly, more advanced Corsair III, a very different king of rebuild which involves not merely a new engine but a new way of thinking about the veritable SLUF.

The Corsair III

'This changes everything,' says LTV's Jim Croslin. 'This will make the airplane supersonic. It has tremendous promise.'

A supersonic SLUF? In level flight?

At the 1984 Farnborough show in England, LTV gave out literature on what it calls the Corsair III—an upgrade for the Air National Guard and for foreign users refitted with the General Electric F110-GE-100 engine, which produces 16,700 lb (7575 kg) dry static thrust and 27,600 lb (12,111 kg) thrust with afterburning. This 'Super Corsair' or Corsair III almost certainly would require a 'start-up' investment by the Air National Guard to prove financially viable. Vought proposes to upgrade all Air Guard A-7Ds with this retrofit to extend the potential service

On a visit to England in 1984, A-7Ds of Lt Col Larry Santerini's 146th TFS, 112th TFG, Pennsylvania Air National Guard appear in Europe One colour scheme. The squadron employed a PA tailcode for several years before shifting to PT. The aircraft are stationed in Pittsburgh (John Dunnell)

RIGHT
A-7D (72-175), coded PT, of the 146th TFS, Pennsylvania ANG, in Europe One paint scheme, visiting Davis-Monthan AFB, Arizona on 20 February 1984 (Douglas E Slowiak)

life of the Guard's A-7 even beyond the current target, the year 2004.

The rebuild to Corsair III standard, again relying at least on the large number of A-7A and A-7B airframes in storage at MASDC (although A-7D and A-7E aircraft would, in fact, be easier to convert) involves fitting a 29.5 inch (.761 m) constant-section plug to extend the fuselage around the wing root area. Another 7.5 inch (.182 m) plug would be added to the rear fuselage to tailor the fuselage internally to the dimensions of the F110 engine and its remote accessory gearbox.

The rear fuselage would be canted upwards five degrees to provide increased ground clearance for the extended tailpipe. The essential shape of the A-7 would remain unchanged but the nose would be more sharply pointed in the manner of the F-8 Crusader, the blunt nose having been originally intended to conserve space on carrier decks.

If an order for the re-engined, supersonic Corsair III could be obtained from the Air National Guard to permit economical 'start-up,' LTV believes that further orders can be obtained from other foreign purchasers, including the same customers to whom it is authorized to show the 'modernized' Corsair.

Apart from the engine change and minor changes

in configuration which would increase the A-7's already respectable fuel capacity (exact figures have not been stated), the proposed Corsair III remains a relatively modest undertaking. 'We might clean up the cockpit a bit,' one company executive is quoted, but there exist no plans for major changes in hydraulics, avionics, or radar.

Furthermore, this re-engined A-7 remains a marketing idea, not cold steel. In July 1985 Vought responded to a USAF request for information on a 1990s close air support/battlefield air interdiction (CAS/BAI) airplane. The company has proposed a supersonic, upgraded A-7D powered by a P&W F100-200 turbofan and equipped with more advanced weapons and sensors. Dubbed A-7 'Strikefighter', the airplane is in competition with modified versions of the F-16, AV-8B and F-20.

Other Futures

The guns are silent.

As this is written, the smoke has cleared over Route Package Six and in other regions where the A-7 Corsair has done battle. The more senior among Corsair aviators are now retired, their fighting behind them, just like the fighting of those semi-retired A-7As and A-7Bs which bask in the sun at MASDC.

But it is not over yet. History has its relentless way of posing new tests. New fighting is no further away than tomorrow's headlines. And even if men can keep their hands off the triggers for a time, new futures for the A-7 are inevitable. Those airframes preserved in the Arizona sunshine have a lot of life remaining in them and somebody is going to find a new use for those airplanes.

The late emergence of the EA-7L electronic-warfare Corsair is but one indicator of the stretching potential of the design. If no A-7M ever appears, it will be surprising. A QA-7B target drone aircraft, converted form those MASDC airframes and meant to satiate the US Navy's endless need for drones built for the sole purpose of being shot down, seems a realistic possibility. The Air National Guard may

LV
AF
70
940

become more deeply enmeshed in electronic warfare and its two-seaters may become EA-7Ks. The possibilities are many.

Meanwhile, USS *Eisenhower* (CVN-69) plies the Mediterranean, an area where the potential for trouble remains strong. Lt Dave Potter of the 'Clinchers' of VA-12 walks the deck, a long port-call at Mallorca just behind, the A-7Es of his squadron and of VA-66 standing ready, an afternoon BARCAP mission coming up as the ship points its prow eastward. So far, nobody has decided to send *Ike* to the Gulf of Sidra which the US regards as international waters and which Colonel Khaddafi of Libya views as his private pond, but it is policymakers who decide such things, not aviators, such a venture is among the possibilities, and memory is fresh of the 1981 encounter between Tomcats and Libyan Sukhoi fighters in those waters. Other potential trouble waits in Lebanon, in the Middle East generally, and up north where the Warsaw Pact's massed armoured forces confront NATO at the Fulda Gap. Dave Potter is easygoing, unphilosophical. When John Konrad went aloft in the first Corsair, Dave was not yet ten years old.

Again, the question.

It has to be asked because so much depends on it. In a world where cessation of hostility is at best a temporary condition, where old men like me send young men like Dave into battle, are the man and machine ready to head once more into the fray?

'I just plain like to fly,' shrugs Dave. 'This is a flyin' airplane.' Some of his counterparts in the US Air Force insist that the A-7D was replaced too soon by the A-10 and readily utter their preference for the Vought product. That doesn't happen in the US Navy, where nobody would pass up a chance at the F/A-18A Hornet, but it remains surprisingly true that Corsair men love their Corsair with a special kind of love and no other collection of metal and plastic is going to be quite the same. Hemingway compared your first airplane to your first woman. 'Are we ready?' Dave nods, getting ready to climb aboard his A-7E for a catapult launch. 'Can we do what needs to be done? I think you asked that once before. You've already printed the answer. You call, we haul.'

In a moment, Dave is taxying up past a six-pack of Tomcats. The A-7 Corsair is still right up there at the front.

The last-active-duty US Air Force unit to operate the A-7D is the 4450th Tactical Group with a tailcode reminding us that its home, Nellis AFB, Nevada, is adjacent to Las Vegas. Low visibility colour scheme on A-7D (70-940), on a visit to Tulsa, Oklahoma in October 1984, is typical of current warpaint
(Norman Taylor)

Glossary

AAA	Anti-aircraft artillery fire. Also: Triple-A
Bingo	Down to fuel limits, i.e. left only with enough fuel to return to base or to tanker
D-M	Davis Monthan Air Force Base, Tucson, Arizona
IR	Infrared
LORAN	Long-range navigation system found in F-4D and F-111A aircraft
SAM	Surface-to-air missile, usually referring to Soviet-made SA-2 Guideline missile
TARPS	Tactical reconnaissance pod carried by F-14A
TRAM	Tactical navigation and bombing system fitted on some A-6E
TFW	Tactical Fighter Wing

Specifications

A-7A

Type: single-seat carrier-based attack aircraft

Powerplant: one 11,350 lb (5150 kg) thrust non-afterburning Pratt & Whitney TF30-P-6 turbofan engine

Performance: maximum speed 578 mph (930 km/h) at sea level; approach speed 140 mph (225 km/h); take-off to 50 ft (15 m) in 5,865 ft (1790 m); combat radius 715 miles (1150 km); maximum ferry range with internal fuel 3,360 miles (5405 km), with four drop tanks 4,100 miles (6,600 km), ceiling 47,000 ft (14325 m)

Weights: empty 15,037 lb (6,821 kg); maximum take-off 32,500 lb (14,750 kg)

Dimensions: wing span 38 ft 9 in (11.8 m); length 46 ft 2 in (14.09 m); height 16 ft 2 in (4.93 m); wing area 375 sq ft (34.83 m^2)

Armament: two Mark 12 20 mm cannons with 680 rounds; provision for various underwing ordnance loads up to 20,000 lb (9100 kg)

A-7D

Type: single-seat attack aircraft

Powerplant: one 14,250 lb (6,465 kg) static thrust non-afterburning Allision TF41-A-1 (Rolls-Royce Spey 168-62) turbofan

Performance: maximum speed 698 mph (1123 km/h) at sea level; take-off run at maximum take-off weight 5,000 ft (1525 m); combat radius 890 miles (1432 km); ferry range with internal fuel 2,281 miles (3671 km), with maximum internal and external fuel, 2,871 miles (4621 km); service ceiling 51,000 ft (15,544 m)

Weights: empty 19,781 lb (8972 kg); maximum take-off, 42,000 lb (19,050 kg)

Dimensions: wing span 38 ft 9 in (11.8 m); length 46 ft $1\frac{1}{2}$ in (14.06 m); height 16 ft $0\frac{3}{4}$ in (4.90 m); wing area, 375 sq ft (34.83 m^2)

Armament: one General Electric M61A1 Vulcan, Gatling-style 20 mm cannon with 1,000 rounds; provision for various underwing ordnance loads up to 20,000 lb (9100 kg)

Appendices

Appendix I. **A-7 Corsairs Manufactured**

Model	*Amount*	*From*	*To*	*Remarks*
A-7A	3	152580	152582	44 converted to A-7P
	4	152647	152650	6 converted to TA-7P
	10	152651	152660	
	25	152661	152685	
	48	153134	153181	
	52	153182	153233	
	40	153234	153273	
	17	154344	154360	
Subtotal	199			
A-7B	57	154361	154417	24 converted to TA-7C
	57	154418	154474	Conversions to A-7P
	48	154475	154522	
	34	154523	154556	
	(17)	(154557)	(154573)	Cancelled batch
	(17)	(154913)	(154929)	Cancelled batch
	(240)	(156178)	(156417)	Cancelled batch
Subtotal	196			
A-7C	7	156734	156740	36 converted to TA-7C
	21	156741	156761	
	39	156762	156800	
Subtotal	67			
YA-7D	5	67-14582	67-14586	Later designated A-7D
Subtotal	5			
A-7D	12	68-8220	68-8231	1 converted to A-7K
	57	69-6188	69-6244	
	128	70-929	70-1056	
	88	71-292	71-379	
	97	72-169	72-265	
	24	73-992	73-1015	
	24	74-1737	74-1760	
	24	75-386	75-409	
Subtotal	454			
A-7E	40	156801	156840	1 converted to YA-7H
	50	156841	156890	
	47	157435	157481	
	56	157482	157537	
	57	157538	157594	
	(54)	(157595)	(157648)	Cancelled batch
	27	158002	158028	
	15	158652	158666	
	15	158667	158681	
	12	158819	158830	
	12	158831	158842	
	48	159261	159308	
	24	159638	159661	
	(12)	(159668)	(159679)	Cancelled batch
	36	159967	160002	

Model	*Amount*	*From*	*To*	*Remarks*
	(4)	(160003)	(160006)	Cancelled batch
	30	160537	160566	
	6	160613	160618	
	30	160710	160739	
	30	160857	160886	
Subtotal	535			
A-7H	6	159662	159667	
	54	159913	159966	
Subtotal	60			
TA-7H	5	161218	161222	
Subtotal	5			
A-7K	12	79-460	79-471	
	12	80-284	80-295	
	6	81-72	81-77	
Subtotal	30			
Total	1,551			

[Note: Some sources list production total as 1,545, which would mean that six aircraft listed are rebuilds from existing airframes]

Appendix 2. **US Air Force A-7D Units**

US Air Force and Air National Guard (ANG) units operating the A-7D as of 31 October 1985.

Unit	*Location*	*Type*	*Tailcode*
Air Force Systems Command			
6512 TS, AFFTC	Edwards AFB, Calif	A-7D	ED
Air Training Command			
Chanute TTC	Chanute AFB, Ill	GA-7D	None
Lowry TTC	Lowry AFB, Colo	GA-7D	None
Sheppard TTC	Sheppard AFB, Texas	GA-7D	None
Tactical Air Command			
23 TFW*	England, AFB, Louisiana	A-7D	EL
354 TFW*	Myrtle Beach AFB, SC and Korat RTAFB, Thailand	A-7D	MB
355 TFW*	Davis-Monthan AFB, Ariz	A-7D	DM
4450 TG	Nellis AFB, Nevada	A-7D	LV
Air National Guard (ANG)			
107 TFS 127 TFW	Selfridge ANGB, Michigan	A-7D	MI
112 TFS 180 TFG	Toledo, Ohio	A-7D	OH
120 TFS 140 TFW	Buckley ANGB, Colorado	A-7D, A-7K	CO
124 TFS 132 TFW	Des Moines, Iowa	A-7D	IA
125 TFS 138 TFG	Tulsa, Oklahoma	A-7D, A-7K	OK
146 TFS 112 TFG	Pittsburgh, Pennsylvania	A-7D	PT
149 TFS 192 TFG	Sandston, Virginia	A-7D, A-7K	None
152 TFTS 162 TFTG	Tucson, Arizona	A-7D, A-7K	AZ
157 TFS 169 TFG	McEntire ANGB, SC	A-7D	SC
162 TFS 178 TFG	Springfield, Ohio	A-7D, A-7K	OH
166 TFS 121 TFW	Rickenbacker ANGB, Ohio	A-7D, A-7K	OH
174 TFS 185 TFG	Sioux City, Iowa	A-7D	IA
175 TFS 114 TFG	Sioux Falls, SD	A-7D, A-7K	SD
188 TFS 150 TFG	Kirtland AFB, NM	A-7D, A-7K	None
198 TFS 156 TFG	Minoz Airport, Puerto Rico	A-7D	PR

*23 TFW, 354TFW, 355 TFW since converted to A-10. GA-7D is non-flyable training airframe.

Appendix 3. **US Navy A-7 Corsair Squadrons**

Squadron	*Nickname*	*Traditional Home Port*
VA-12	Clinchers	NAS Cecil Field, Florida
VA-15	Valions	Cecil
VA-22	Fighting Redcocks	NAS Lemoore, California
VA-25	Fist of the Fleet	Lemoore
VA-27	Royal Maces	Lemoore
VA-37	Bulls	Cecil
VA-45	Blackbirds	Cecil
VA-46	Clansmen	Cecil
VA-56	Champions	NAS Atsugi, Japan
VA-66	Waldomen	Cecil
VA-72	Blue Hawks	Cecil
VA-81	Sunliners	Cecil
VA-82	Marauders	Cecil
VA-83	Rampagers	Cecil
VA-86	Sidewinders	Cecil
VA-87	Golden Warriors	Cecil
VA-93	Ravens	Atsugi
VA-94	Mighty Shrikes	Lemoore
VA-97	Warhawks	Lemoore
VA-105	Gladiators	Cecil
VA-122	Flying Eagles	Lemoore
VFA-125	Rough Riders	Lemoore
VA-127	Royal Blues	Lemoore
VA-146	Blue Diamonds	Lemoore
VA-147	Argonauts	Lemoore
VA-153	Blue Tail Flies	Lemoore
VA-174	Hellrazors	Cecil
VA-192	Golden Dragons	Lemoore
VA-195	Dam Busters	Lemoore
VA-203	Blue Dolphins	NAS Jacksonville, Florida
VA-204	River Rattlers	NAS New Orleans, Louisiana
VA-205	Green Falcons	NAS Atlanta, Georgia
VA-215	Barn Owls	Lemoore
VA-303	Golden Hawks	NAS Alameda, California
VA-304	Firebirds	Alameda
VA-305	Lobos	NAS Point Mugu, California
VAQ-34	(Not recorded)	NAS Miramar, California
VX-5	Vampires	NAS China Lake, California

Appendix 4. **Disposition of the Naval Reserve A-7B Force May 1983**

VA-203 **Blue Dolphins** Cecil Field		**VA-204** **River Rattlers** New Orleans		**VA-205** **Green Falcons** Atlanta	
153394	AF-300	154547	AF-400	154469	AF-500
154556	301	154448	401	154413	501
154375	302			154509	502
154451	303	154415	403	154372	503
154475	304	154388	404	154381	504
154551	305	154468	405	154498	505
154452	306	154443	406	154466	506
154395	307	154397	407	154481	507
154368	310	154409	410	154478	510
154371	311	154491	411	154484	511
154396	312	154490	412	154494	512
154366	313	154465	413	154472	513

VA-203 **Blue Dolphins** Cecil Field		**VA-204** **River Rattlers** New Orleans		**VA-205** **Green Falcons** Atlanta	
154463	AF-314	154453	AF-414	154512	AF-514
		154538	?		

VA-303 **Golden Hawks** Alameda		**VA-304** **Firebirds** Alameda		**VA-305** **Lobos** Point Mugu	
154389	ND-300	154362	ND-400	154554	ND-500
154438	301	154370	401	154535	501
154488	302	154505	402	154502	502
154552	303	154460	403	154474	503
154431	304	154445	404		
154433	305	154456	405	154449	505
154550	306	154406	406	154440	506
154476	307	154462	407	154439	507
154485	310	154549	410	154416	510
154516	311	154454	411	154411	511
154520	312	154479	412		
				154390	513
154529	314	154527	414	154382	ND-514
154548	315	154545	ND-415		
154523	ND-316				

NAEC
Lakehurst

154373

NARF
Jacksonville

154420 (?)
154553 (?) was AF-414 VA-204

BUNO	MODEX	VA	BUNO	MODEX	VA
154362	ND 400	304	154460	ND 403	304
366	AF 313	203	462	ND 407	304
368	AF 310	203	463	AF 314	203
370	ND 401	304	465	AF 413?	204
371	AF 311	203	466	AF 506	205
372	AF 503	205	468	AF 405	204
373	NAEC Lakehurst		469	AF 500	205
375	AF 302	203	472	AF 513	205
381	AF 504	205	474	ND 503	305
382	ND 514	305	475	AF 304	203
388	AF 404	204	476	ND 307	303
389	ND 300	303	478	AF 510	205
390	ND 513	305	479	ND 412	304
395	AF 307	203	481	AF 507	205
396	AF 312	203	482	AF 400	204
397	AF 407	204	484	AF 511	205
			485	ND 310	303
406	ND 406	304	488	ND 302	303
409	AF 410	204	490	AF 412	204
411	ND 511	305	491	AF 411	204
413	AF 501	205	493	AF 300	203
415	AF 403	204	494	AF 512	205
416	ND 510	305	498	AF 505	205
420	(? NARF JAX)		502	ND 502	305
431	ND 304	303	505	ND 402	304
433	ND 305	303	509	AF 502	205
438	ND 301	303	512	AF 514	205
439	ND 507	305	516	ND 311	303

BUNO	MODEX	VA
440	ND 506	305
443	AF 406	204
445	ND 404	304
448	AF 401	204
449	ND 505	305
451	AF 303	203
452	AF 306	203
453	AF 414	204
454	ND 411?	304
154456	ND 405	304

	BUNO	MODEX	VA
	520	ND 312	303
	523	ND 316	303
	527	ND 414	304
	529	ND 314	303
	535	ND 501	305
	538	AF 4xx	204
	545	ND 415	304
	547	AF 400	204
	548	ND 315	303
	549	ND 410	304
	550	ND 306	303
	551	AF 305	203
	552	ND 303	303
(NARF)	553	AF 414	204?
	554	ND 500	305
	154556	AF 301	203

In the spring of 1983 RADM Robert F. Dunn, Chief of Naval Reserve, testified that of 77 A-7Bs assigned to the Reserve all but 19 were grounded with engine problems.

Basis of above listing is a 1 JAN 80 inventory of A-7Bs. At least two of these have been stricken in crashes. Modexes given are believed current.

Appendix 5. **US Navy Conversions to TA-7C**

BUNO	VOUGHT NO	RECEIVED VOUGHT	FAB SEQ	NEW NO
154361	B-1	15 Jul 75	6	TB-4
154377	B-17	24 Nov 75	8	TB-8
154379	B-19	29 Jul 76	23	TB-19
154402	B-42	22 Jun 76	18	TB-16
154404	B-44	28 Jan 76	11	TB-10
154407	B-47	23 Apr 76	14	TB-13
154410	B-50	27 Sep 76	30	TB-23
154412	B-52	25 Aug 76	29	TB-22
154424	B-64	8 Jan 76	9	TB-9
154425	B-65	31 Jul 76	25	TB-20
154437	B-77	24 Sep 75	7	TB-7
154450	B-90	28 Mar 76	13	TB-12
154455	B-95	26 Aug 75	4	TB-6
154458	B-98	24 Aug 76	27	TB-21
154464	B-104	27 Jun 75	2	TB-2
154467	B-107	20 Feb 76	12	TB-11

BUNO	VOUGHT NO	RECEIVED VOUGHT	FAB SEQ	NEW NO
154471	B-111	22 Jul 76	21	TB-18
154477	B-117	28 Feb 75	1	TB-1
154489	B-129	14 Jun 76	17	TB-15
154500	B-140	23 Jun 76	19	TB-17
154507	B-147	20 May 76	16	TB-14
154536	B-176	4 Oct 76	31	TB-24
154537	B-177	15 Jul 75	5	TB-5
154544	B-184	21 Nov 74	3	TB-3
156737	C-4	6 Jan 76	20	TE-3
156738	C-5	23 Mar 76	26	TE-6
156740	C-7	6 Jan 76	15	TE-2
156741	C-8	24 Jun 77	42	TE-18
156743	C-10	19 Jan 77	33	TE-9
156744	C-11	5 Apr 77	37	TE-13
156745	C-12	22 June 77	41	TE-17
156746	C-13	4 Nov 77	47	TE-23
156747	C-14	4 Nov 77	48	TE-24
156748	C-15	15 Sep 75	10	TE-1
156750	C-17	8 Jul 77	43	TE-19
156751	C-18	18 Jul 77	44	TE-20
156753	C-20	22 Feb 78	54	TE-30
156757	C-24	25 Feb 76	24	TE-5
156761	C-28	14 May 76	28	TE-7
156765	C-32	12 Dec 77	52	TE-28
156766	C-33	30 Jan 76	22	TE-4
156767	C-34	20 Jul 77	46	TE-22
156768	C-35	11 Nov 77	49	TE-25
156770	C-37	22 May 78	57	TE-33
156773	C-40	23 May 77	39	TE-15
156774	C-41	18 Aug 78	59	TE-35
156777	C-44	21 Nov 77	51	TE-27
156779	C-46	22 Mar 78	55	TE-31
156782	C-49	22 Mar 78	56	TE-32
156784	C-51	25 May 77	40	TE-16
156786	C-53	19 Jan 77	35	TE-11
156787	C-54	8 Feb 78	53	TE-29
156788	C-55	18 Nov 77	50	TE-26
156789	C-56	20 Jul 77	45	TE-21
156790	C-57	28 Apr 77	38	TE-14
156791	C-58	24 Aug 78	60	TE-36
156793	C-60	20 Jun 78	58	TE-34
156794	C-61	17 Feb 77	36	TE-12
156795	C-62	19 Jan 77	32	TE-8
156800	C-67	19 Jan 77	34	TE-10

Index